swarm

volume 1

wildwood river press

2018

Copyright ©2018 Wildwood River Press

Art & book design by Kathy McTavish

Printed in the United States
ISBN: 978-1-947787-07-0

This activity is made possible in part by the voters of Minnesota through a grant from the Arrowhead Regional Arts Council, thanks to appropriations from The McKnight Foundation and the Minnesota State Legislature's general and arts and cultural heritage funds. Funding also provided by Northern Lights.mn and the Jerome Foundation. Art(ists) On the Verge (AOV) is an annual, intensive, mentor-based fellowship program for 5 Minnesota-based, emerging artists or artist groups working experimentally at the intersection of art, technology, and digital culture with a focus on network-based practices that are interactive and/or participatory.

Wildwood River Press

2 Chester Parkway
Duluth, Minnesota 55805
wildwoodriver.com

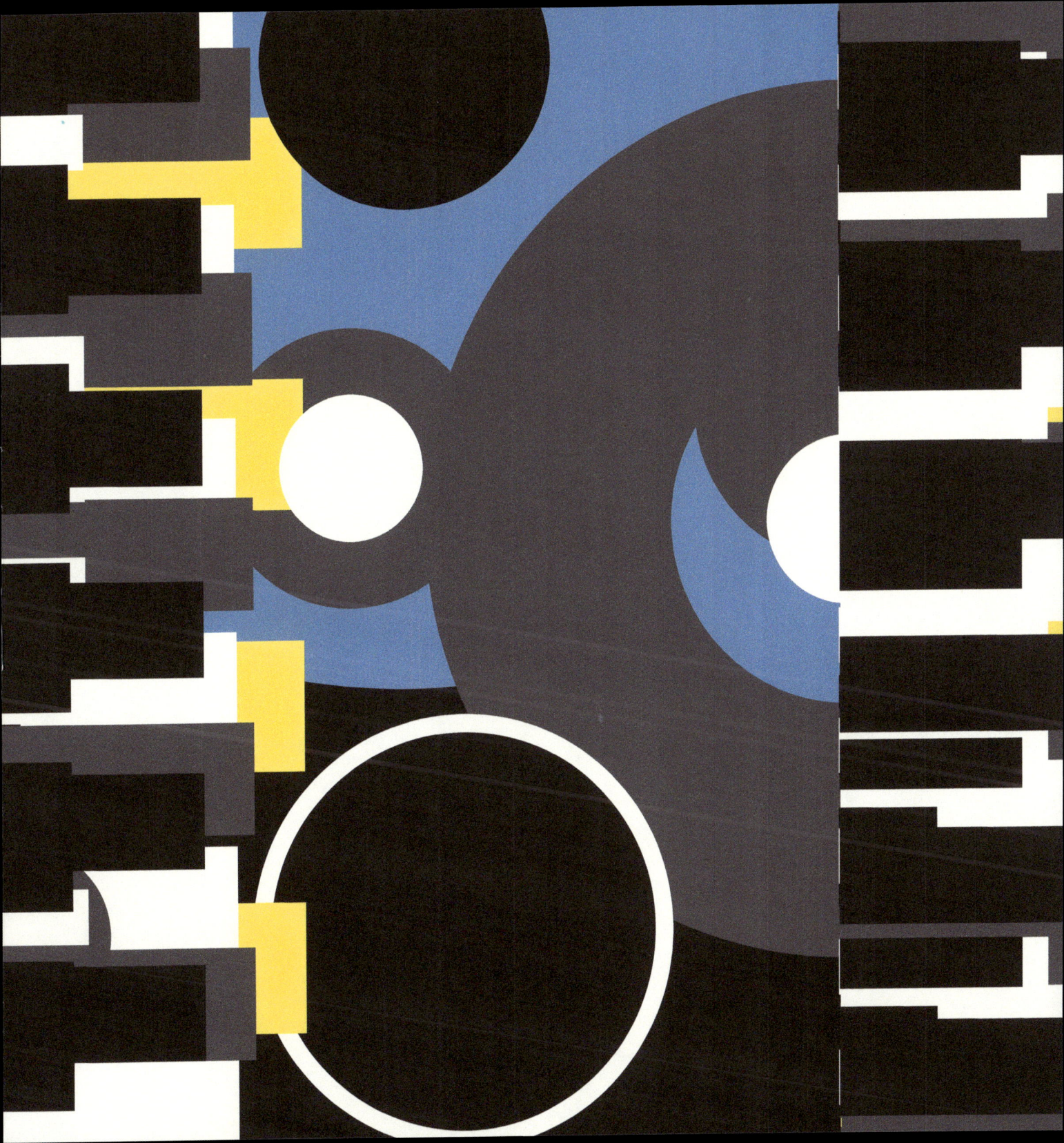

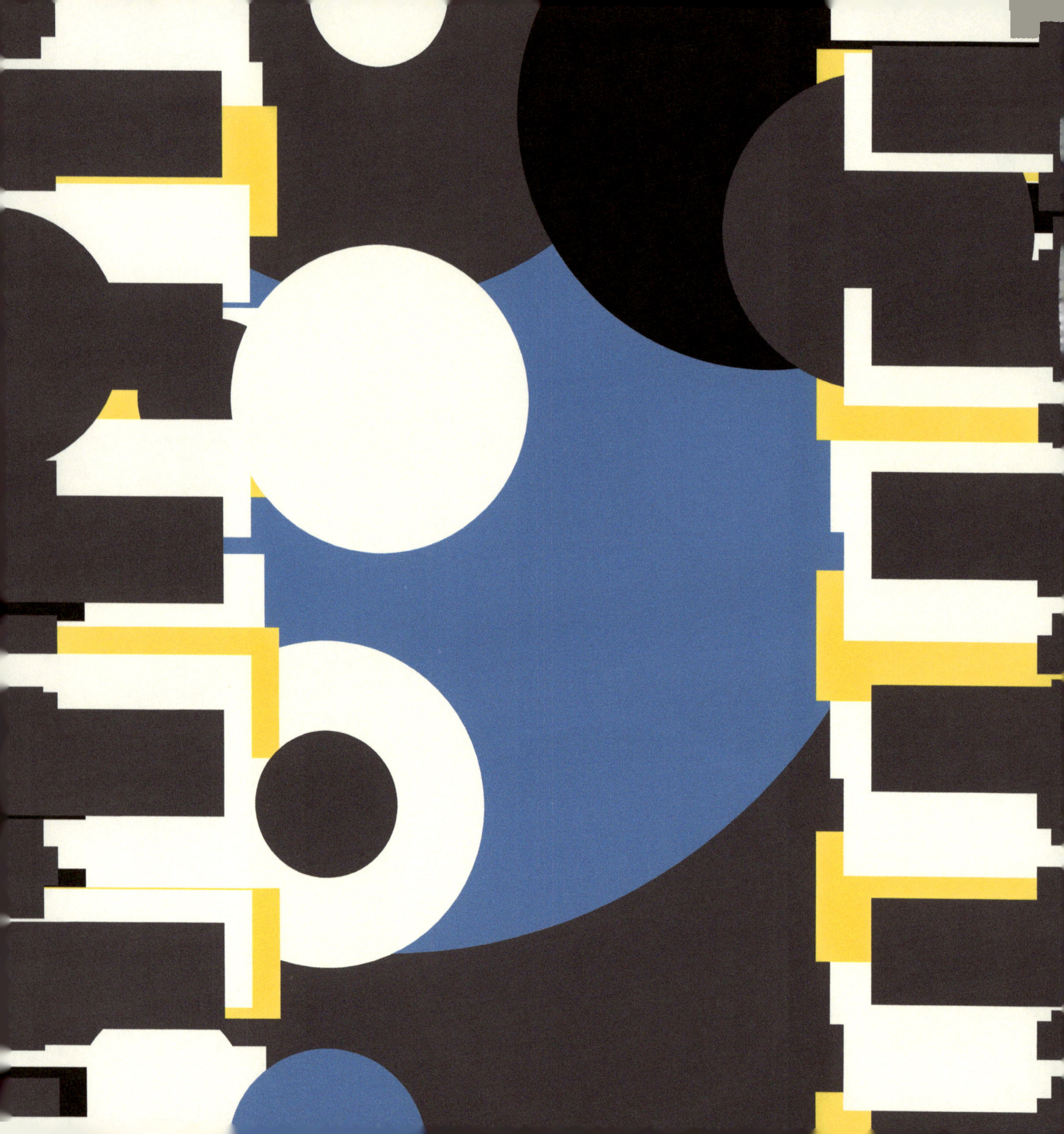

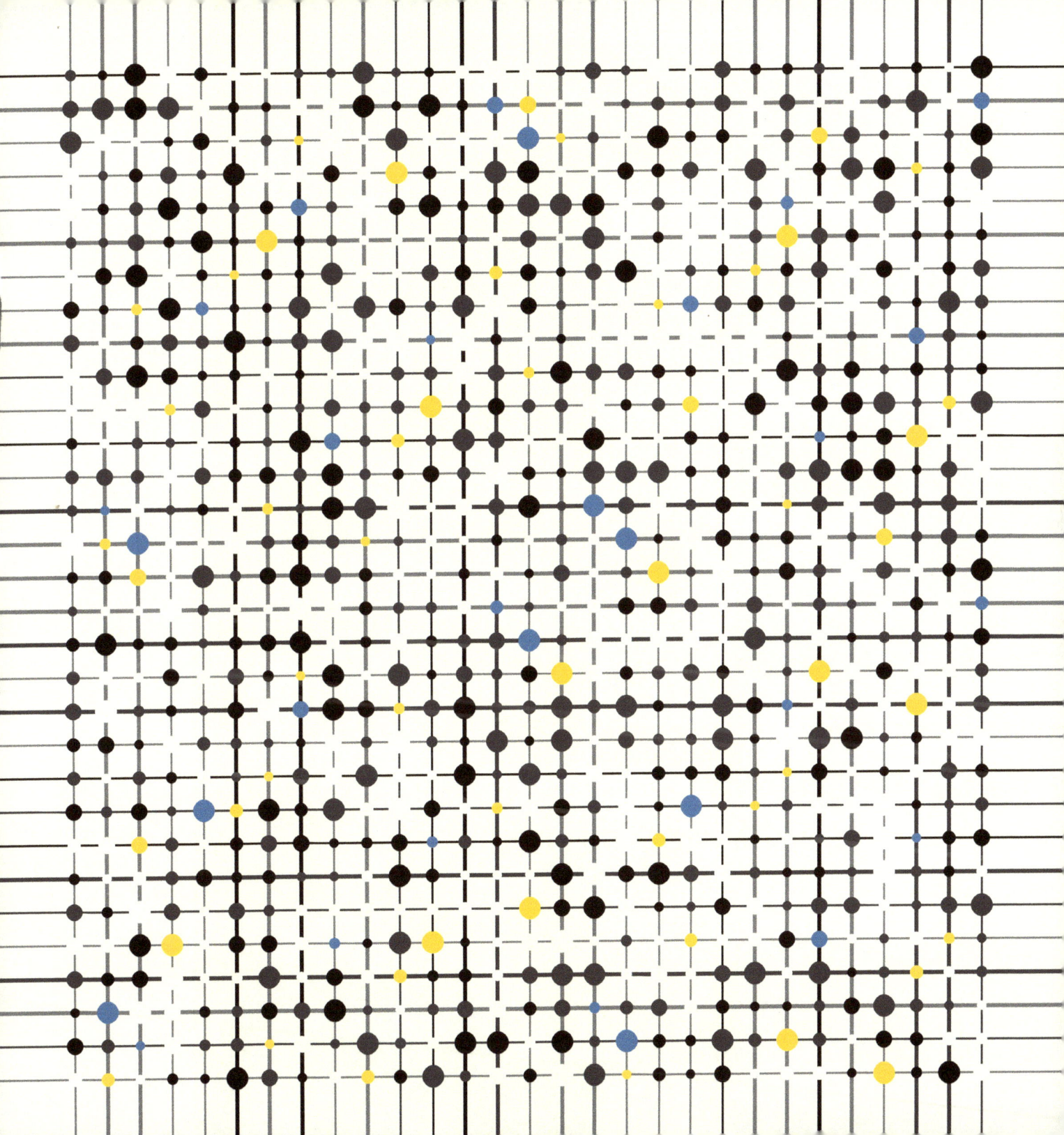

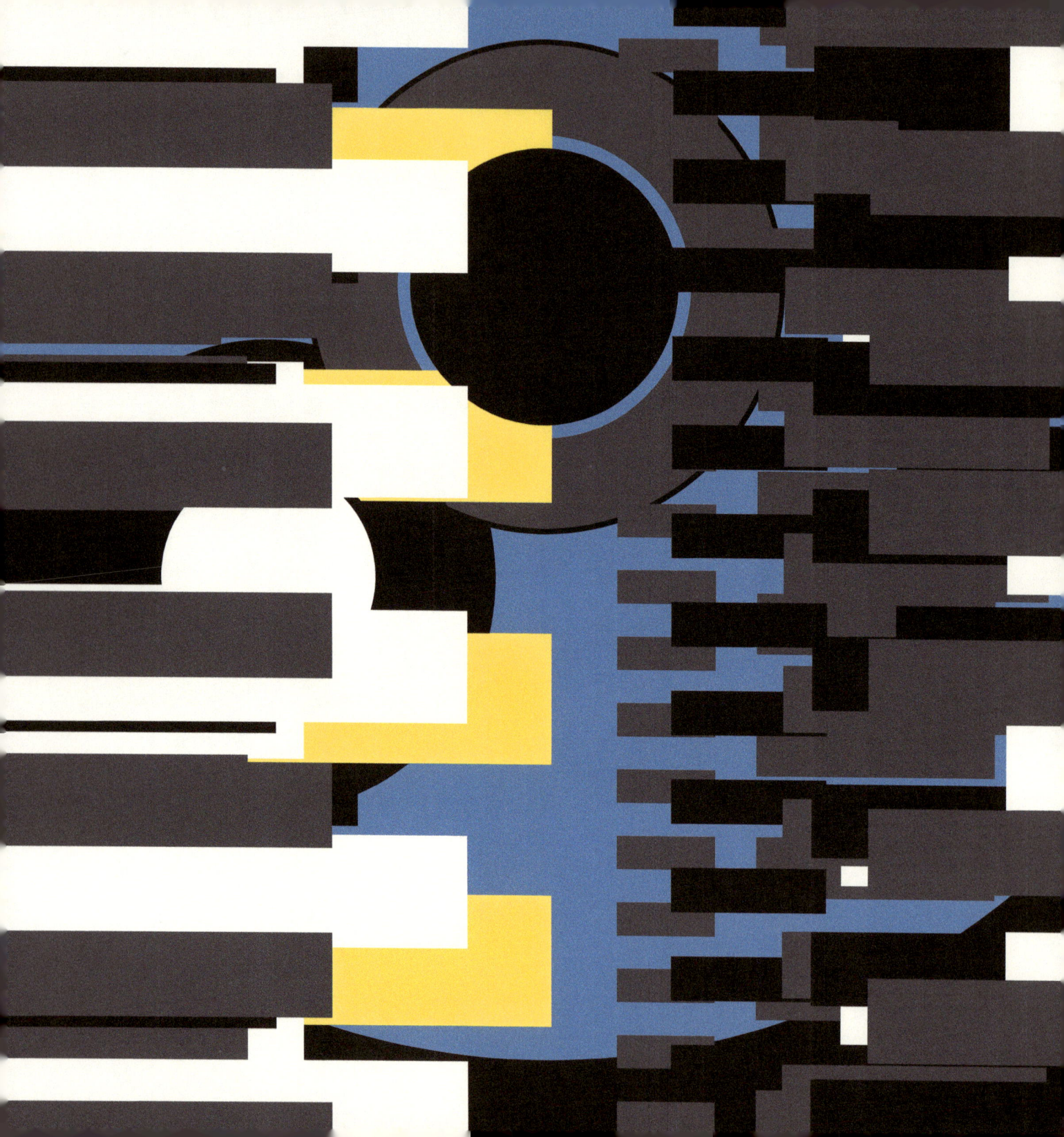

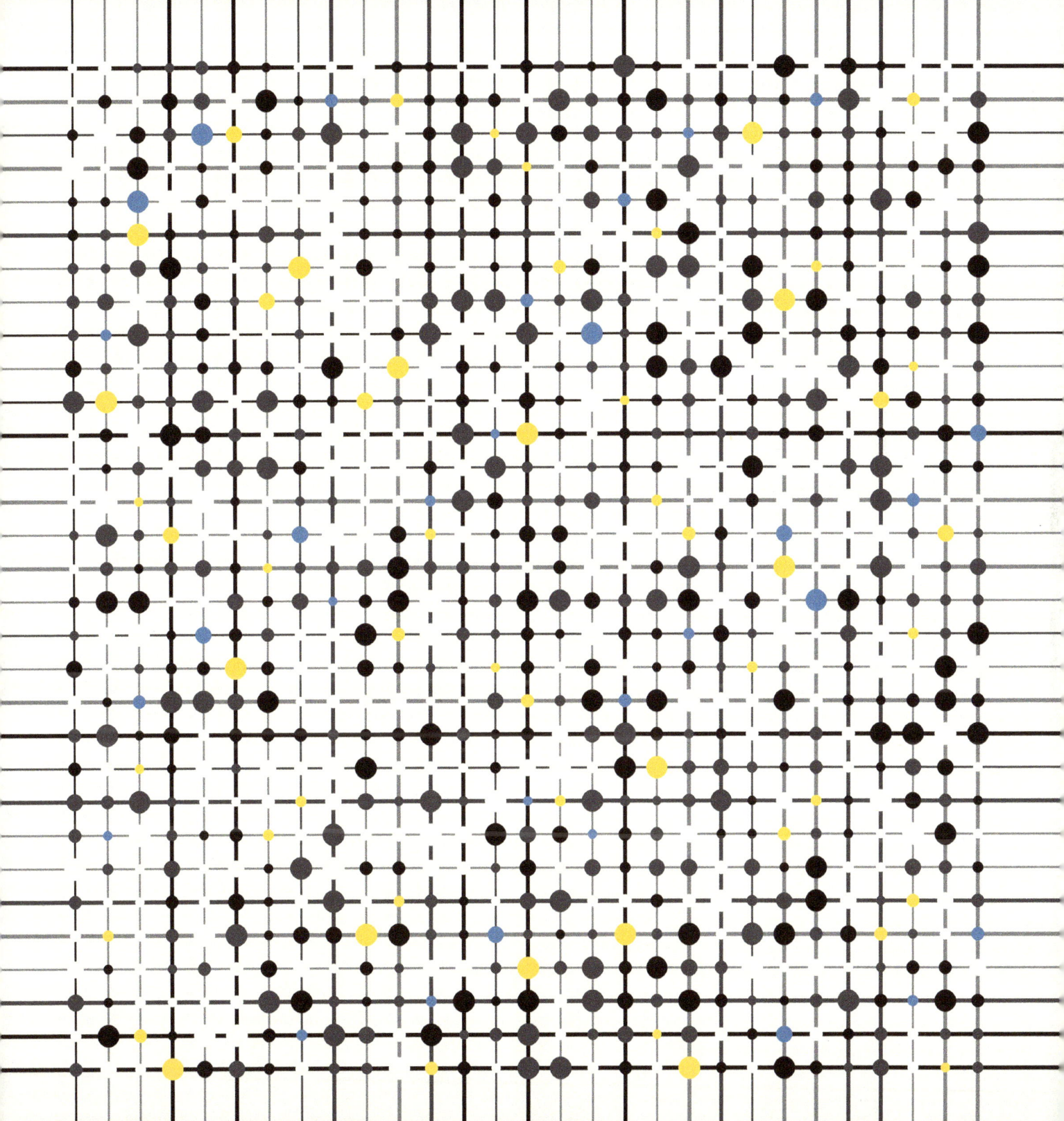

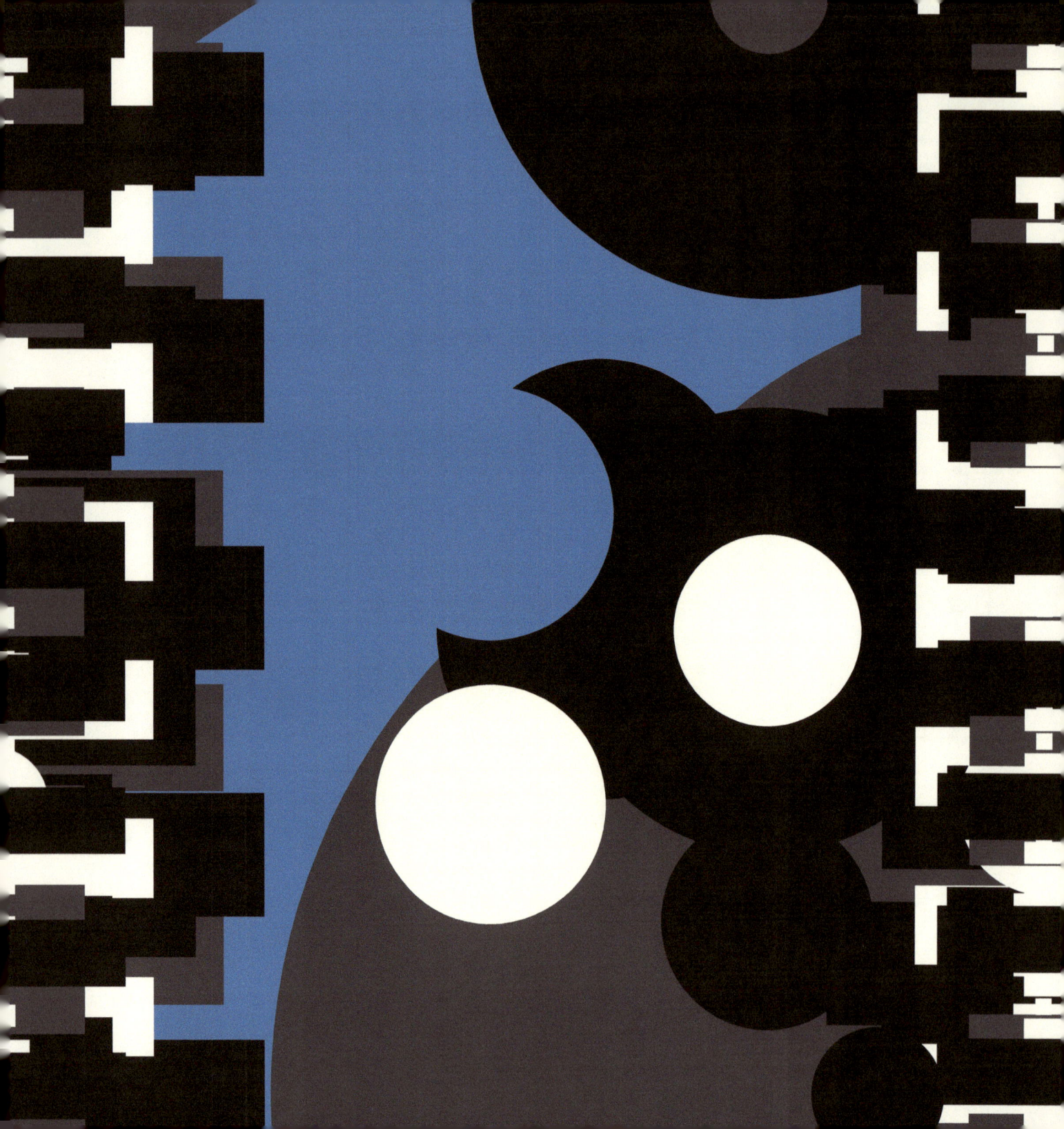

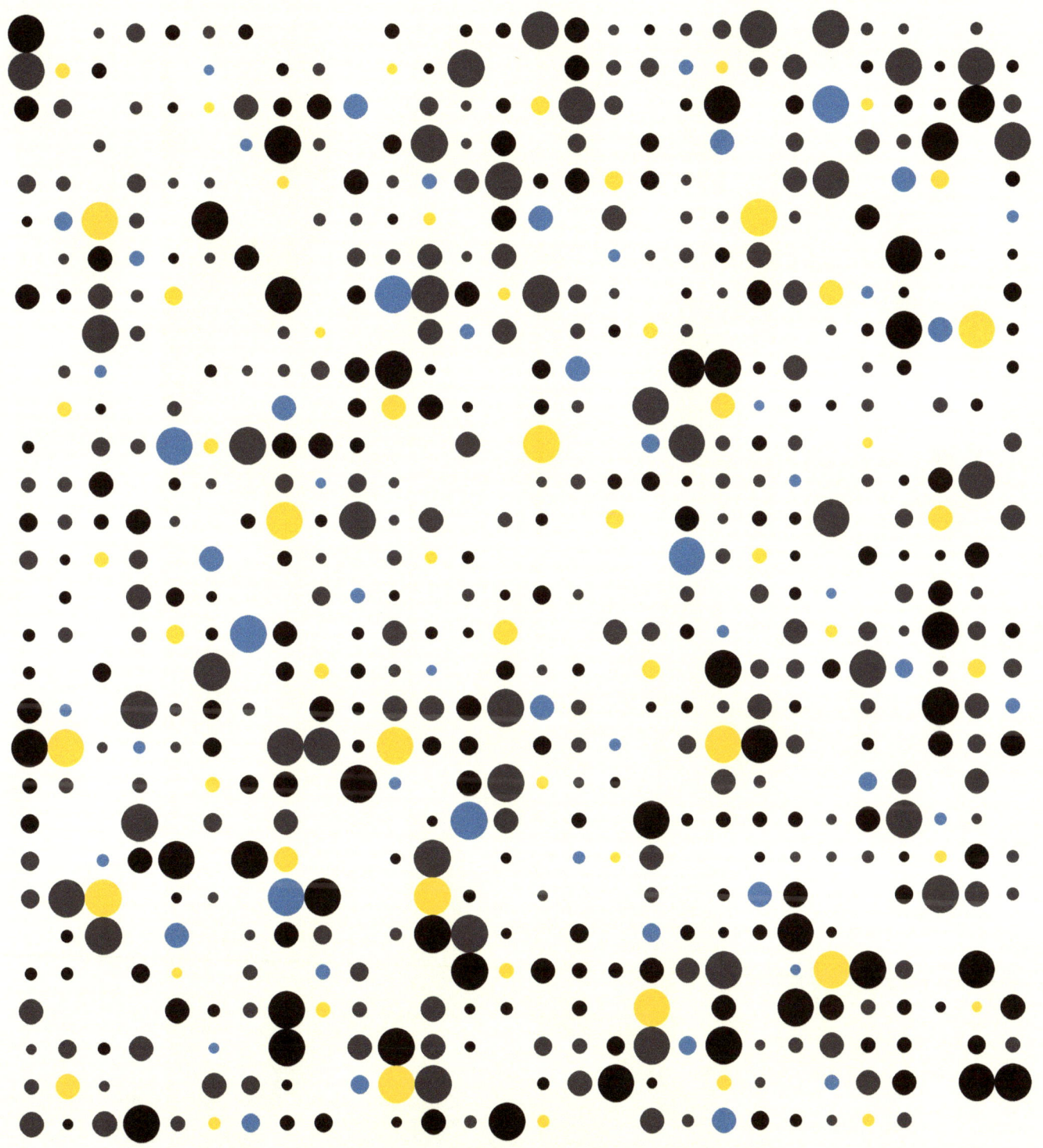

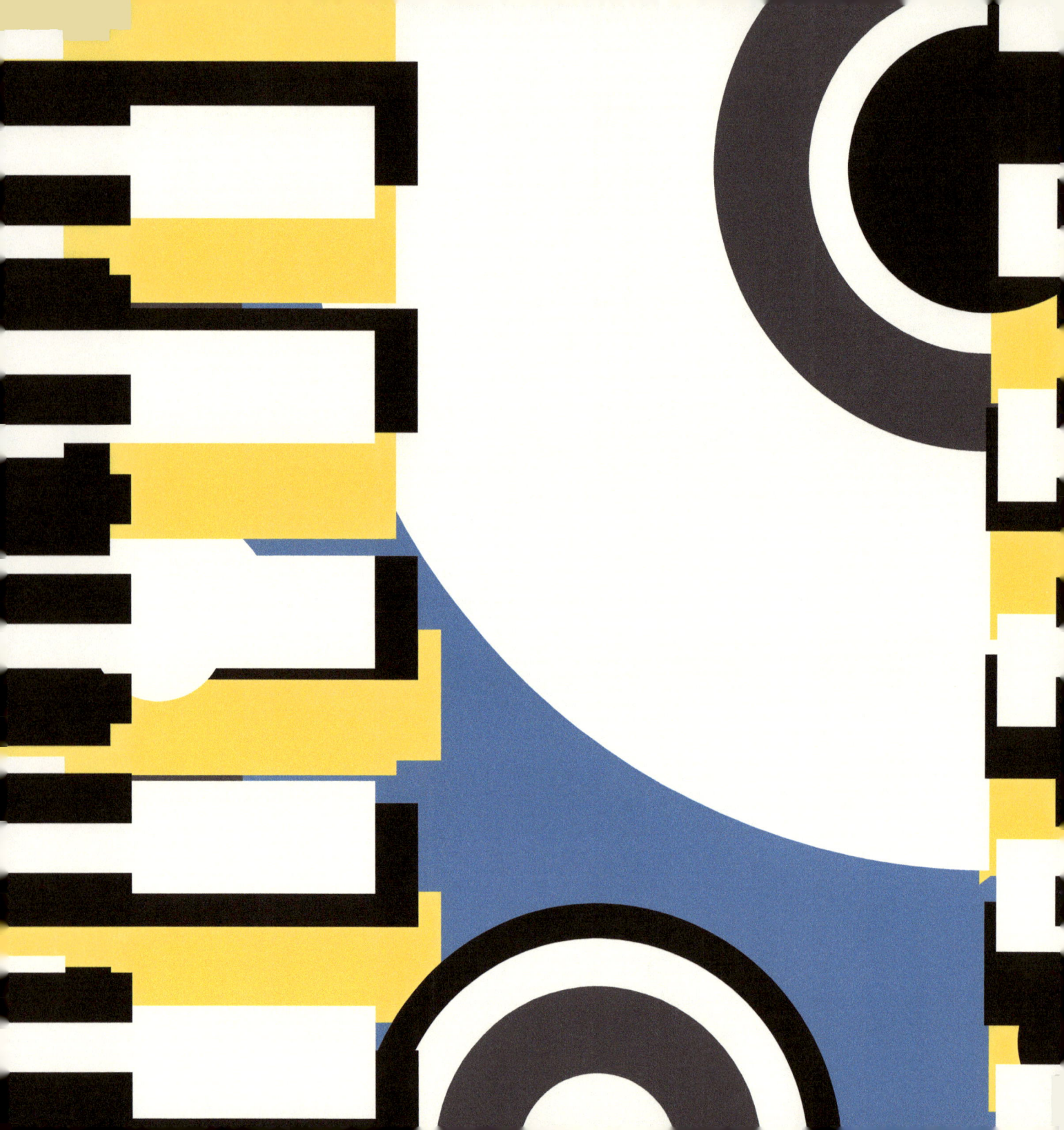

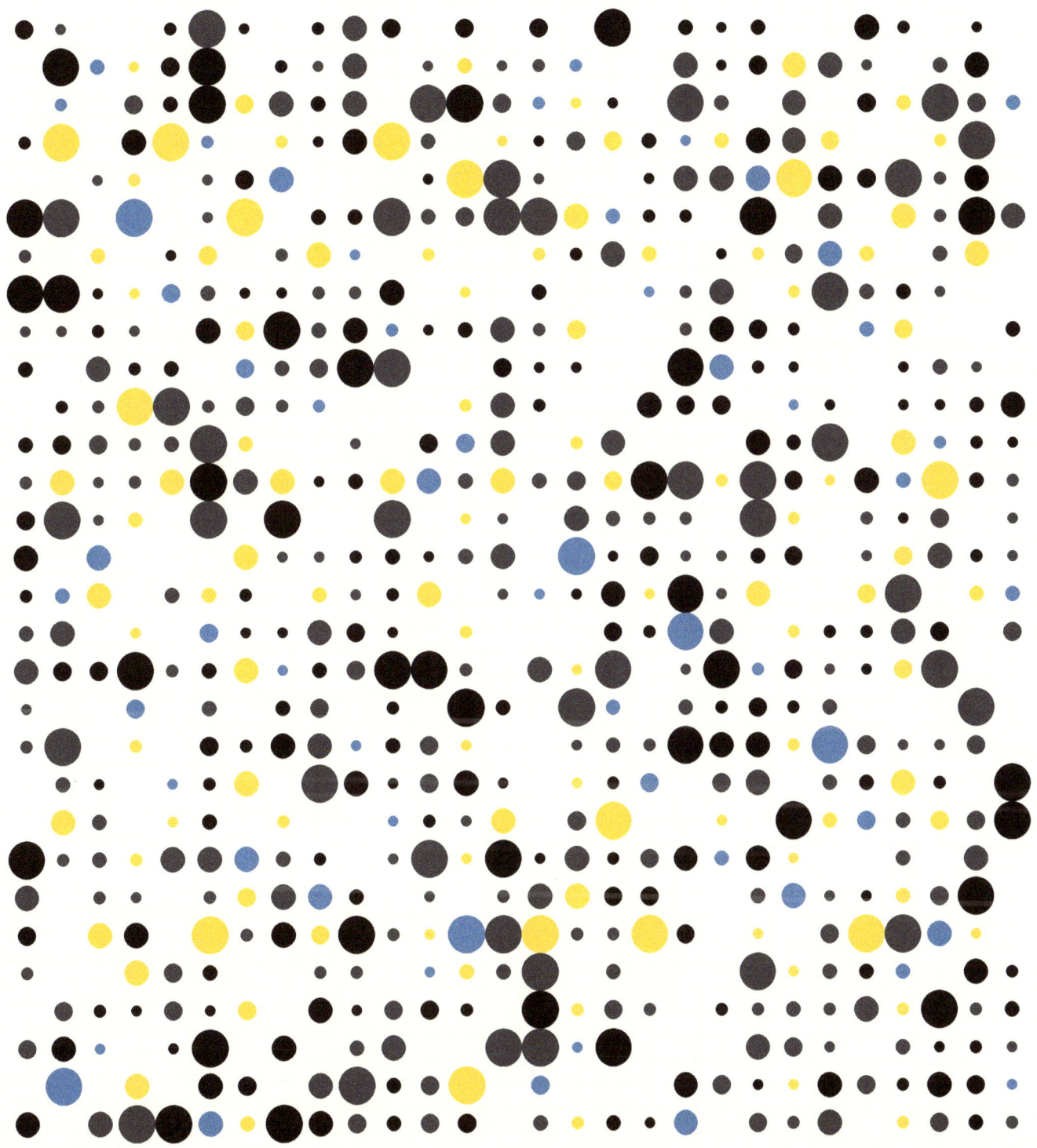

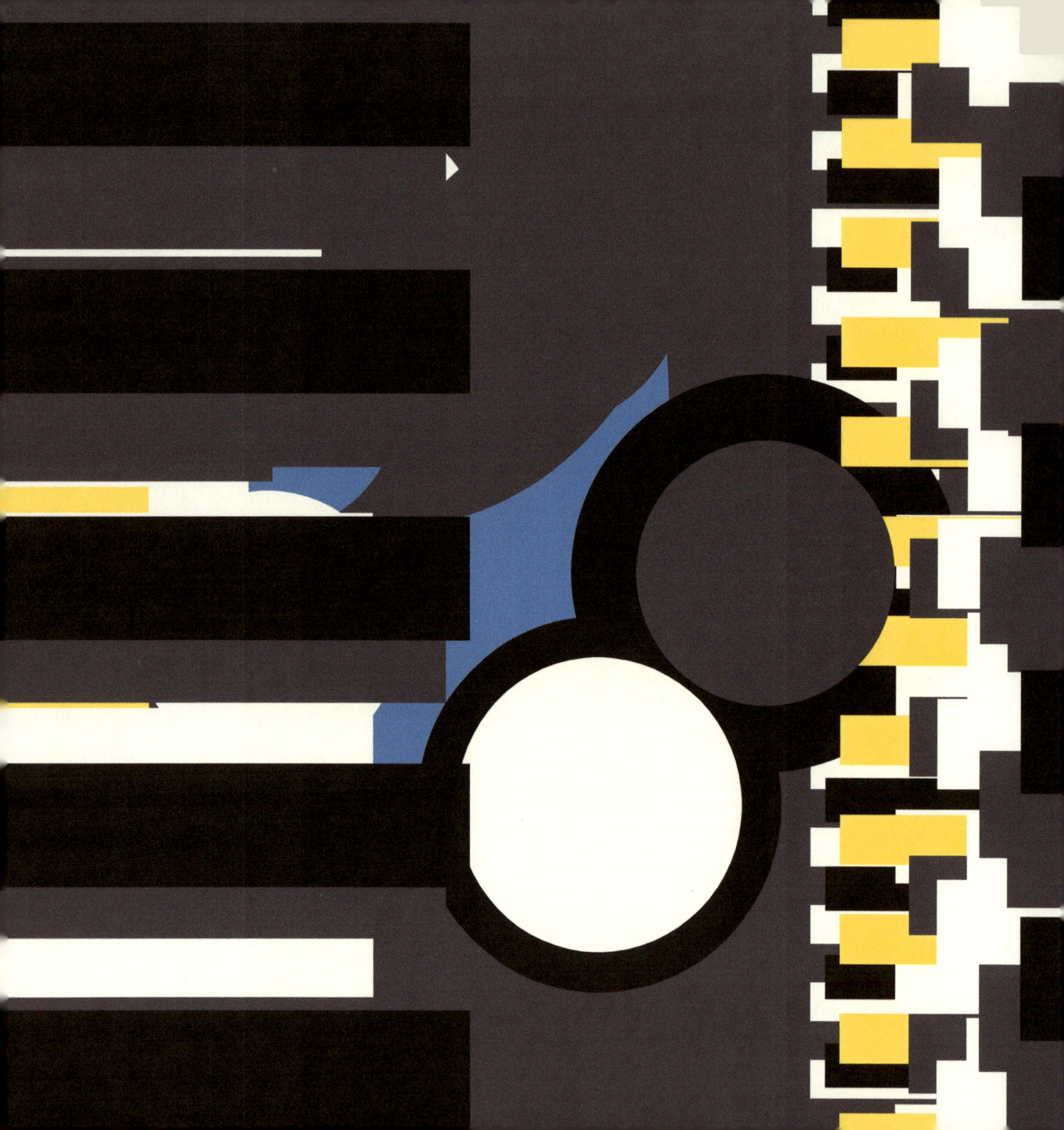

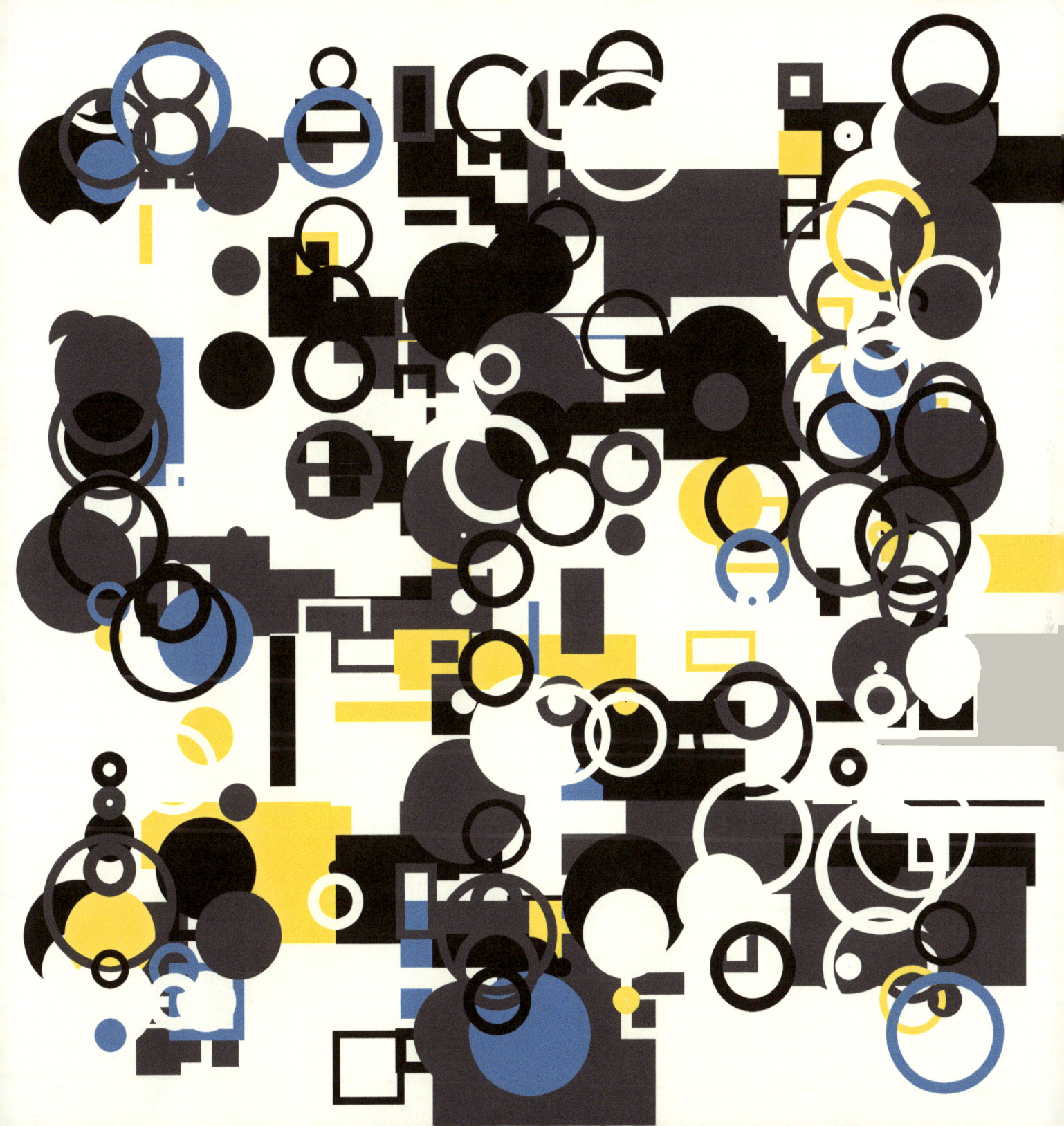

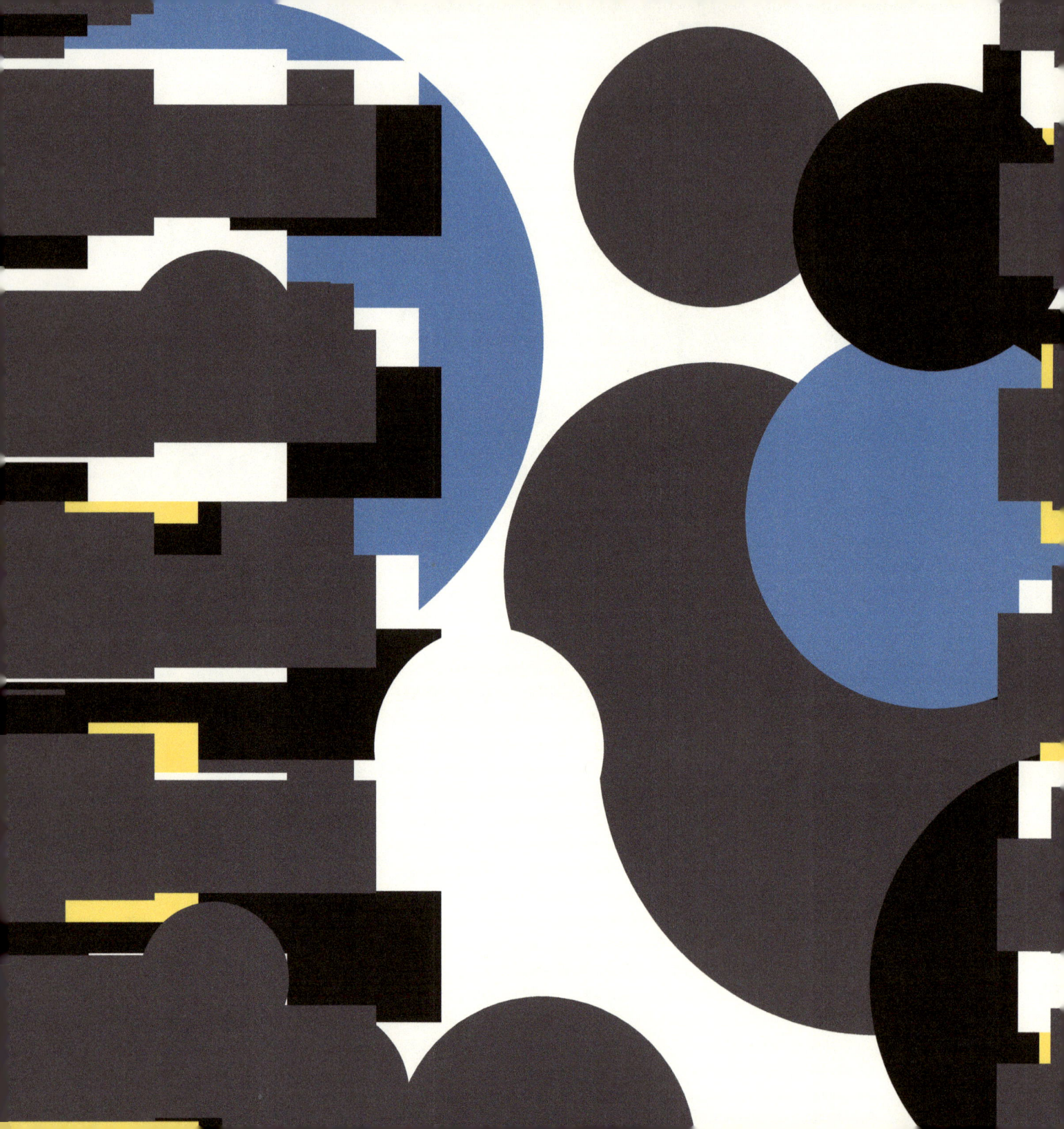

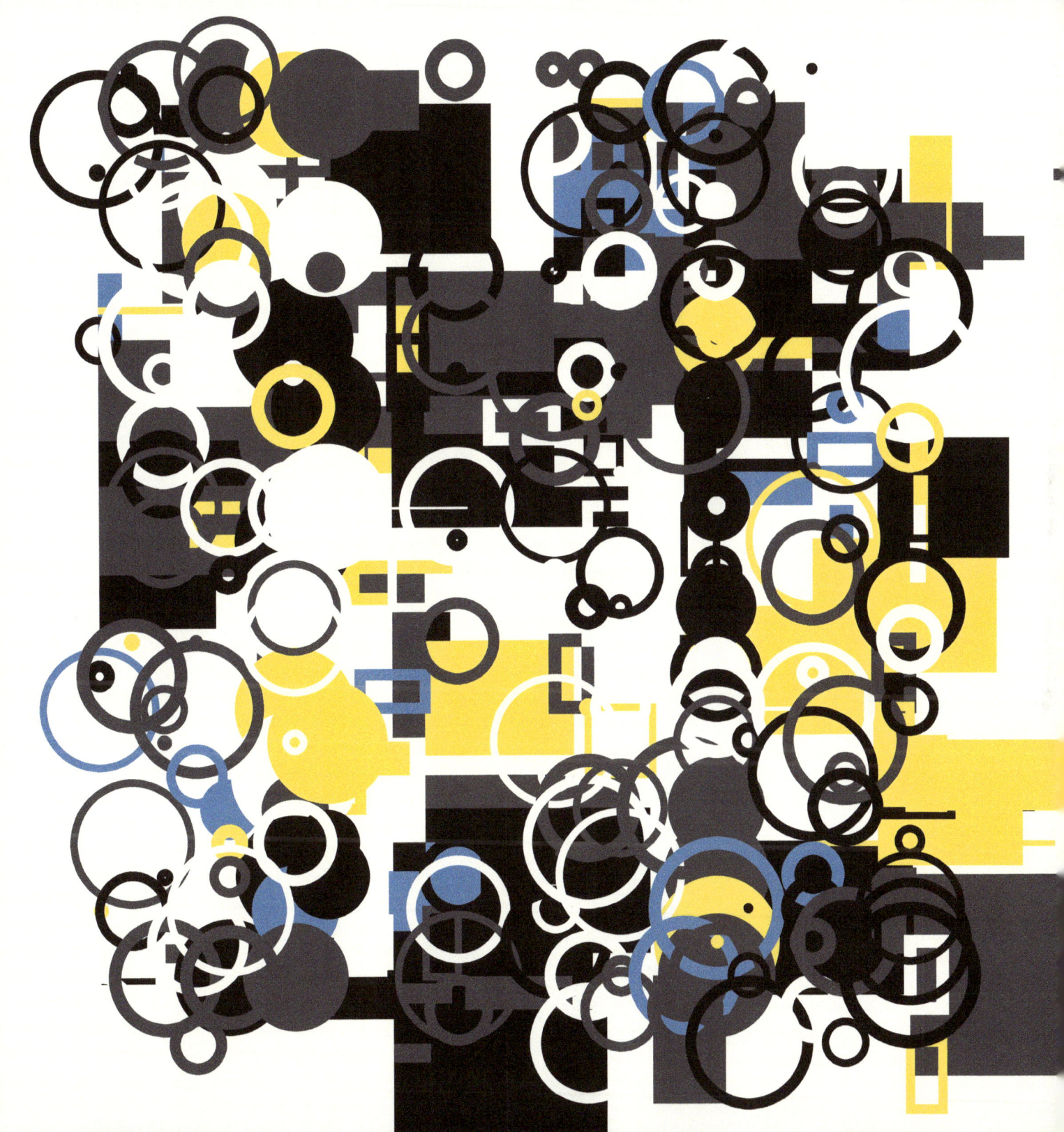

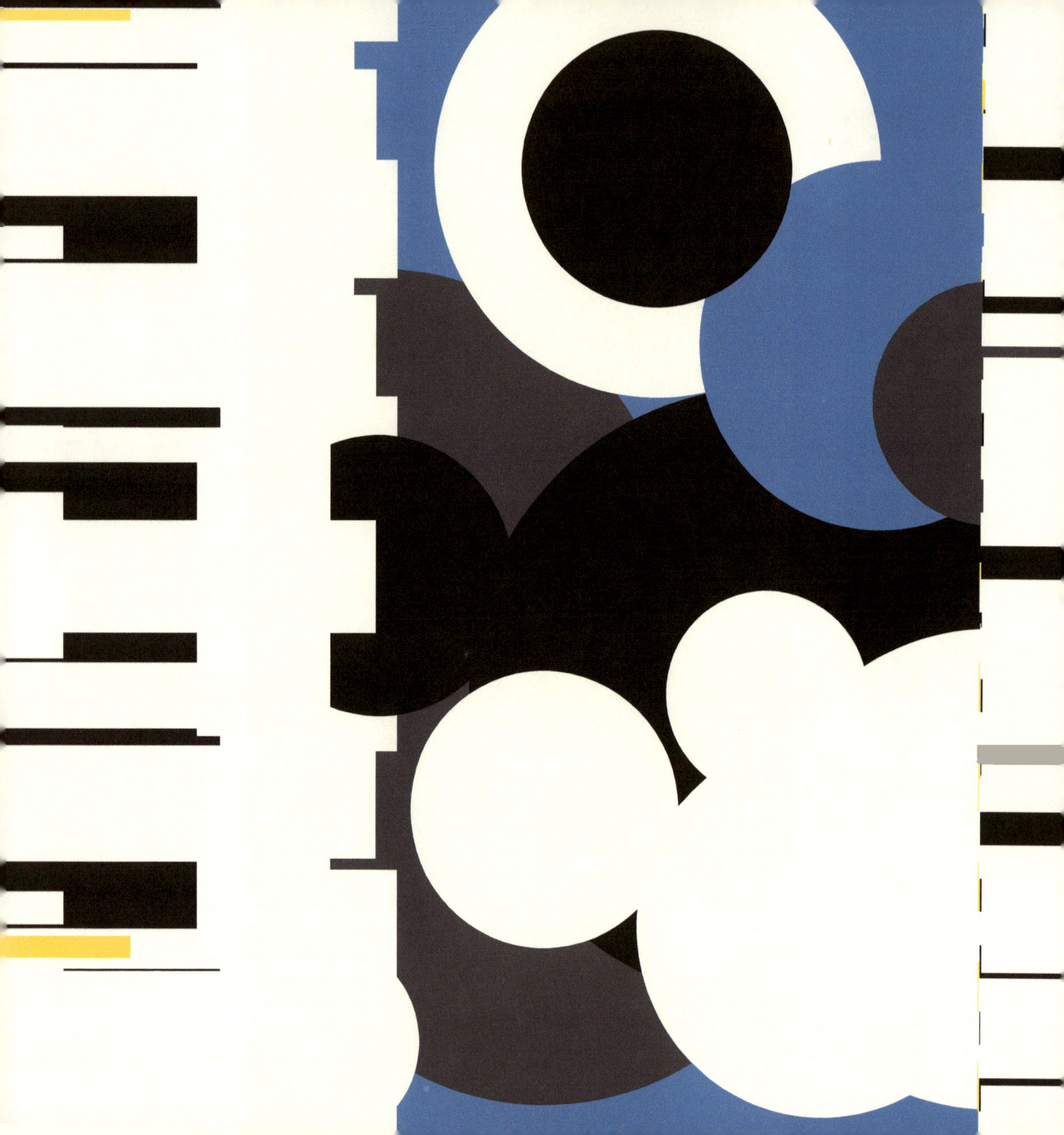

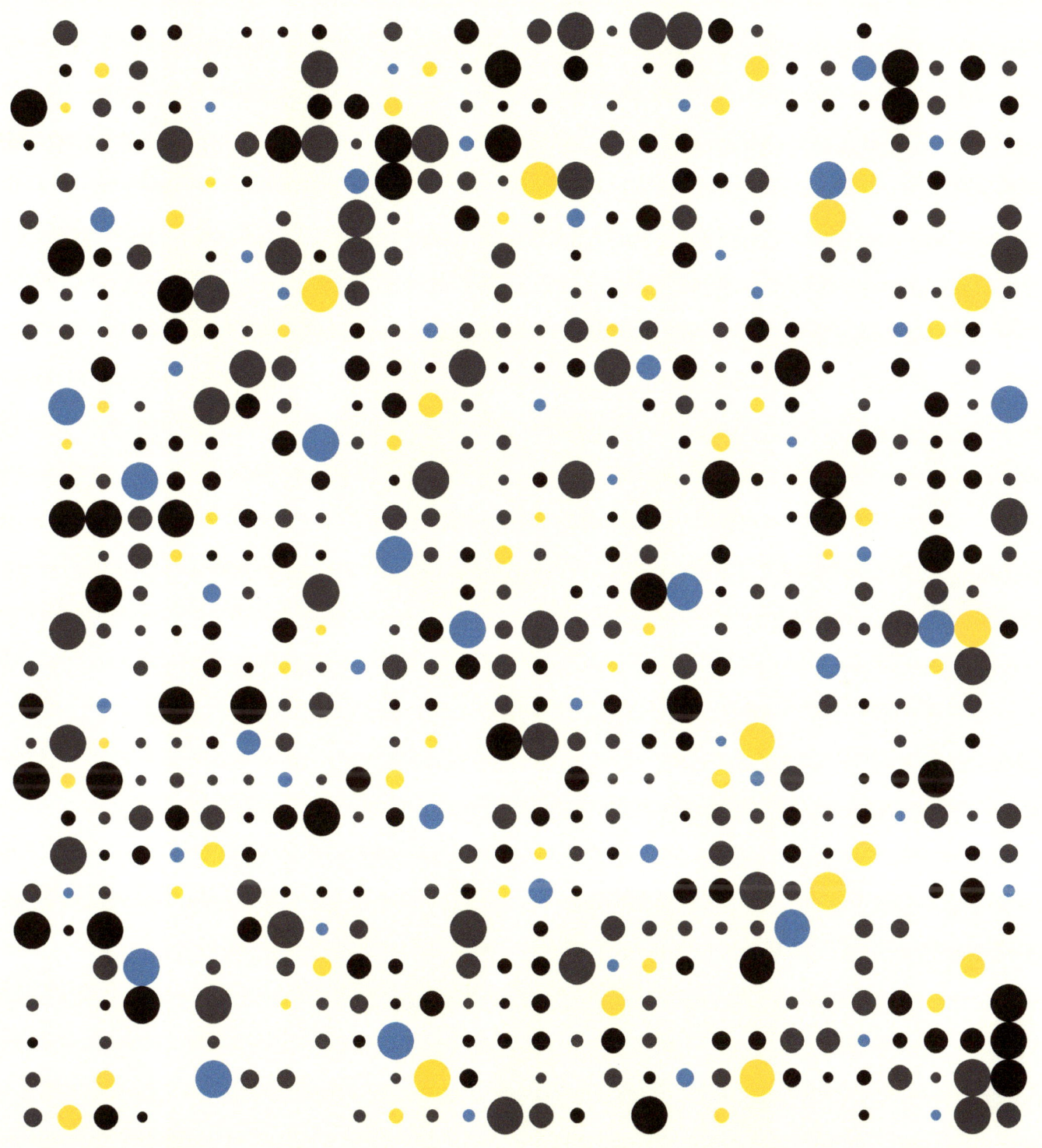

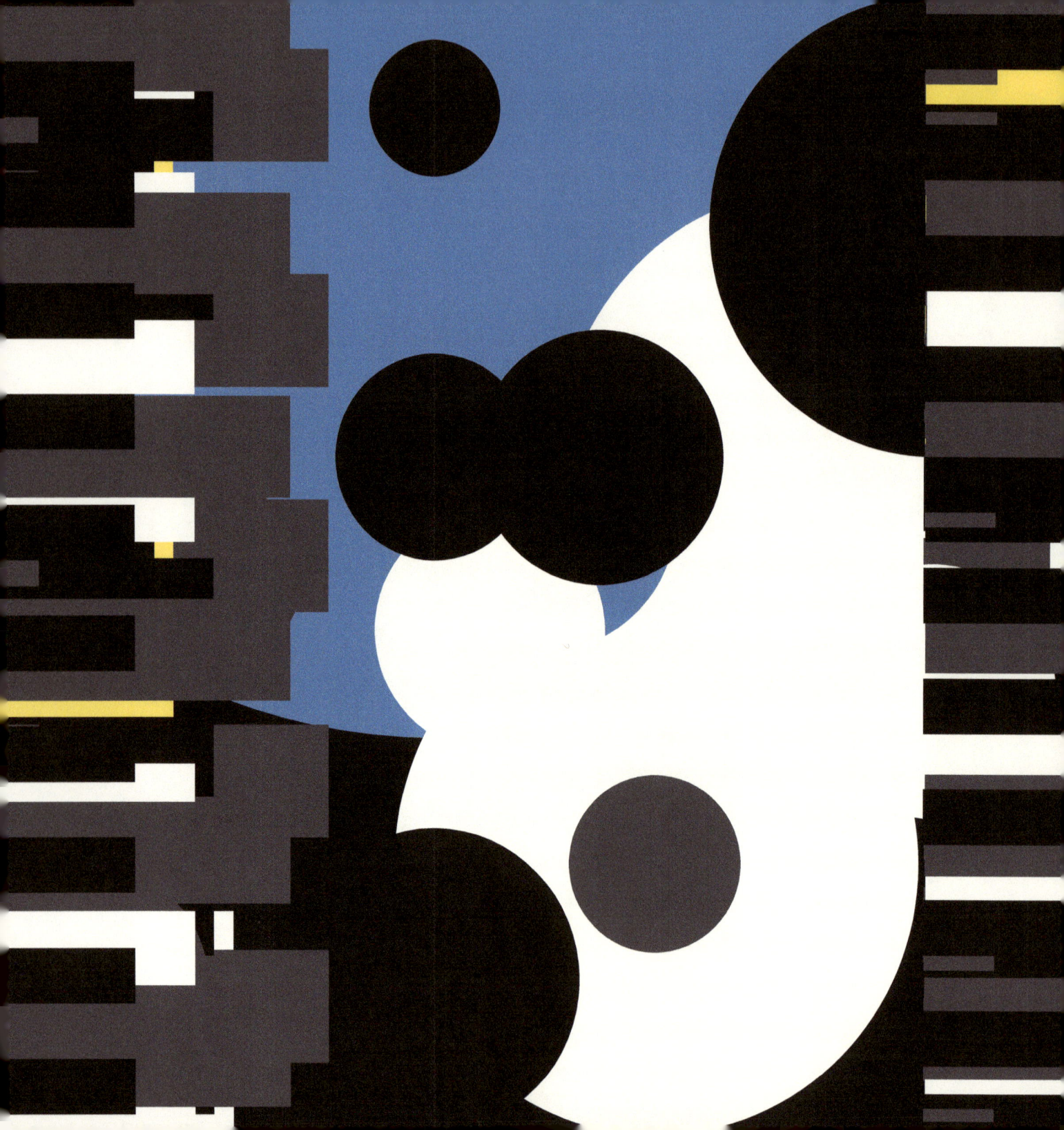

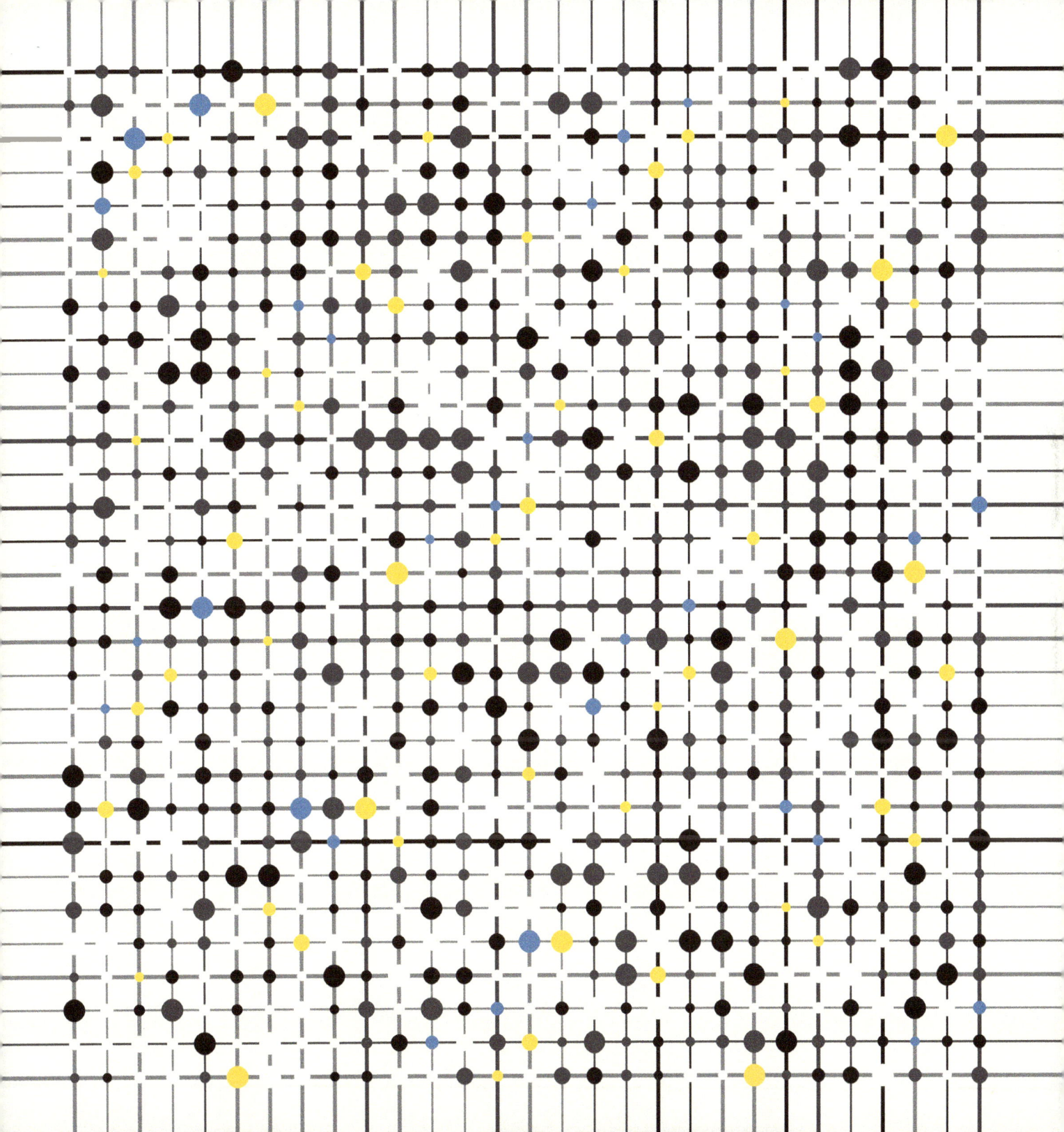

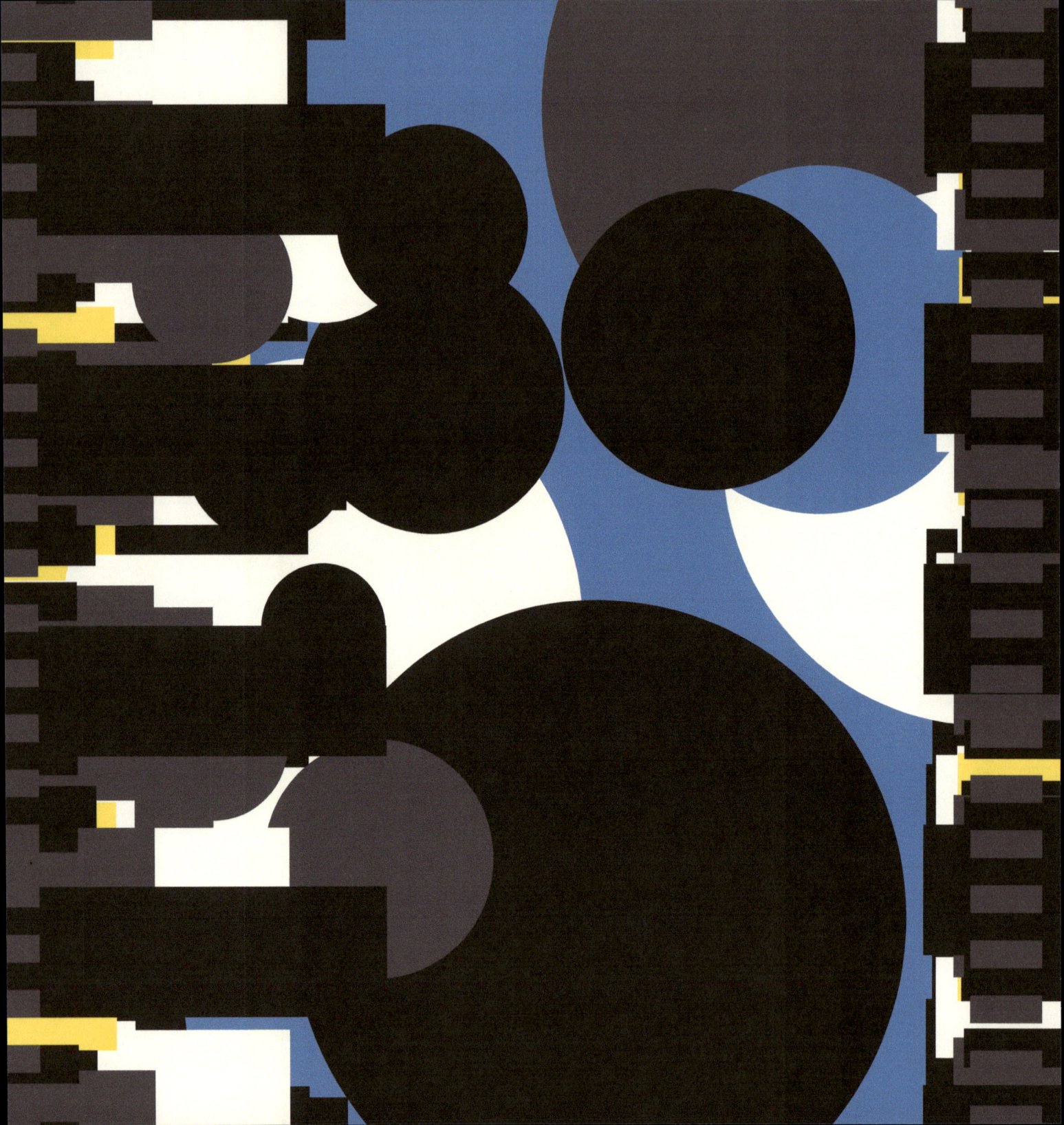

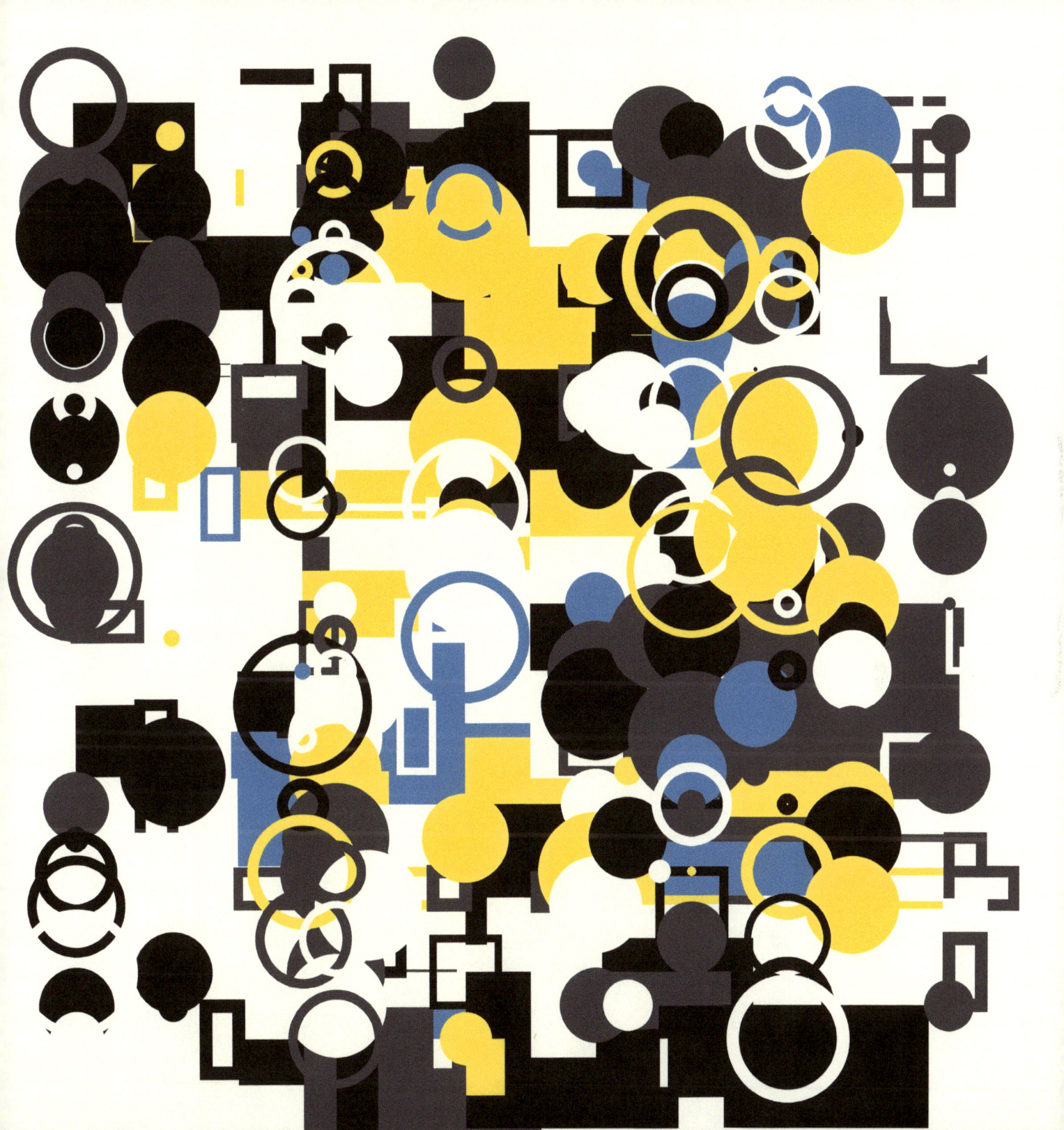

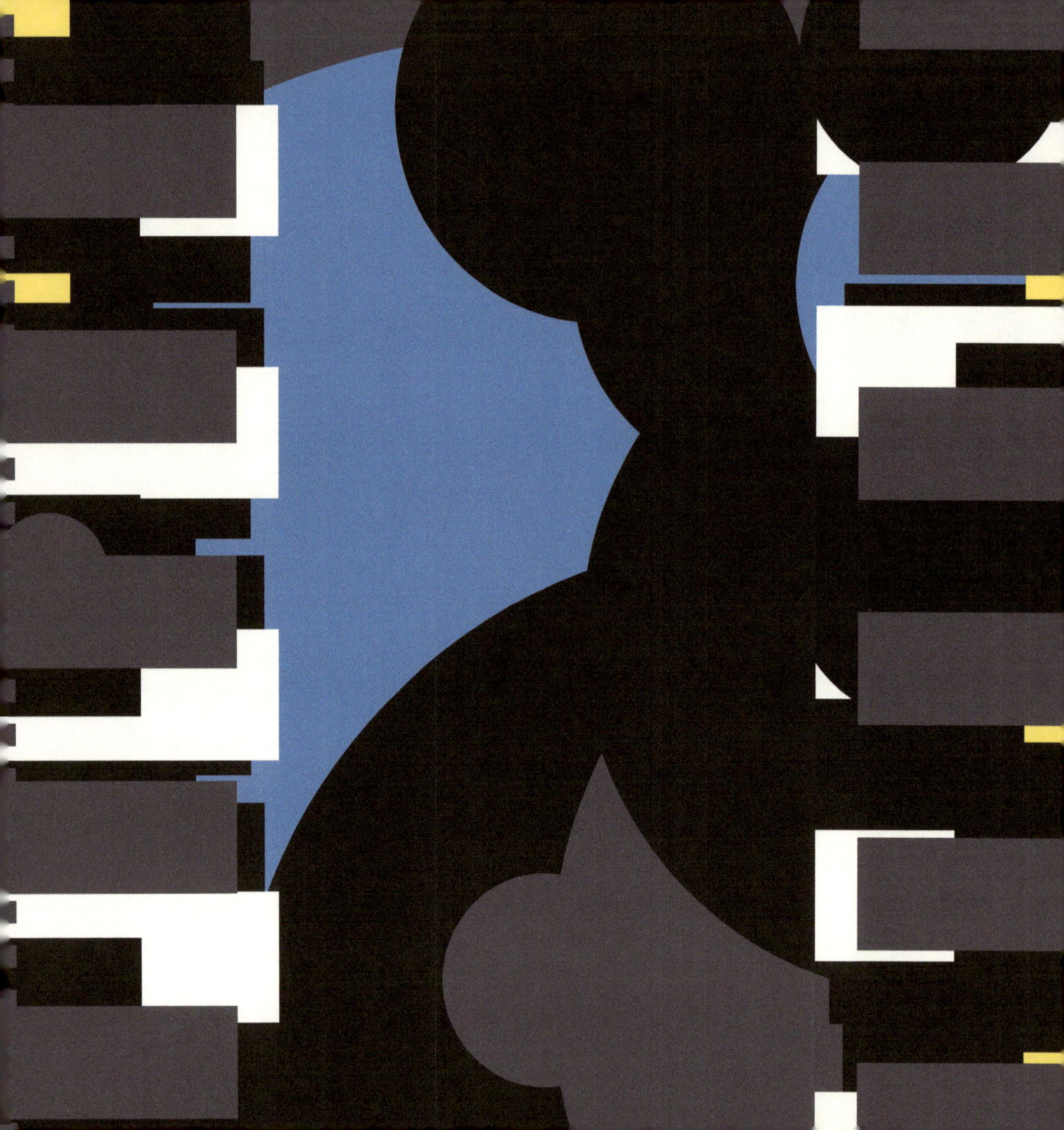

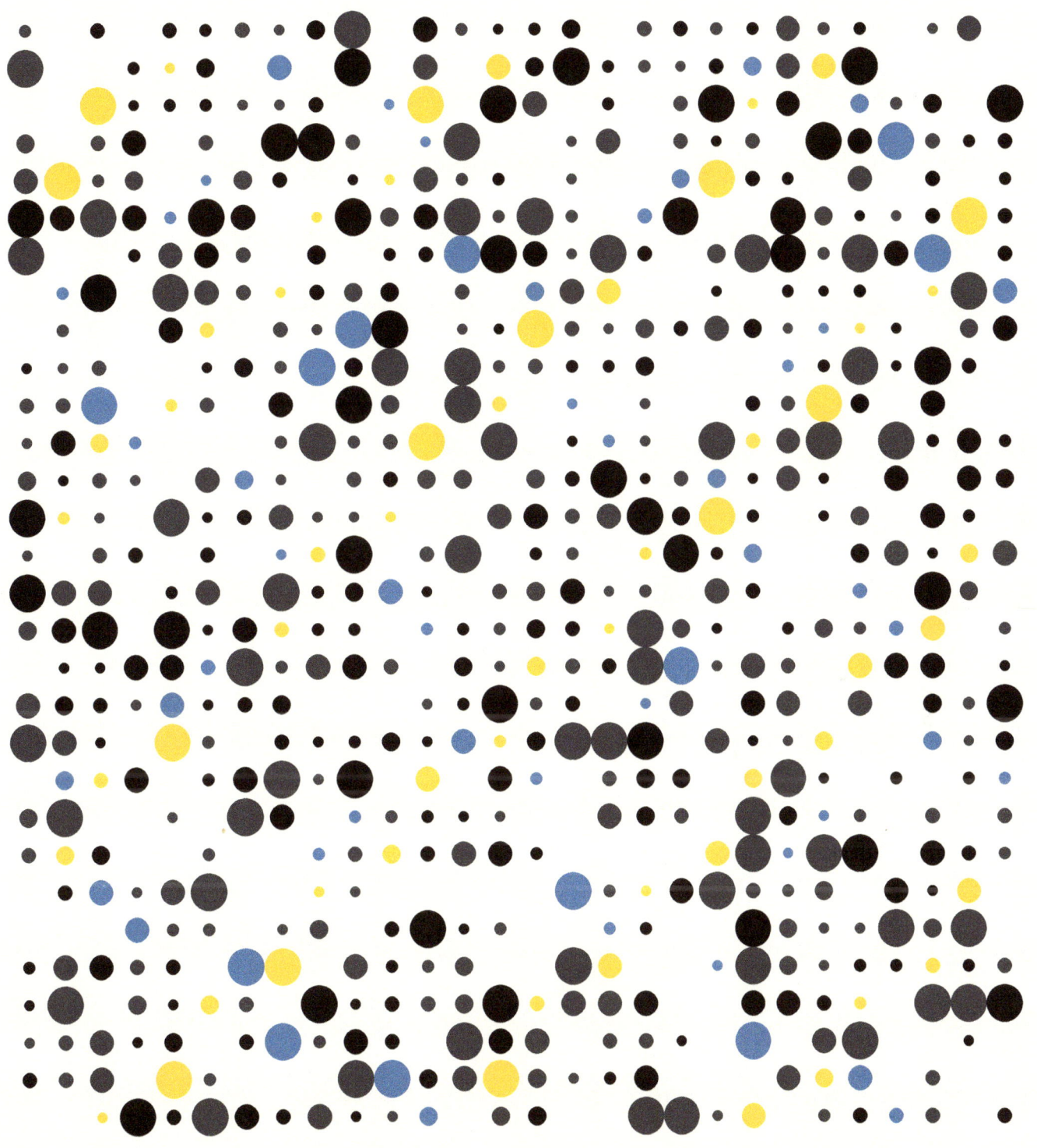

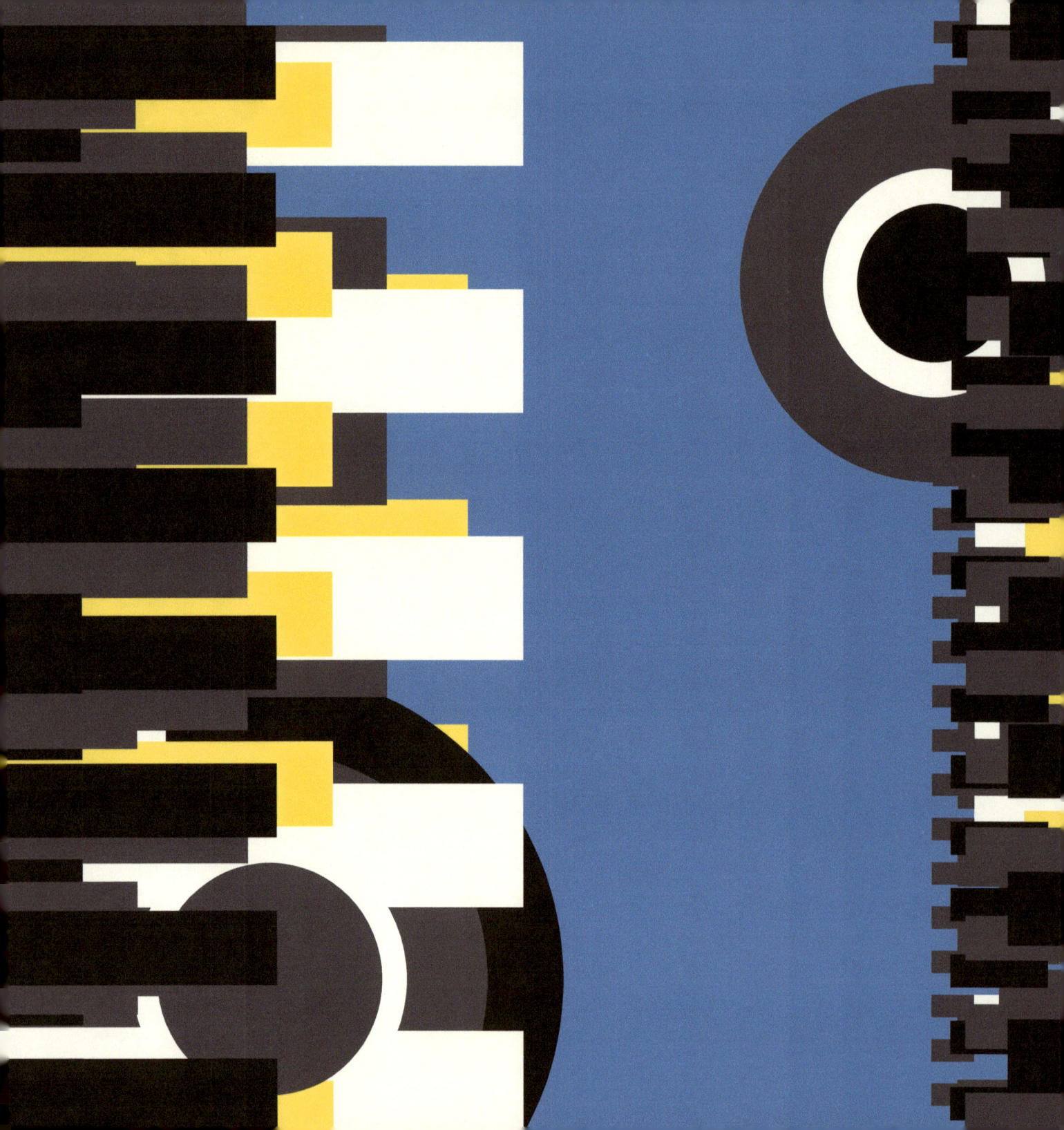

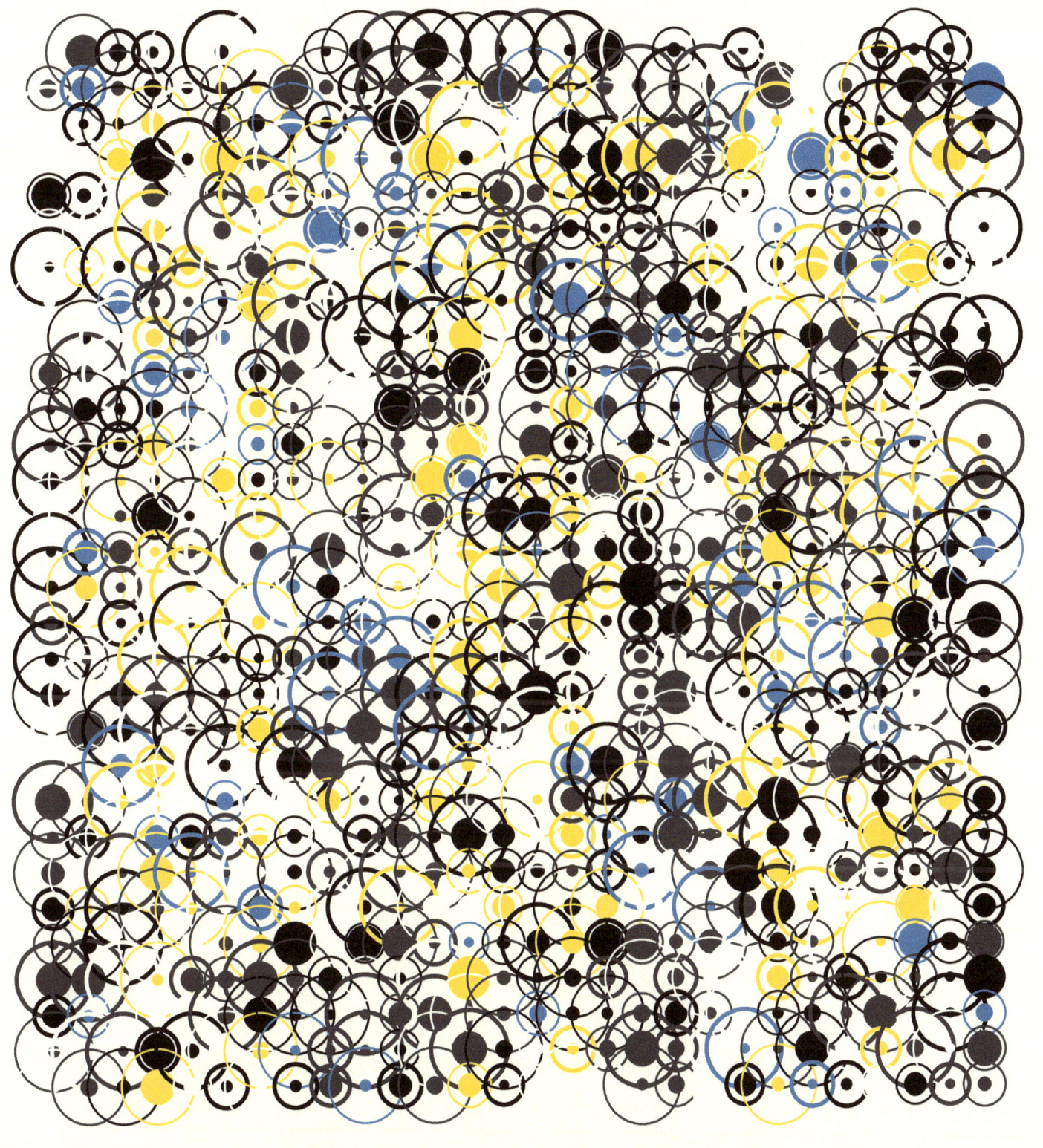

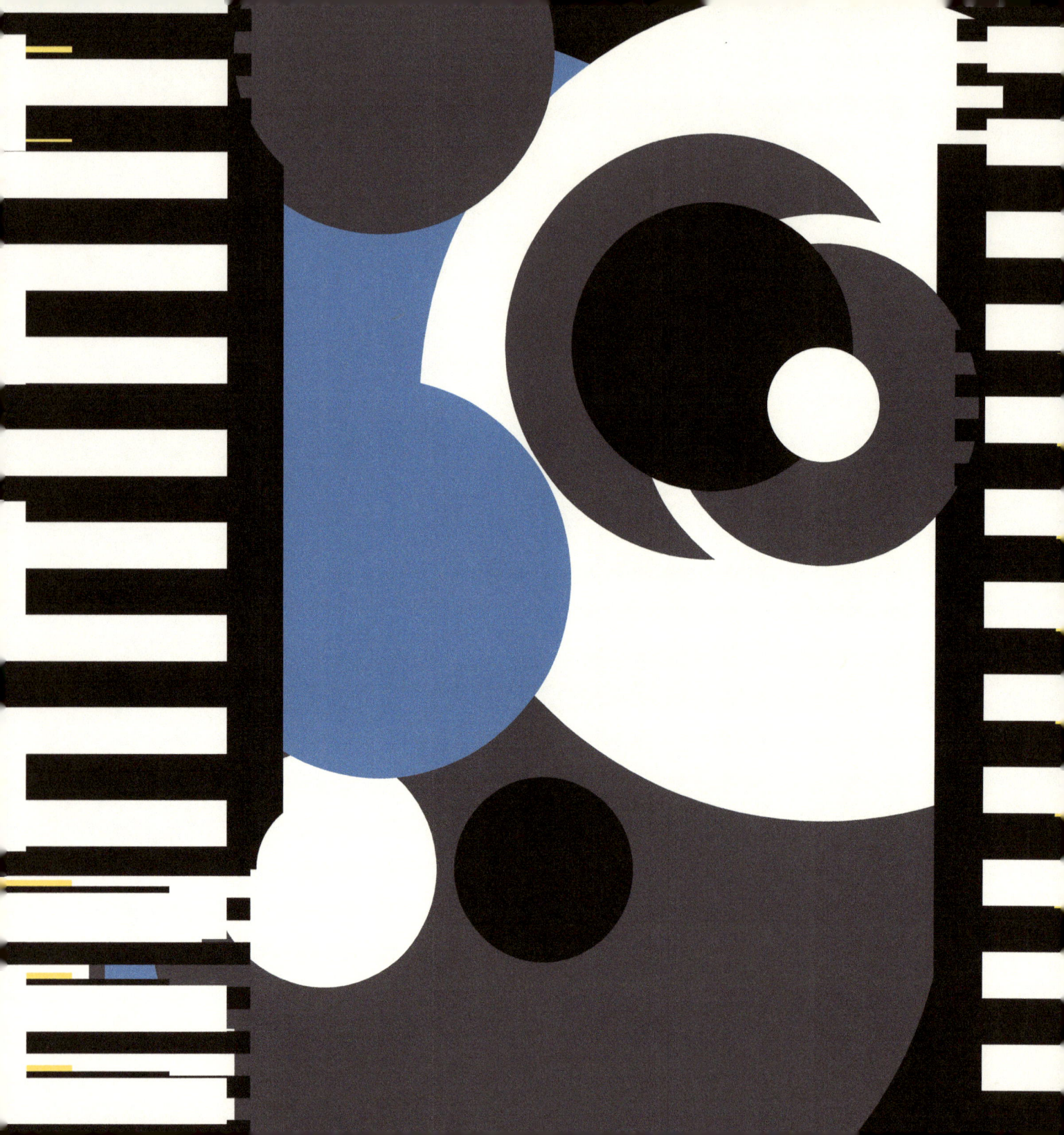

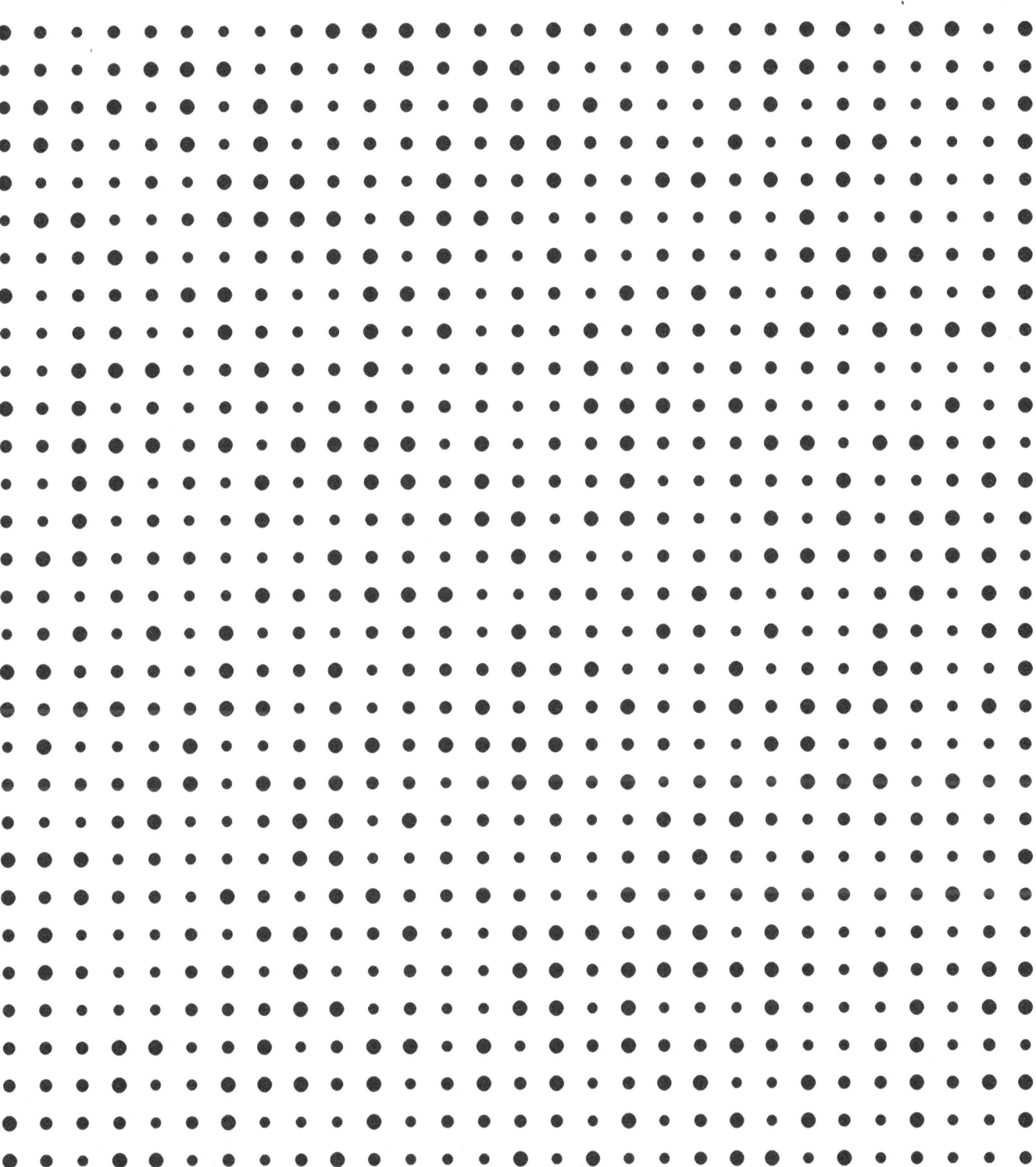

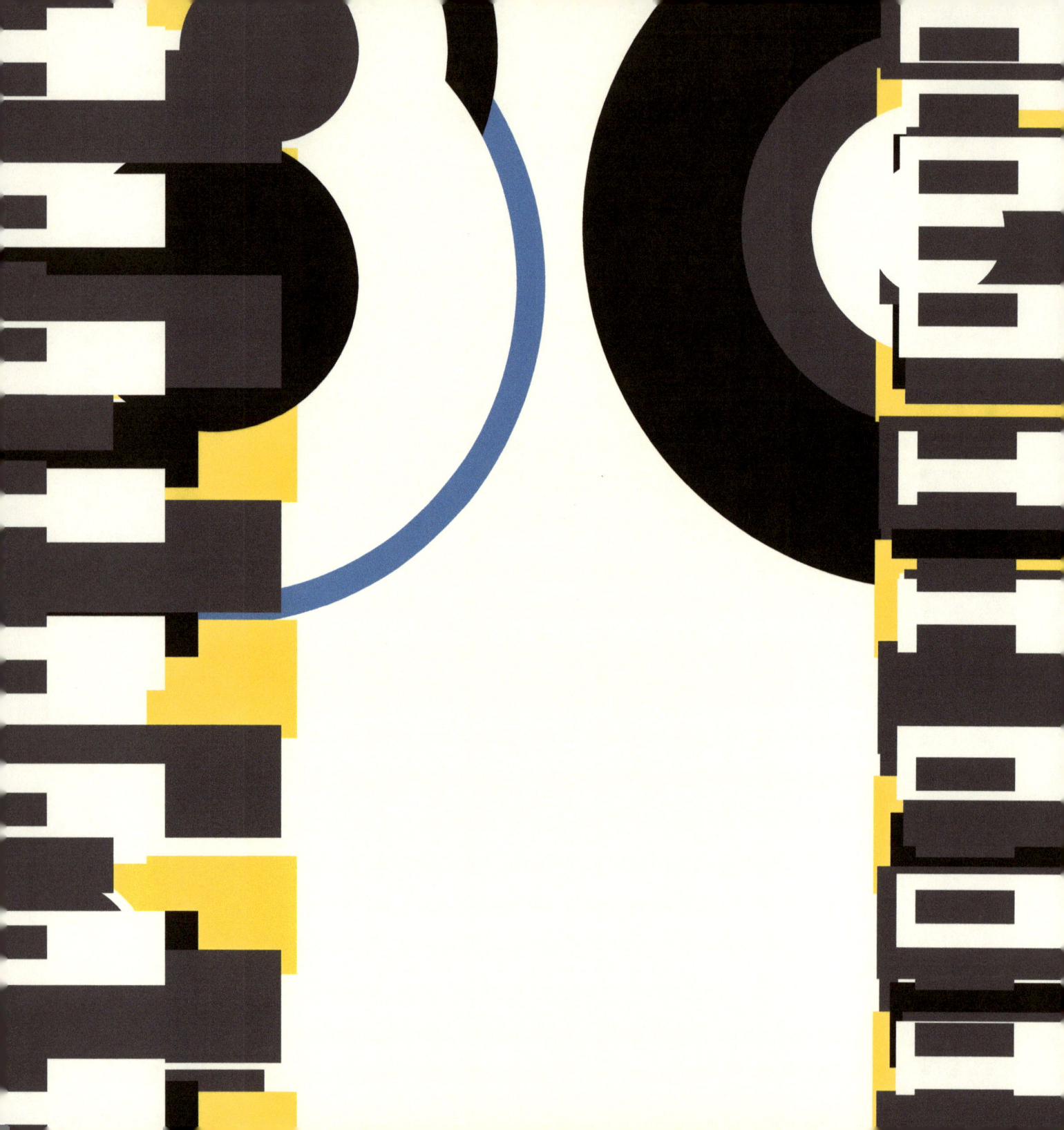

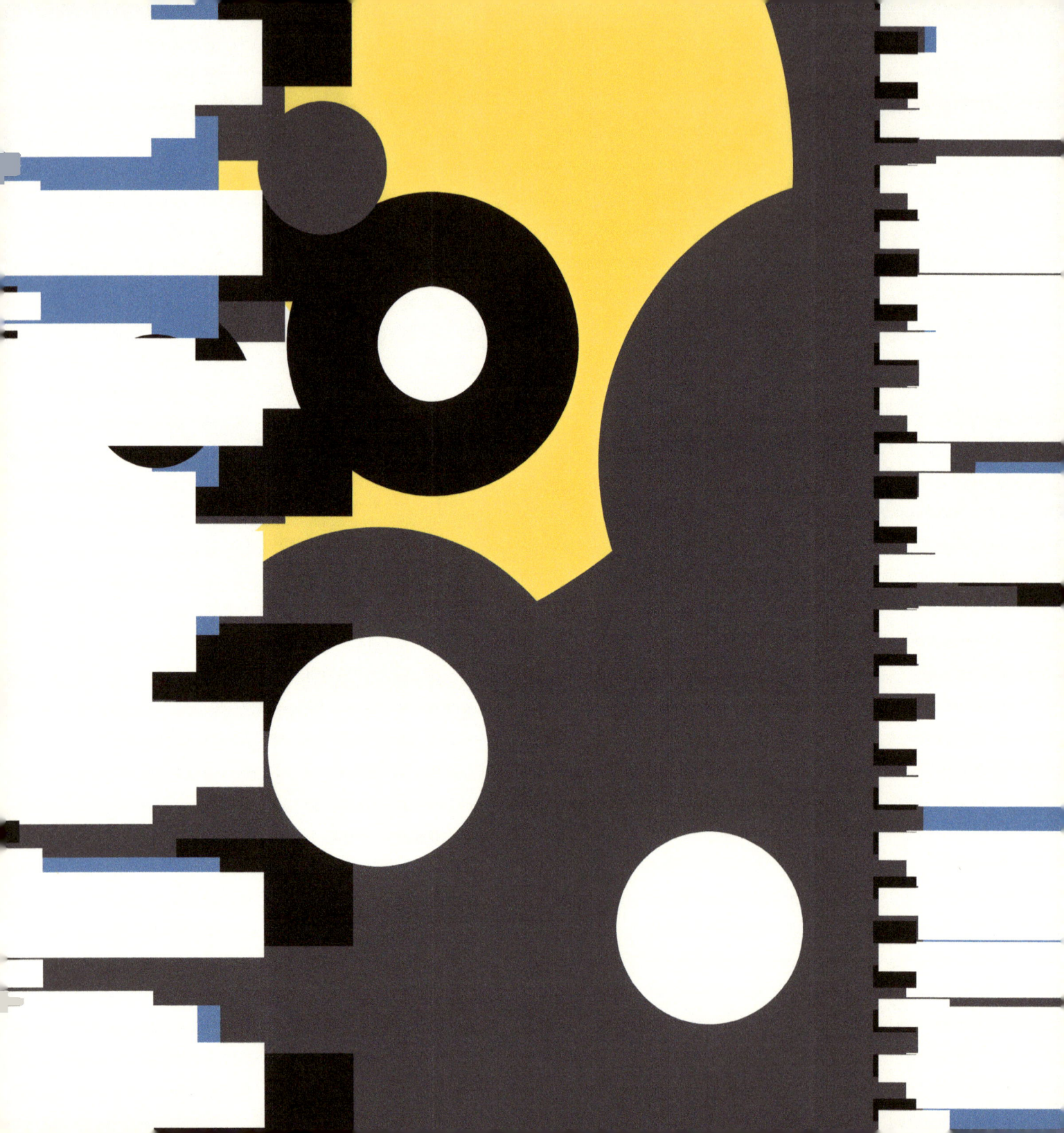

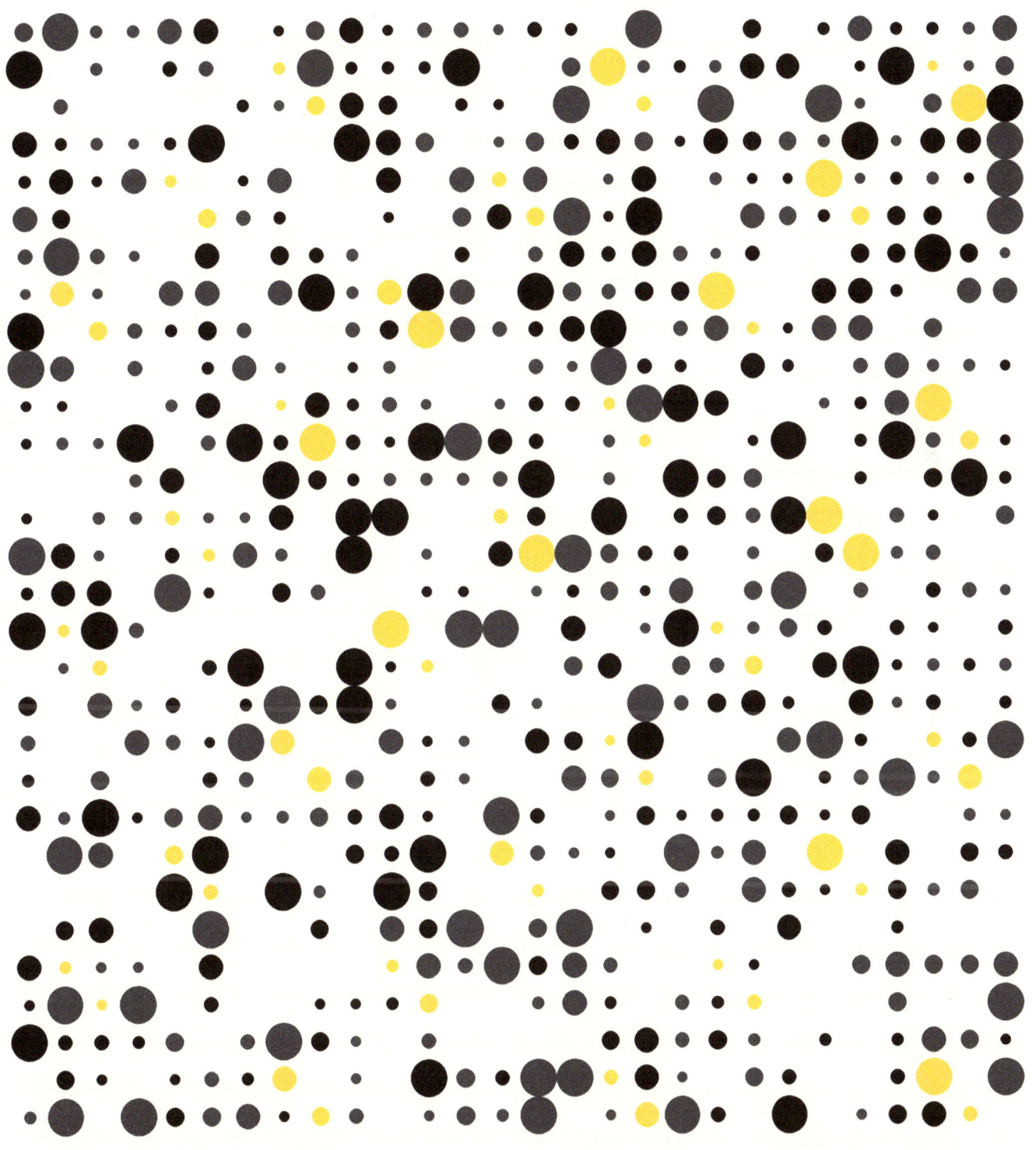

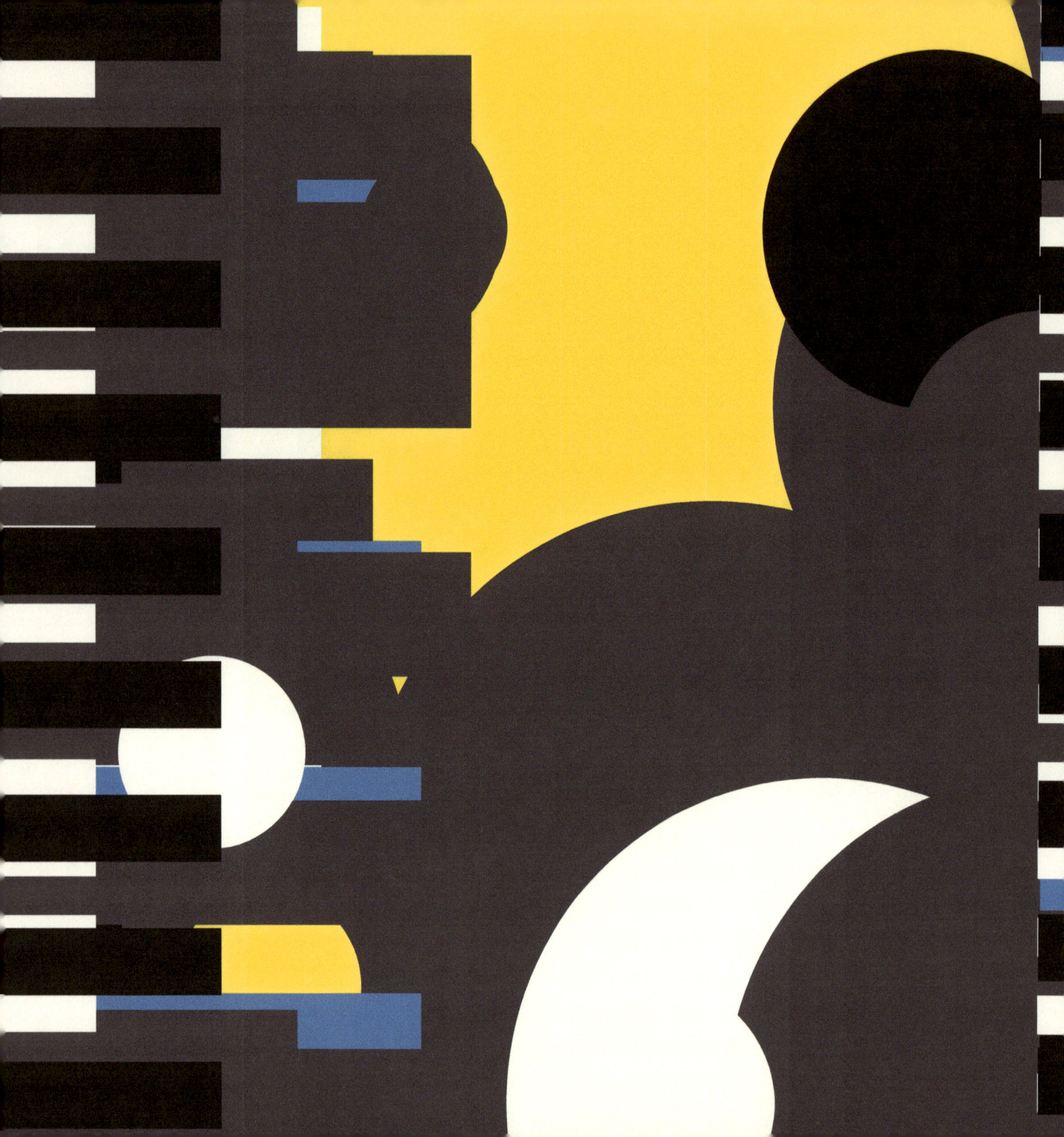

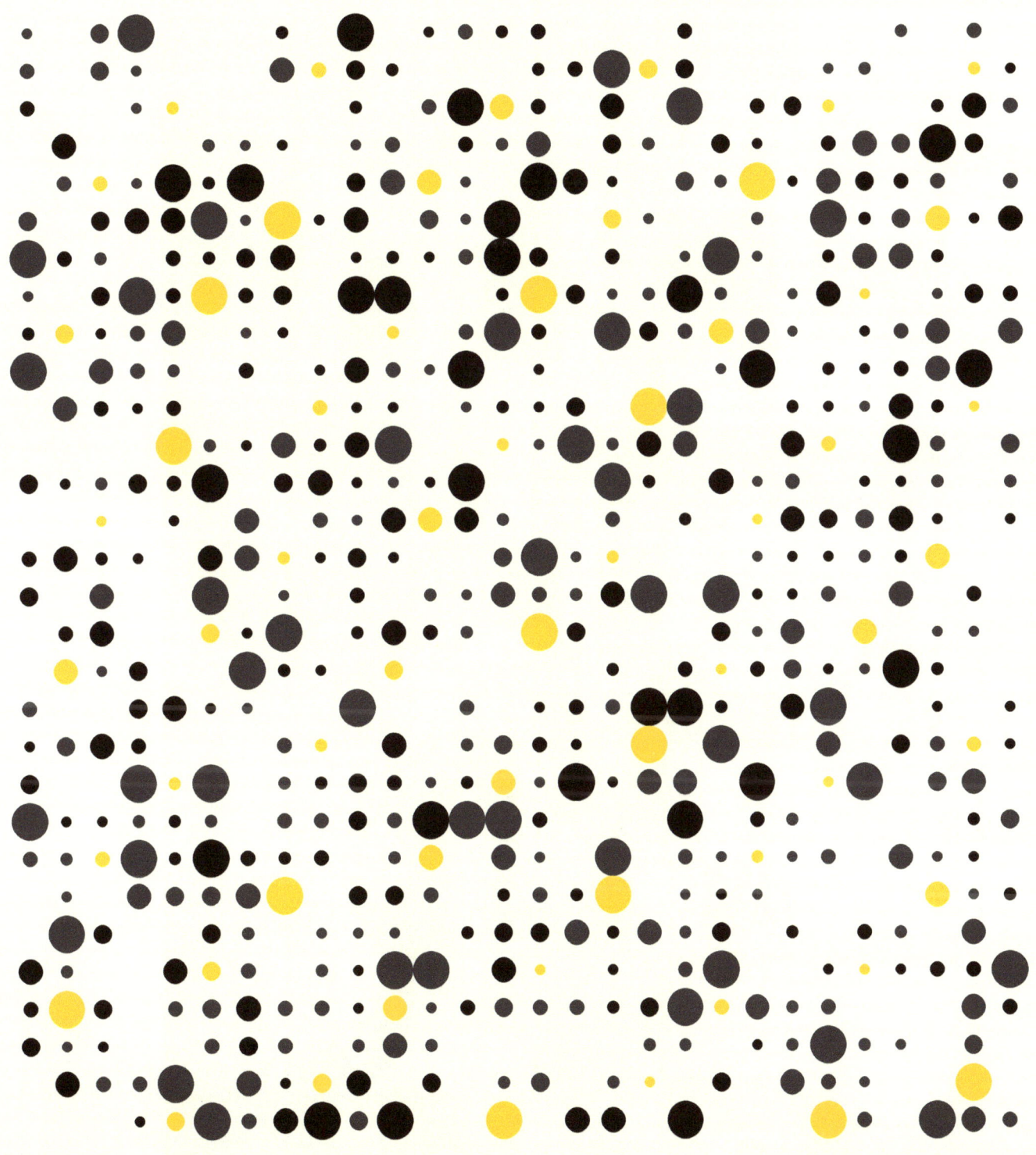

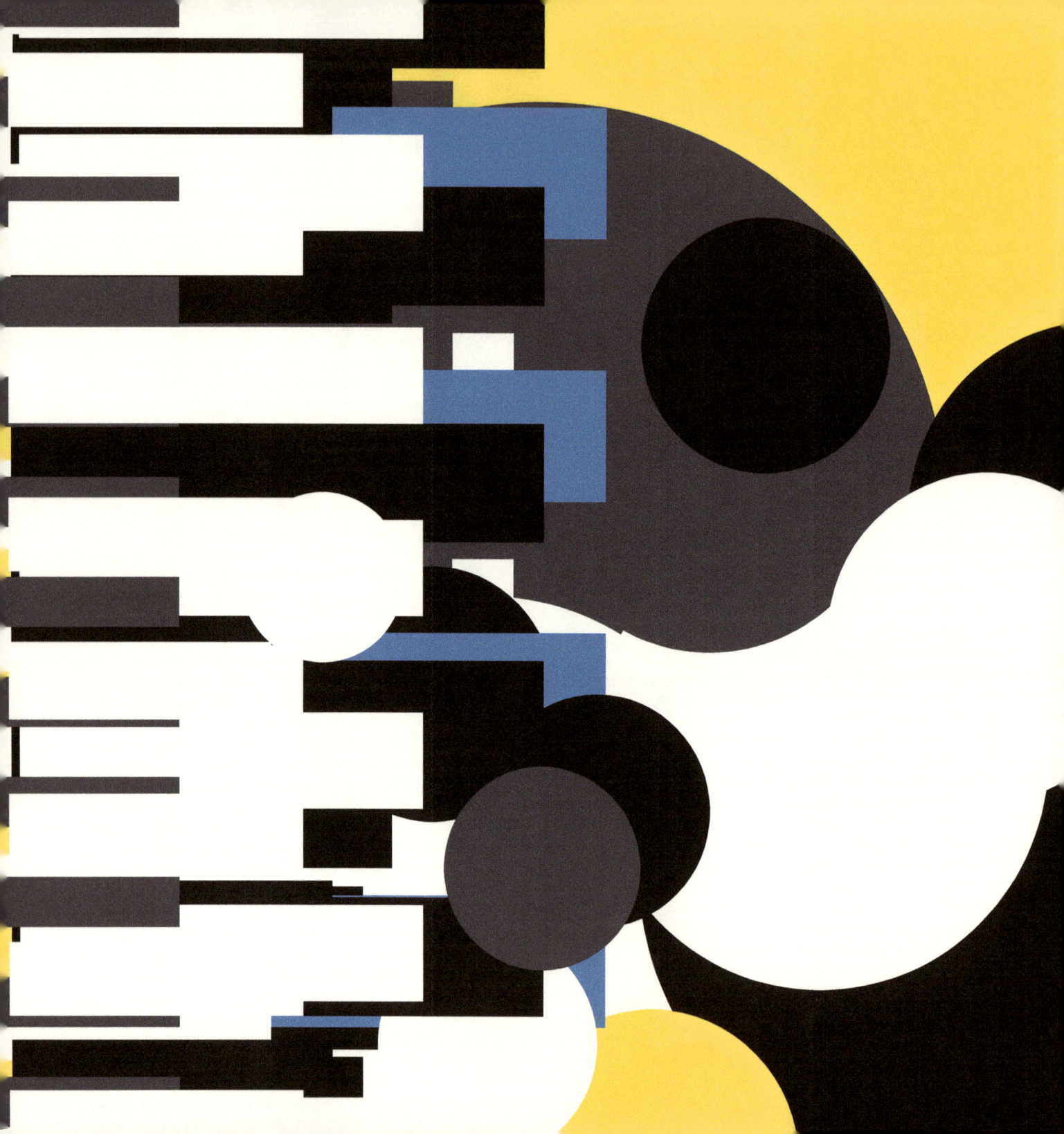

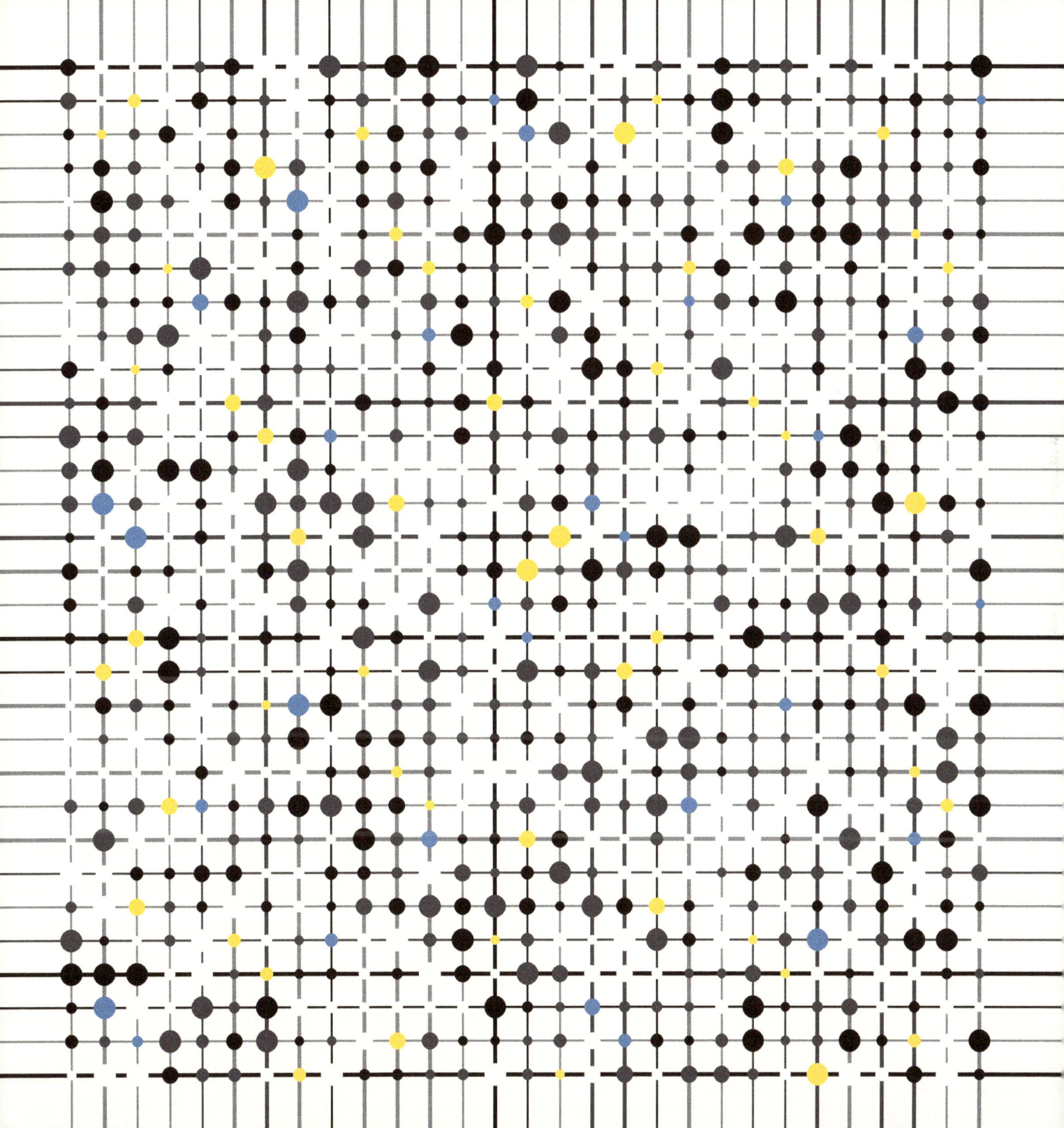

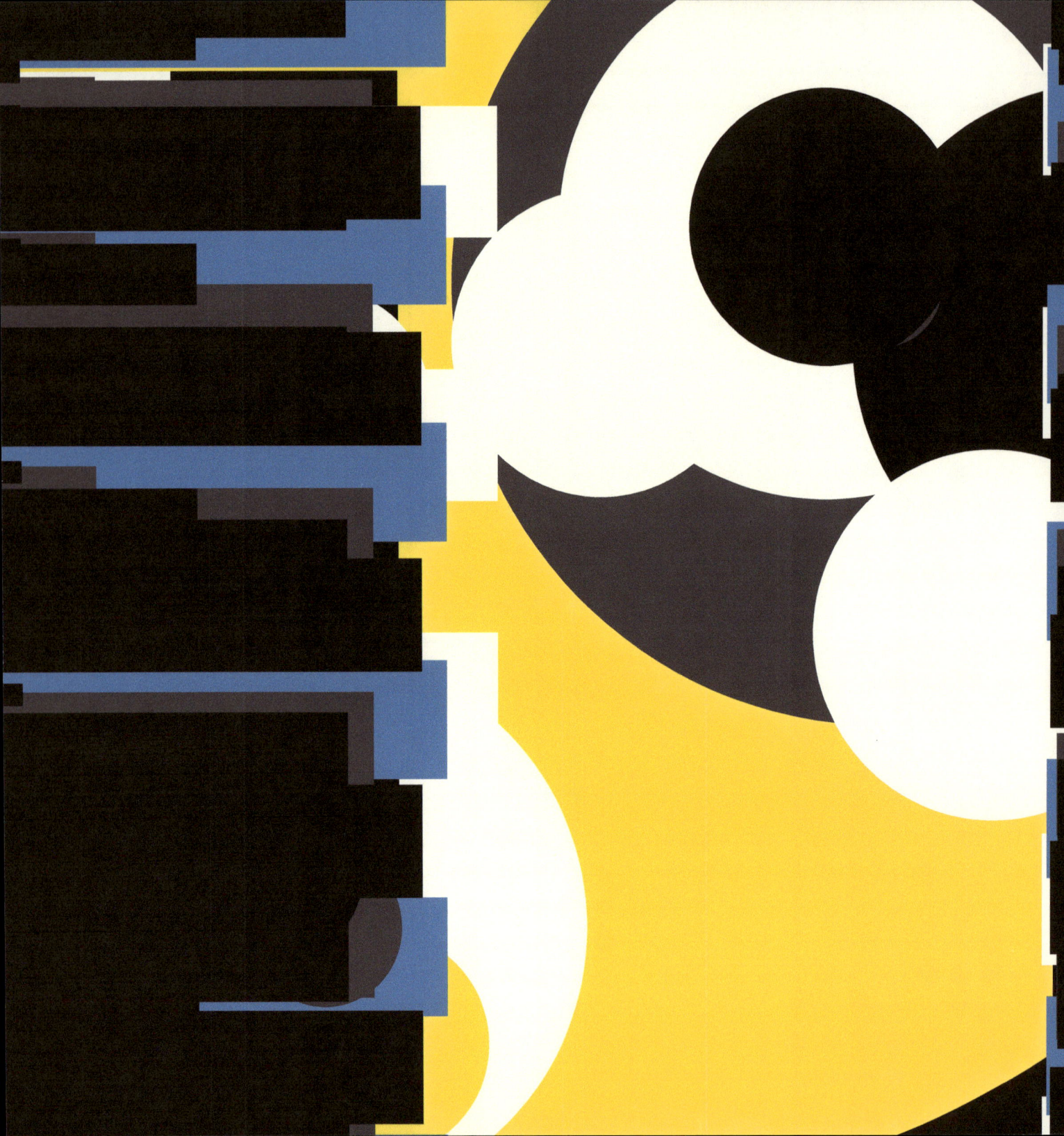

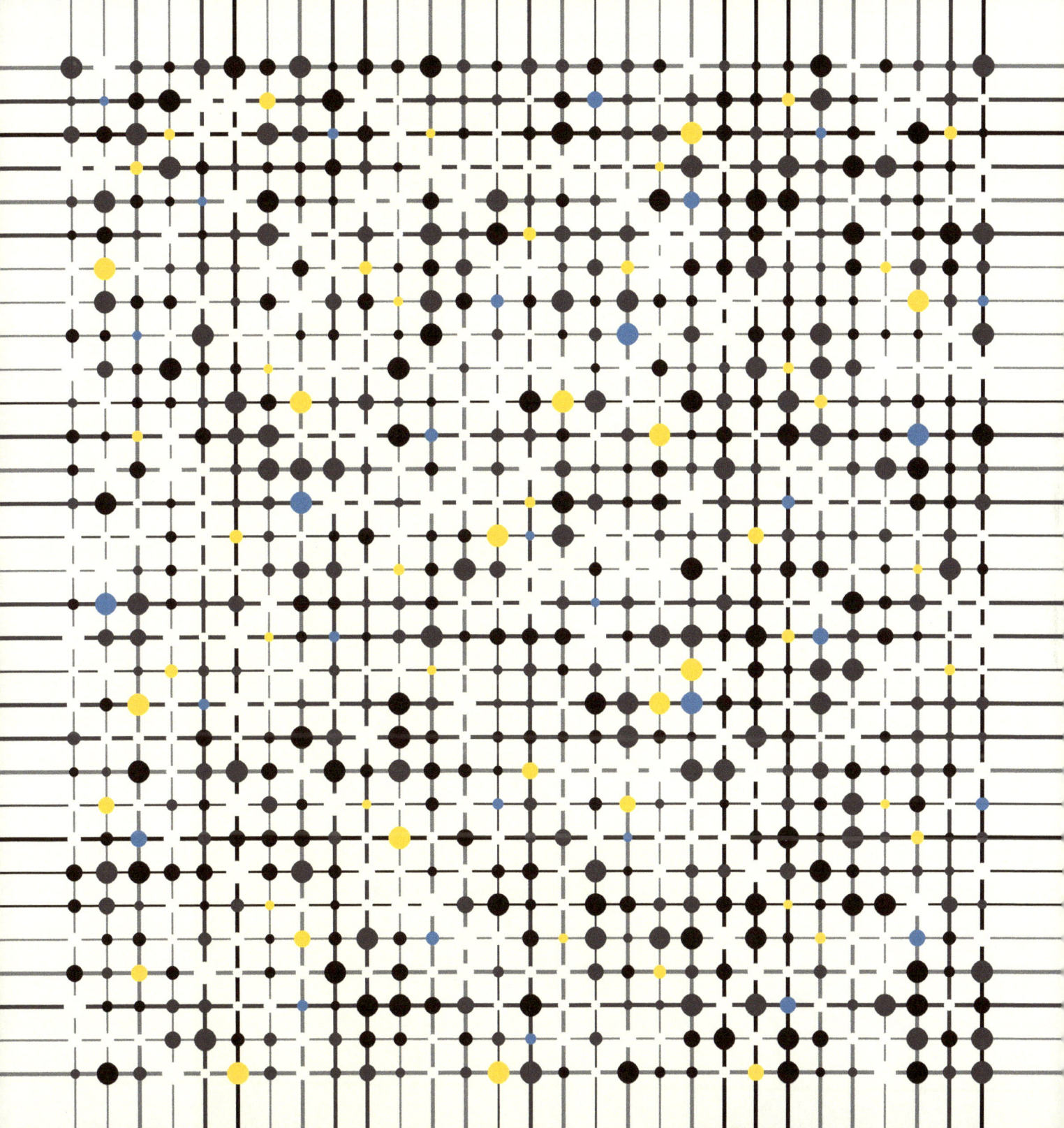

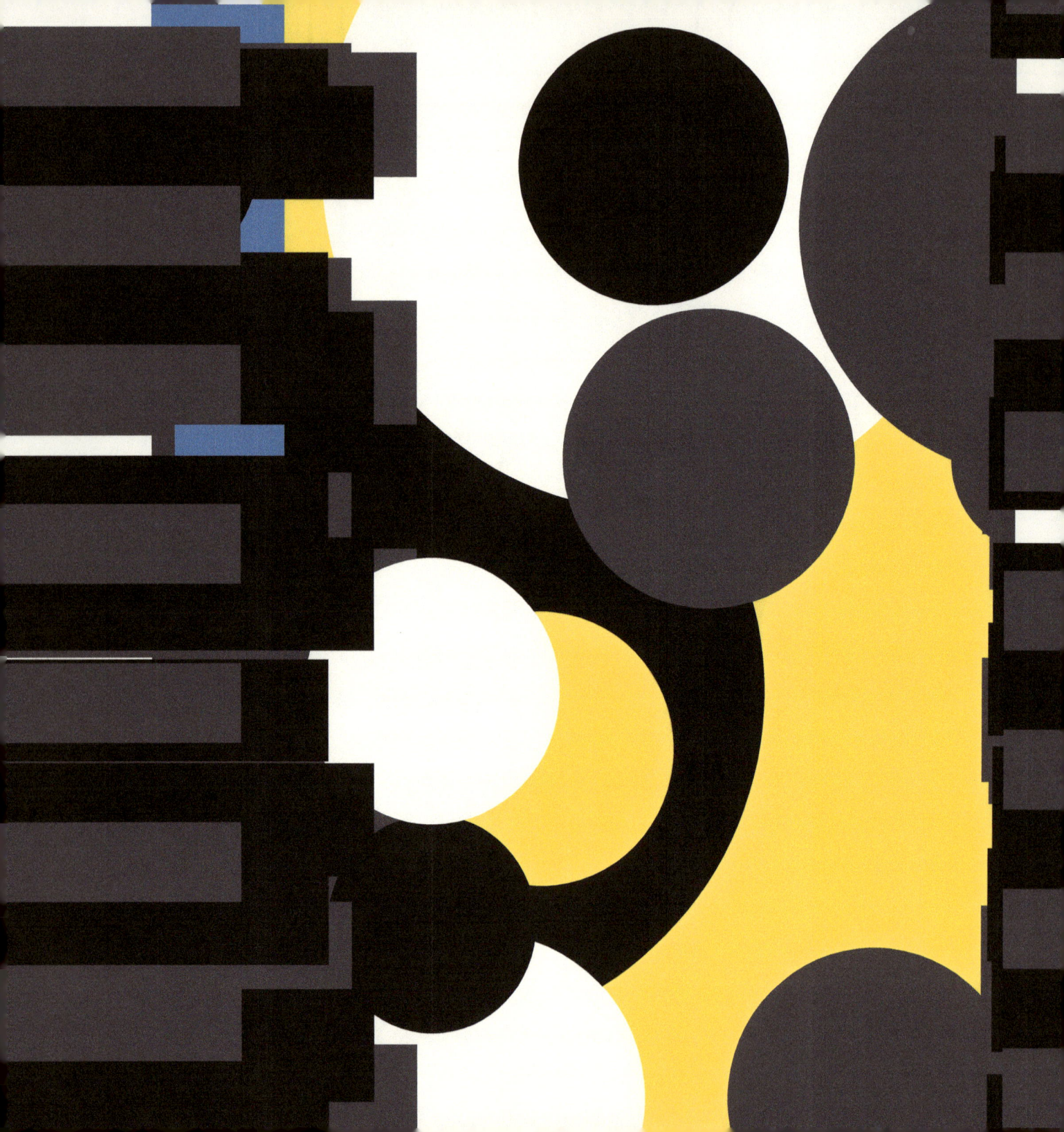

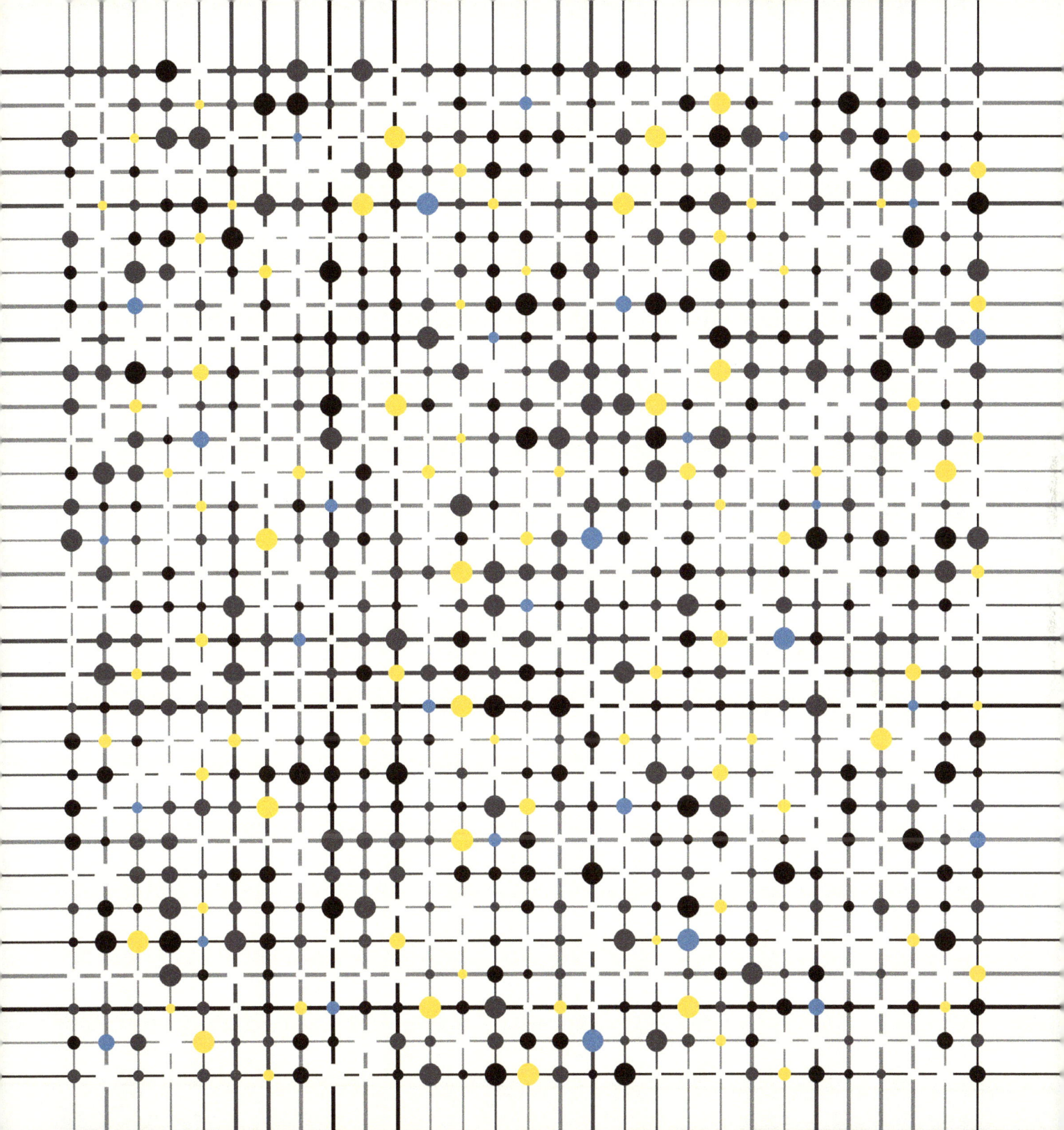

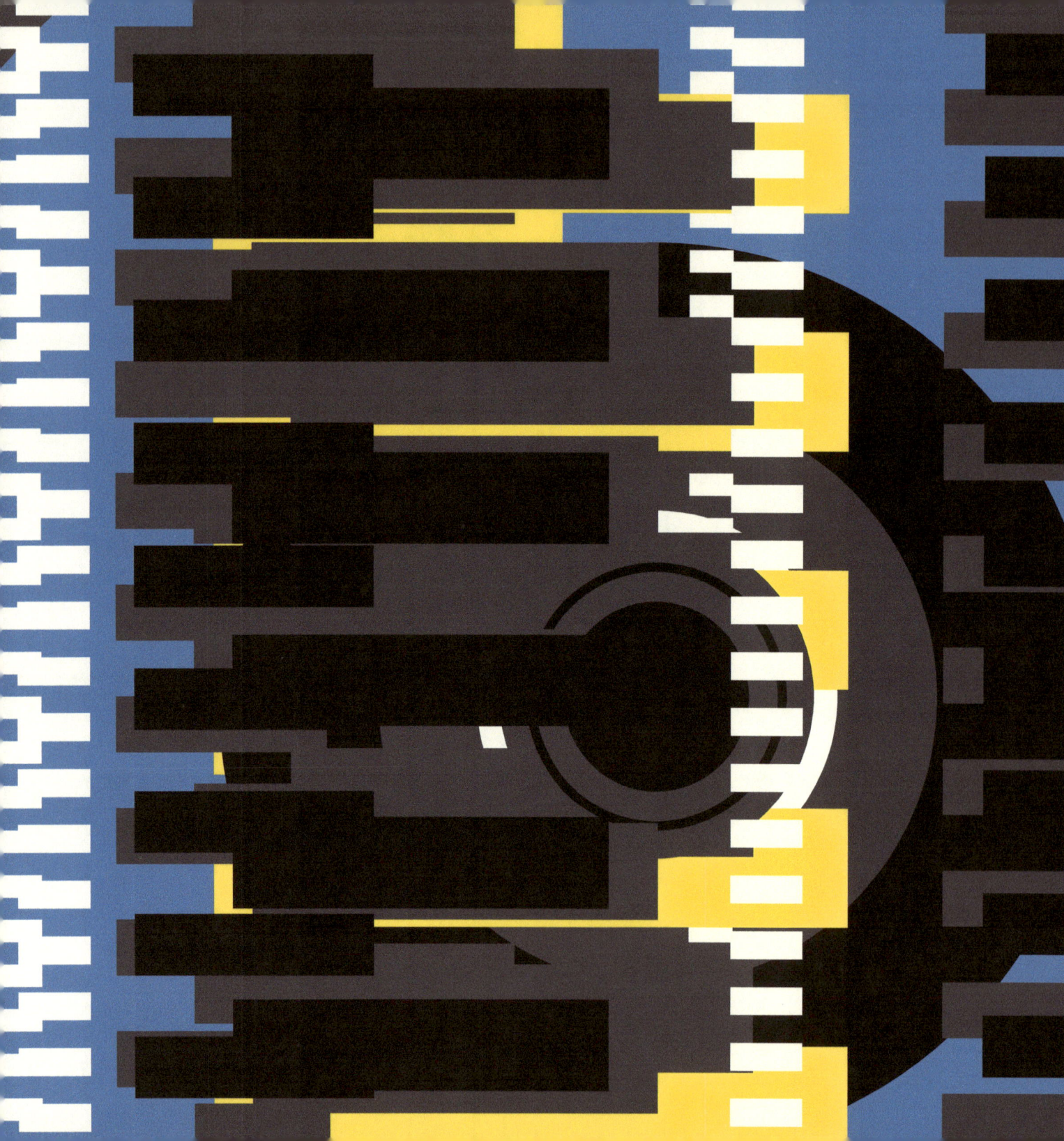

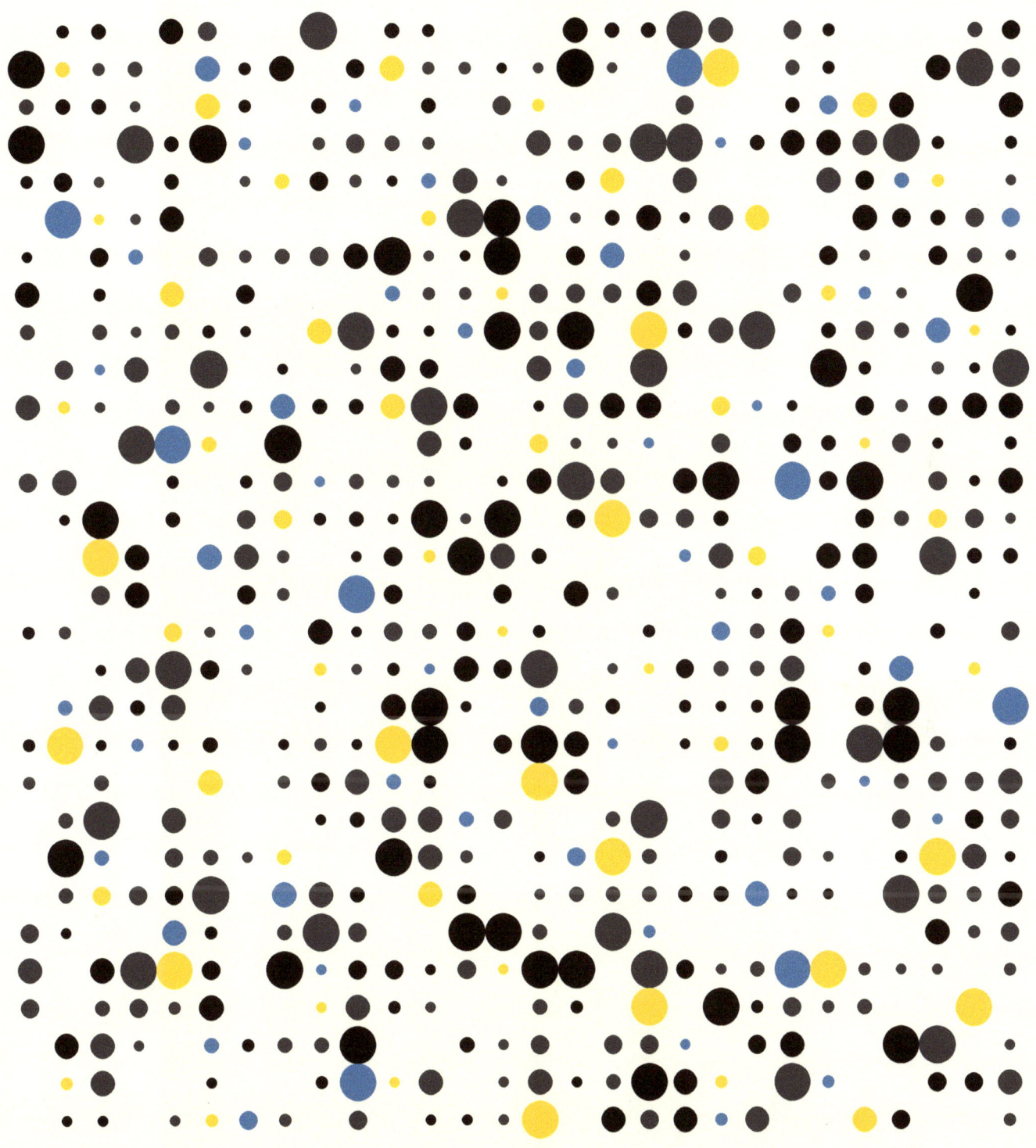

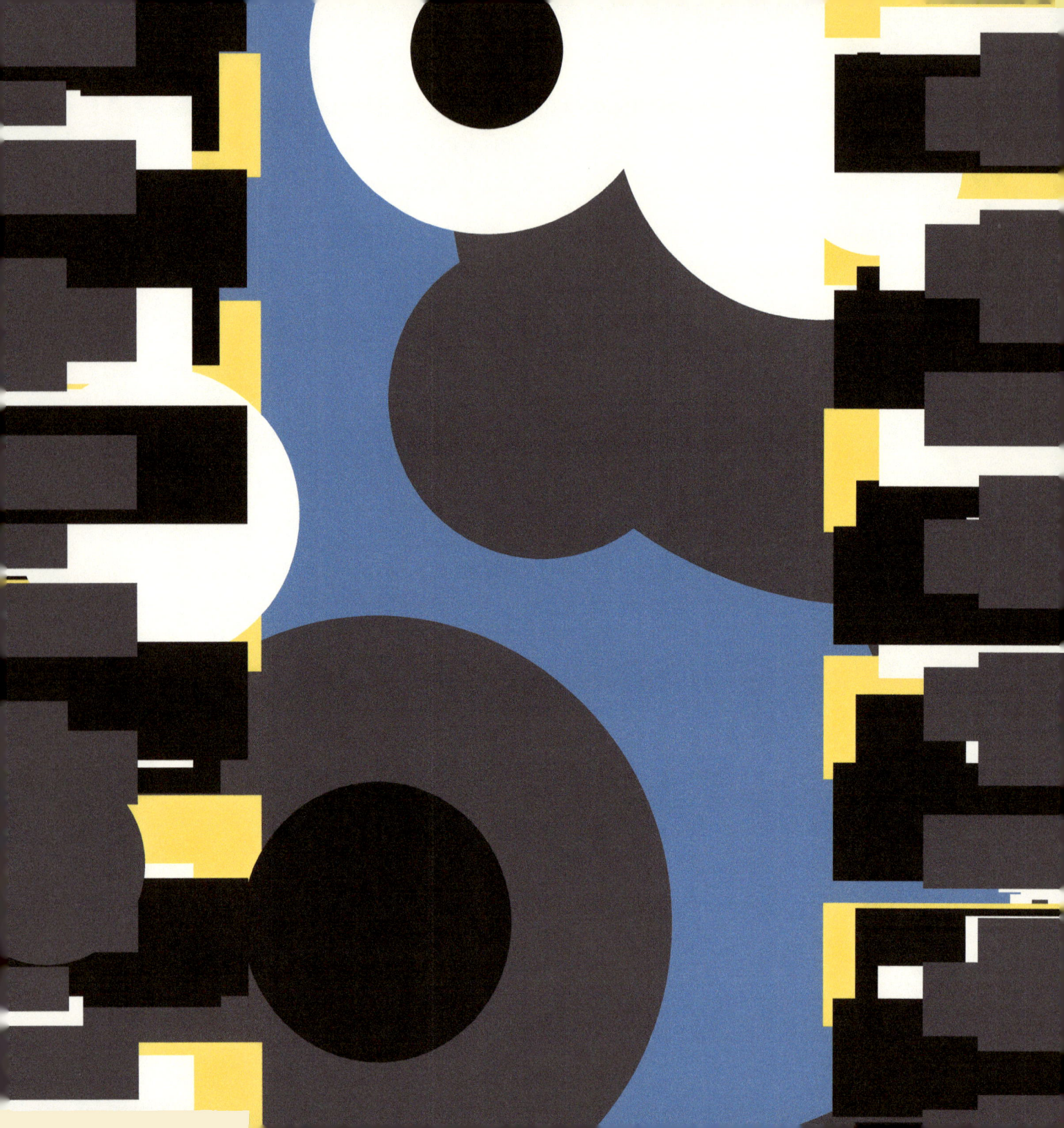

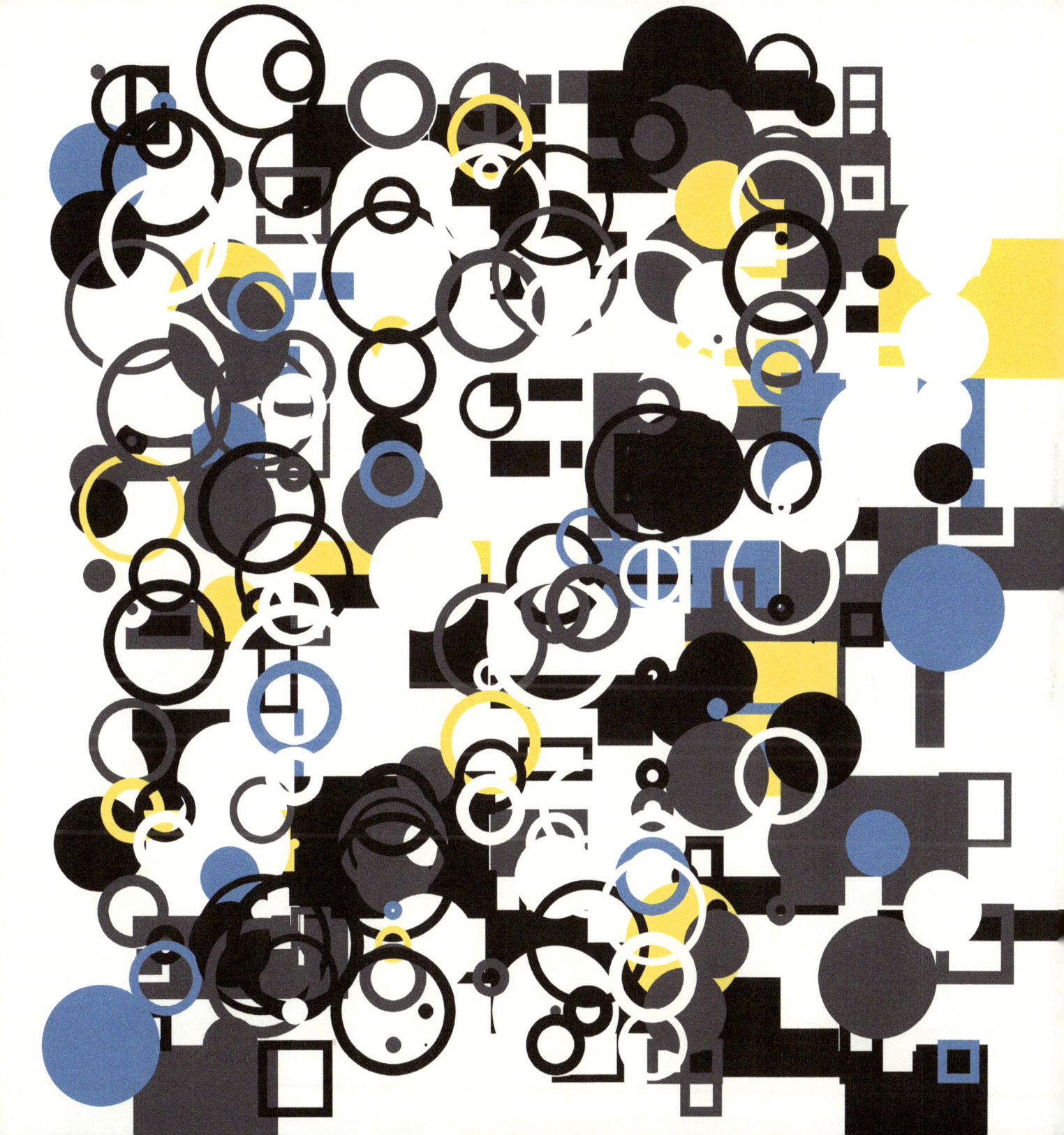

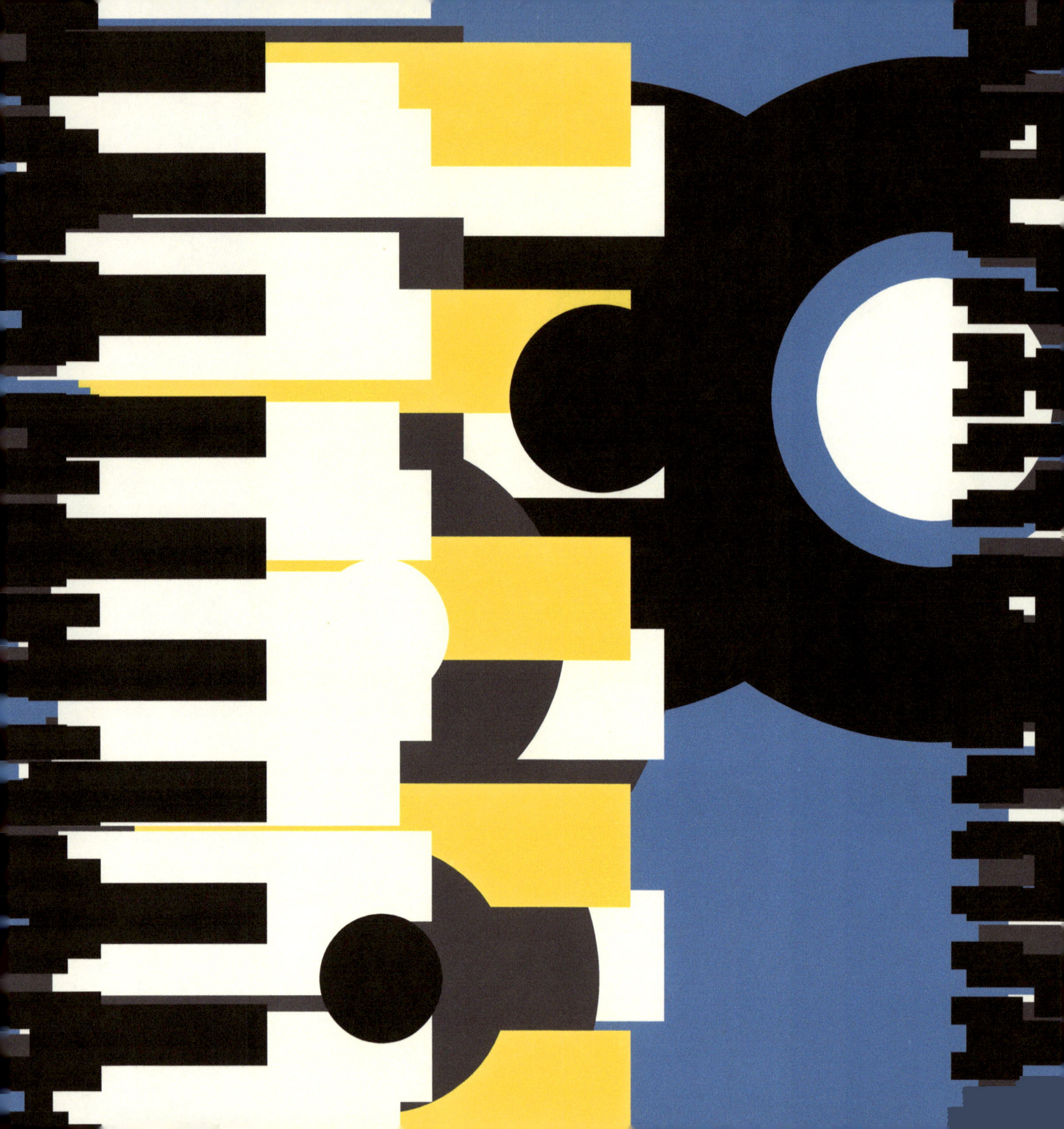

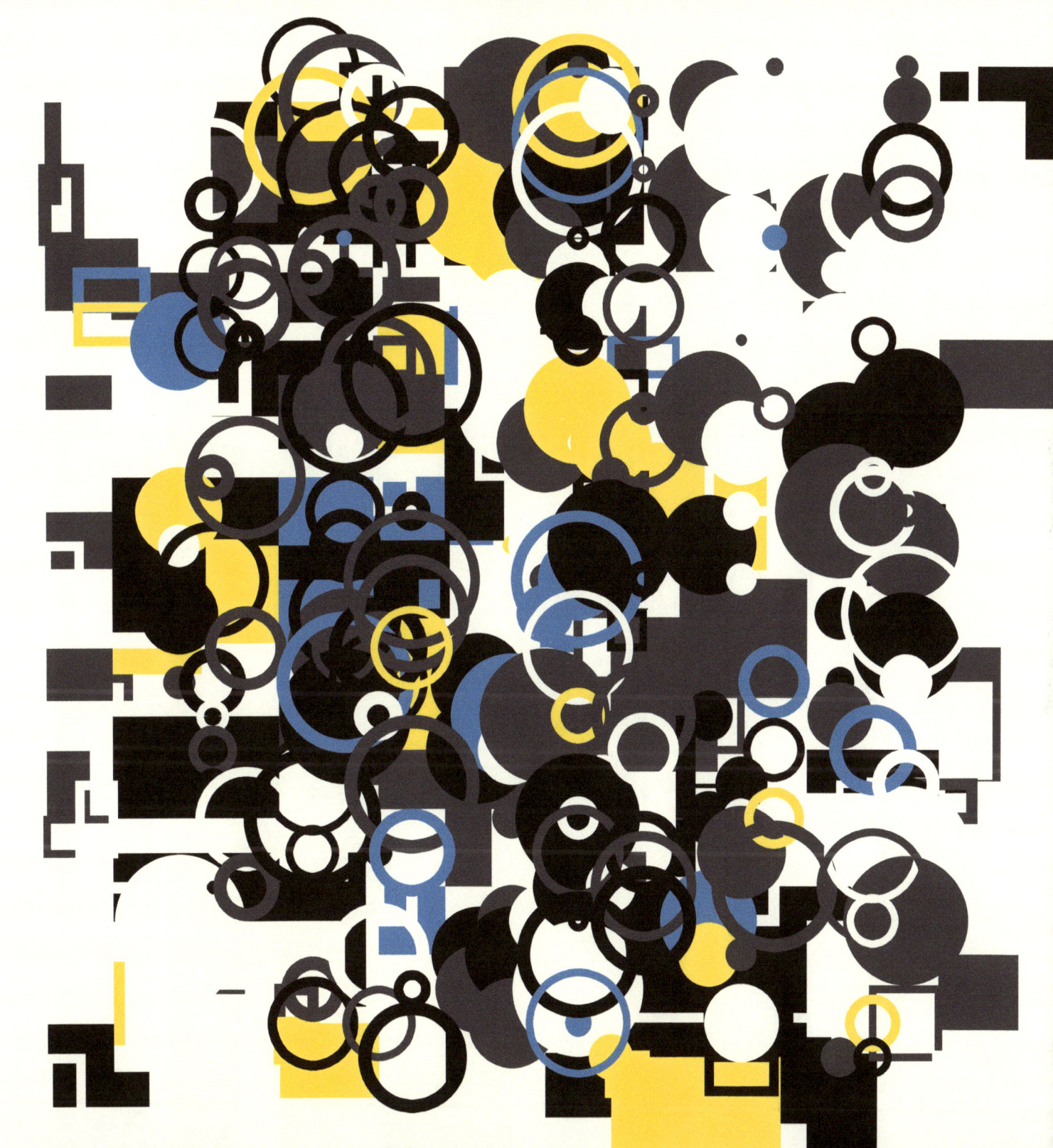

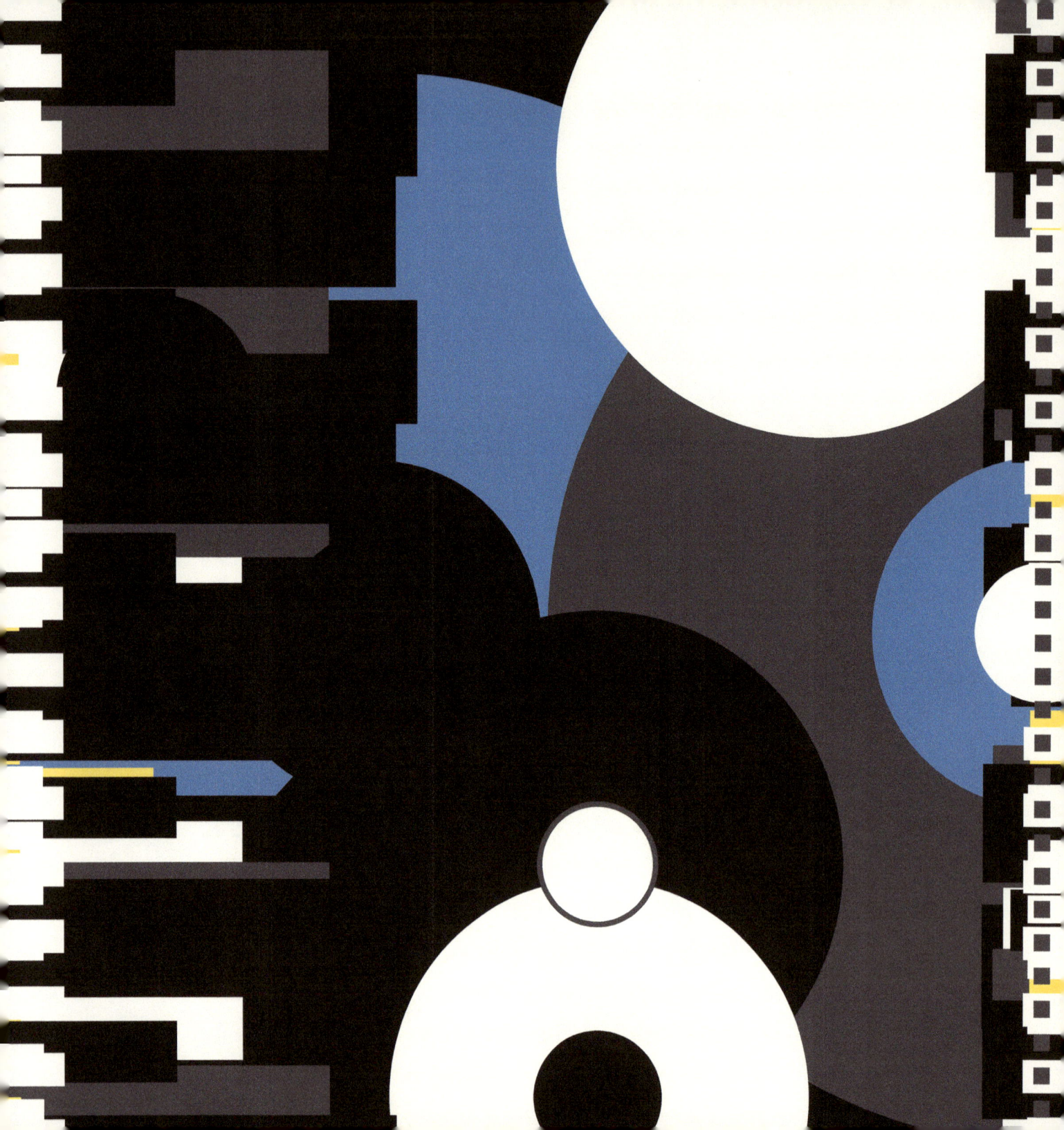

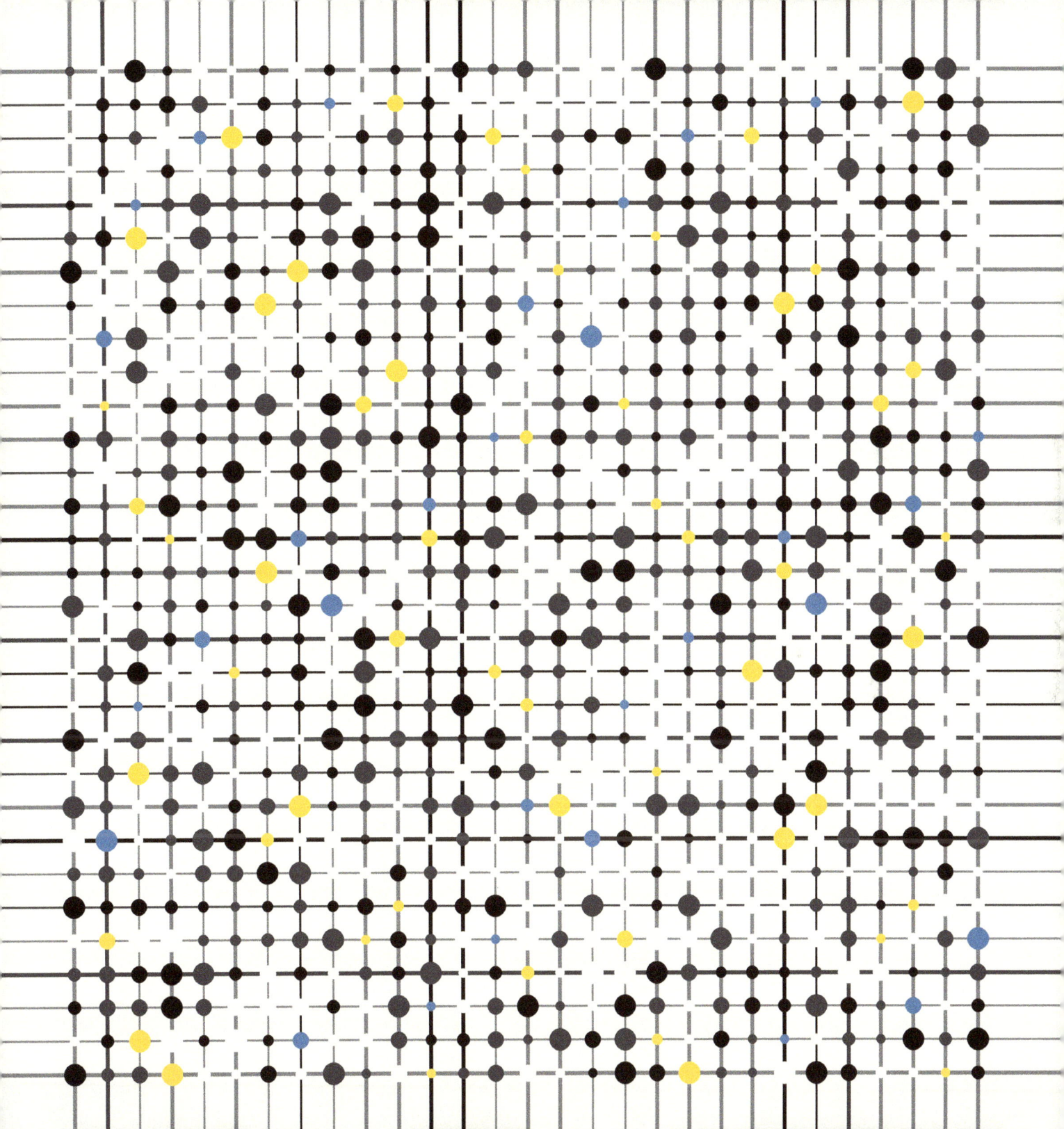

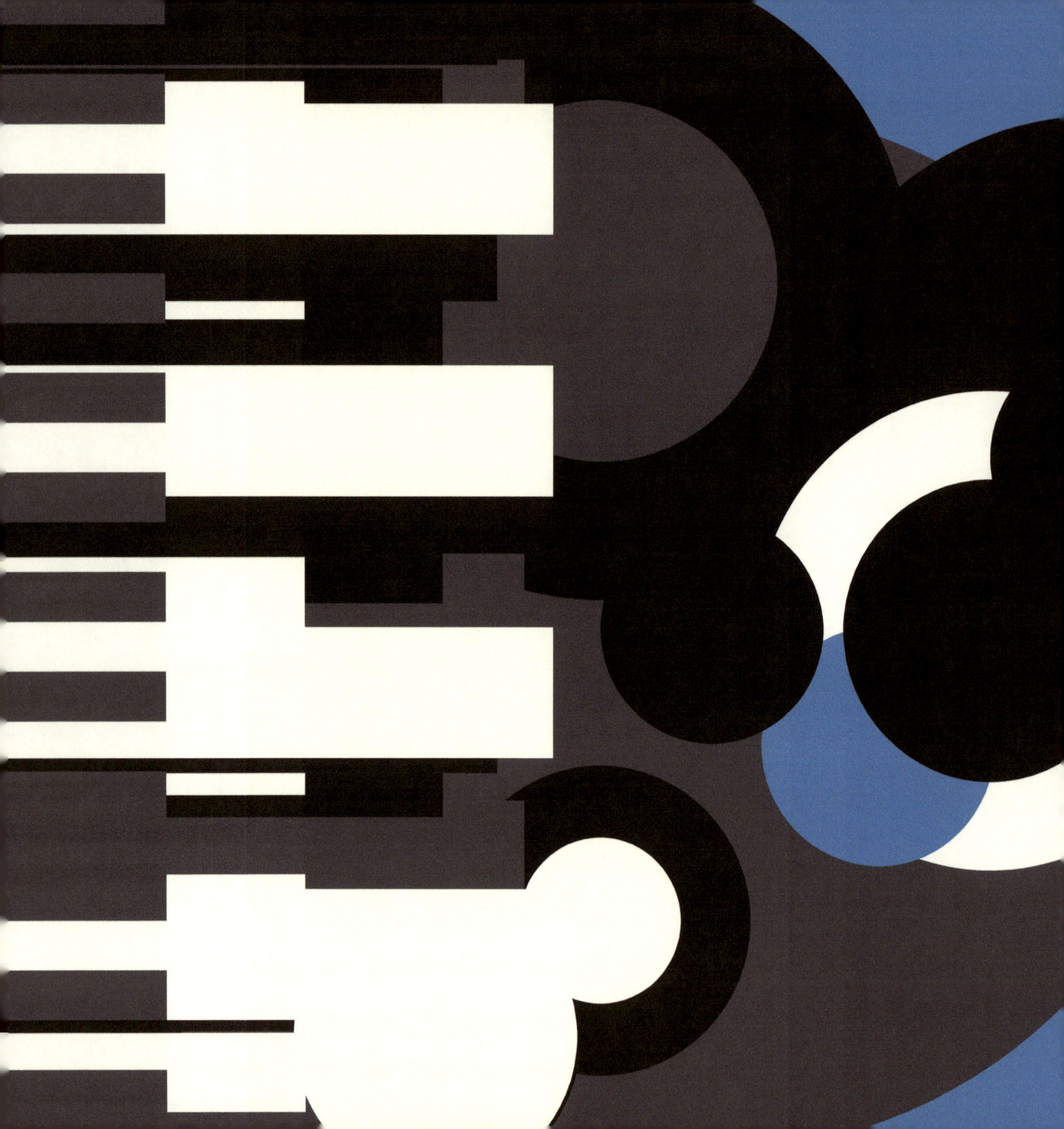

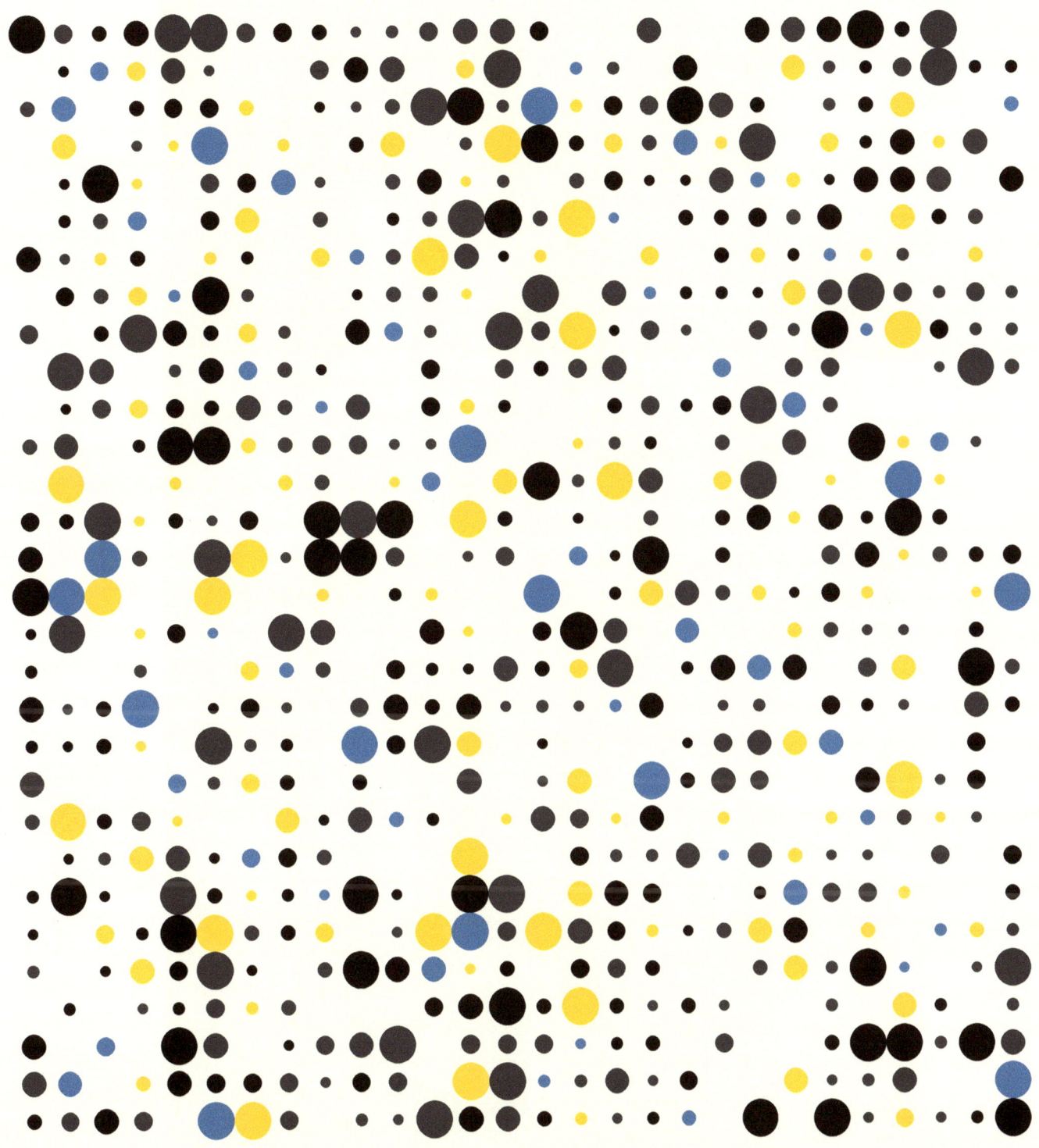

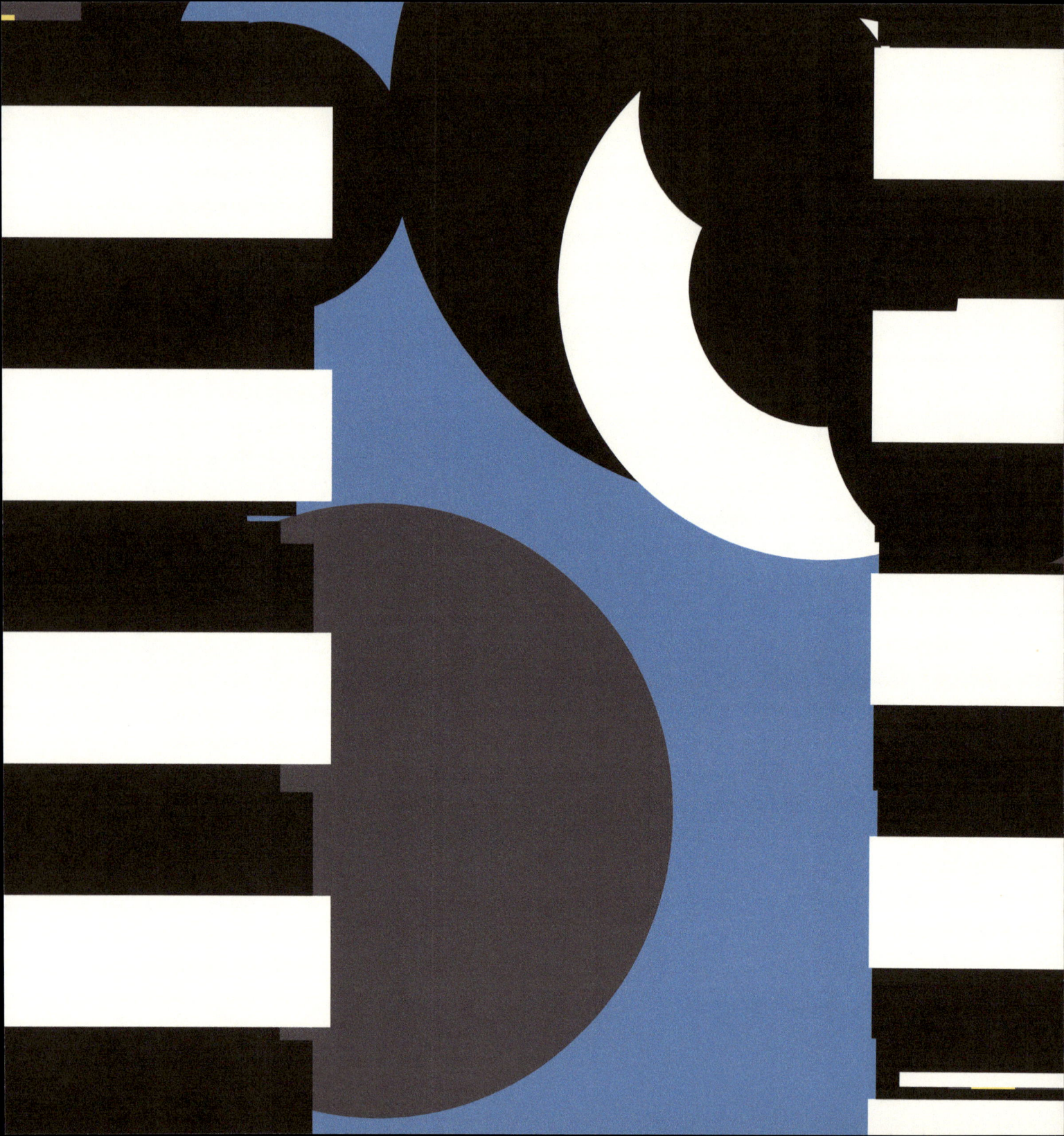

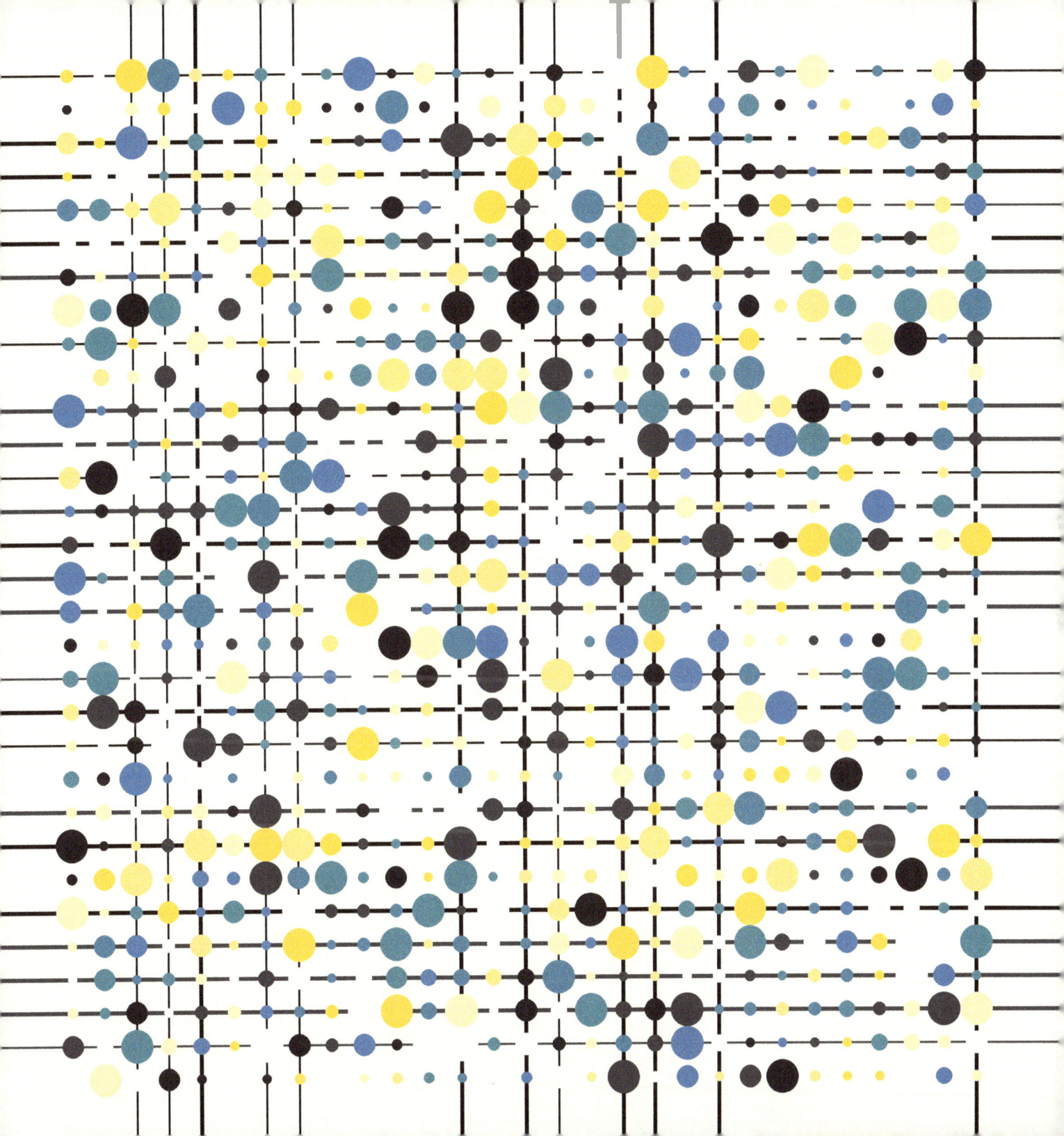

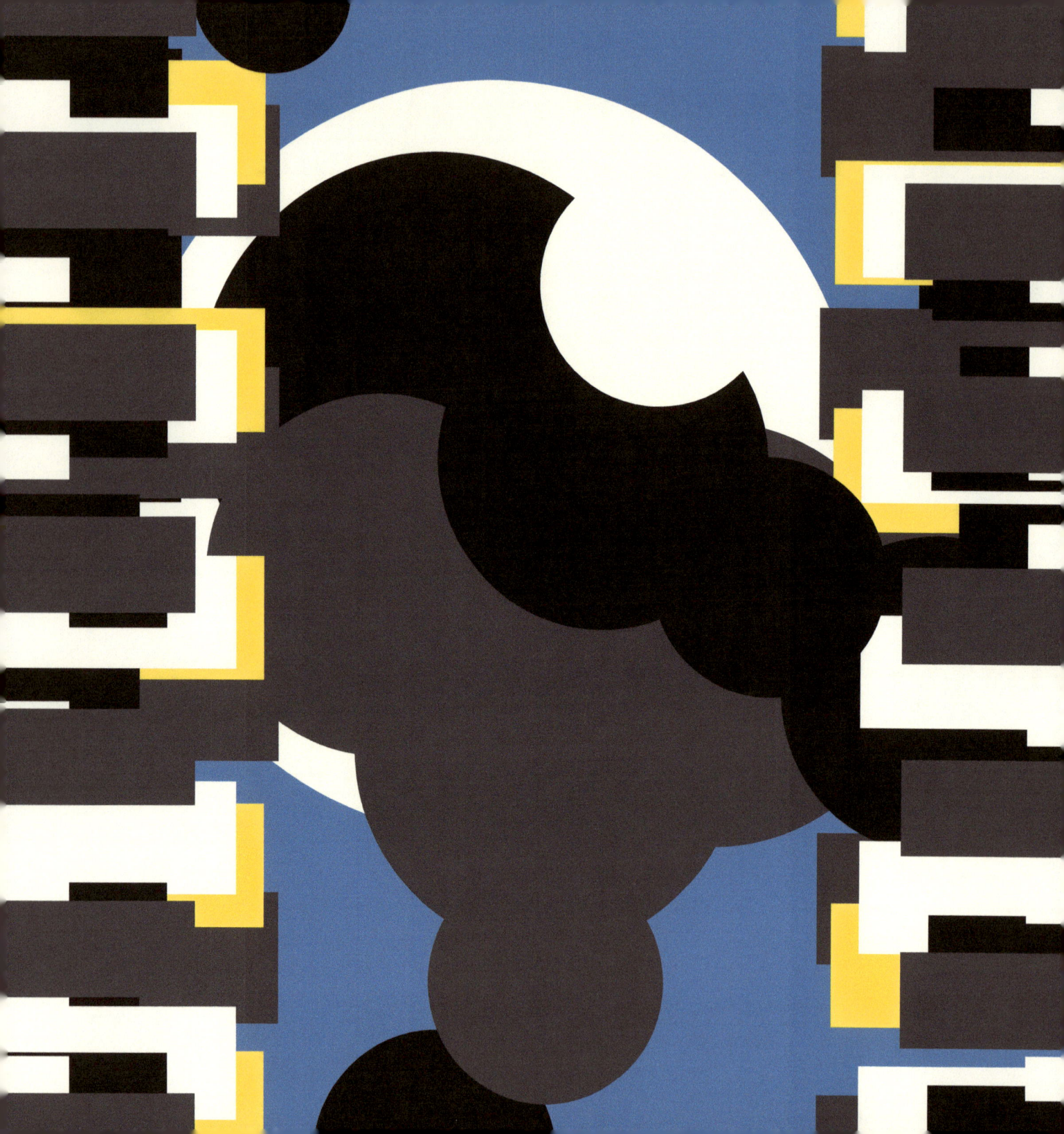

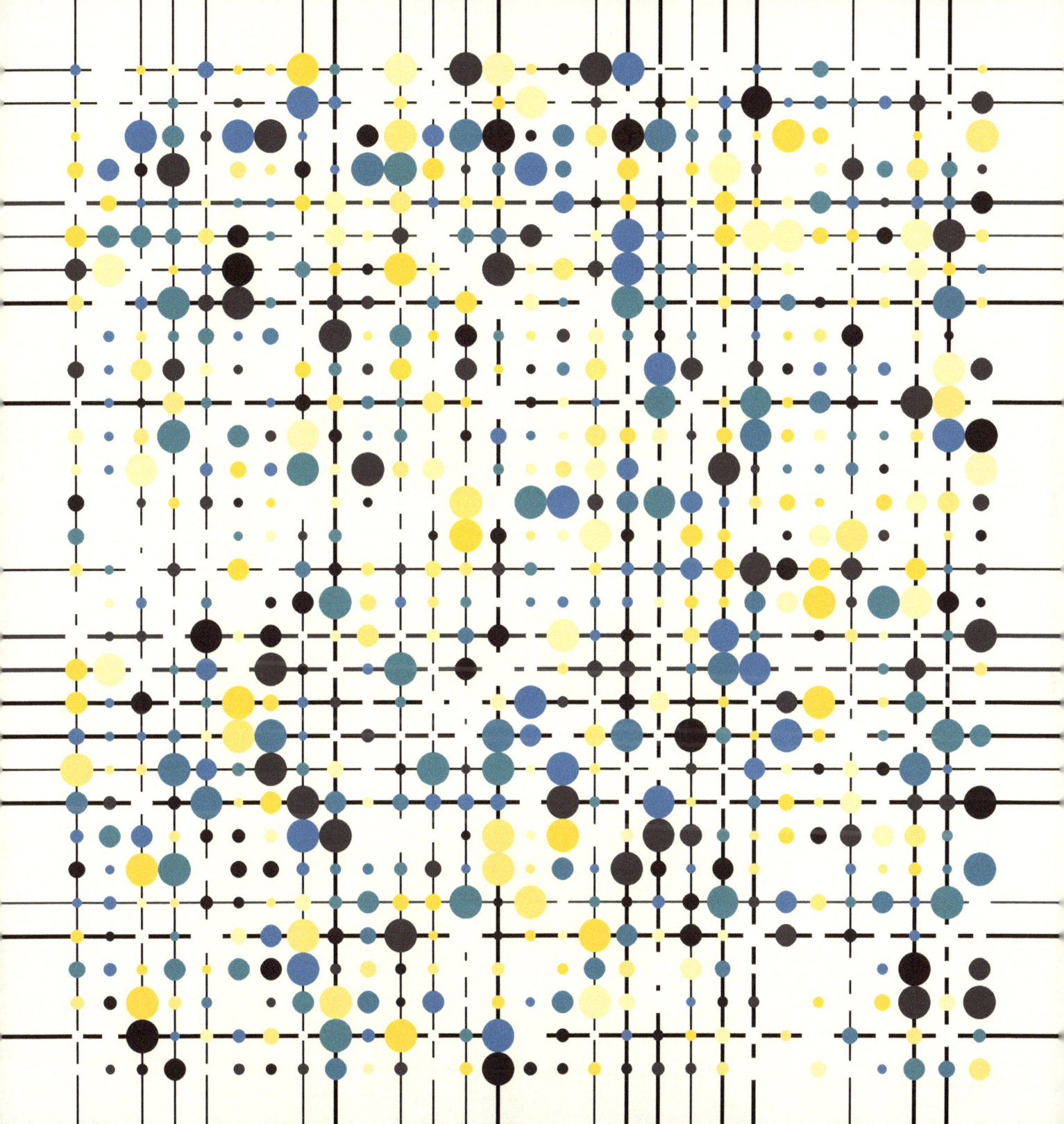

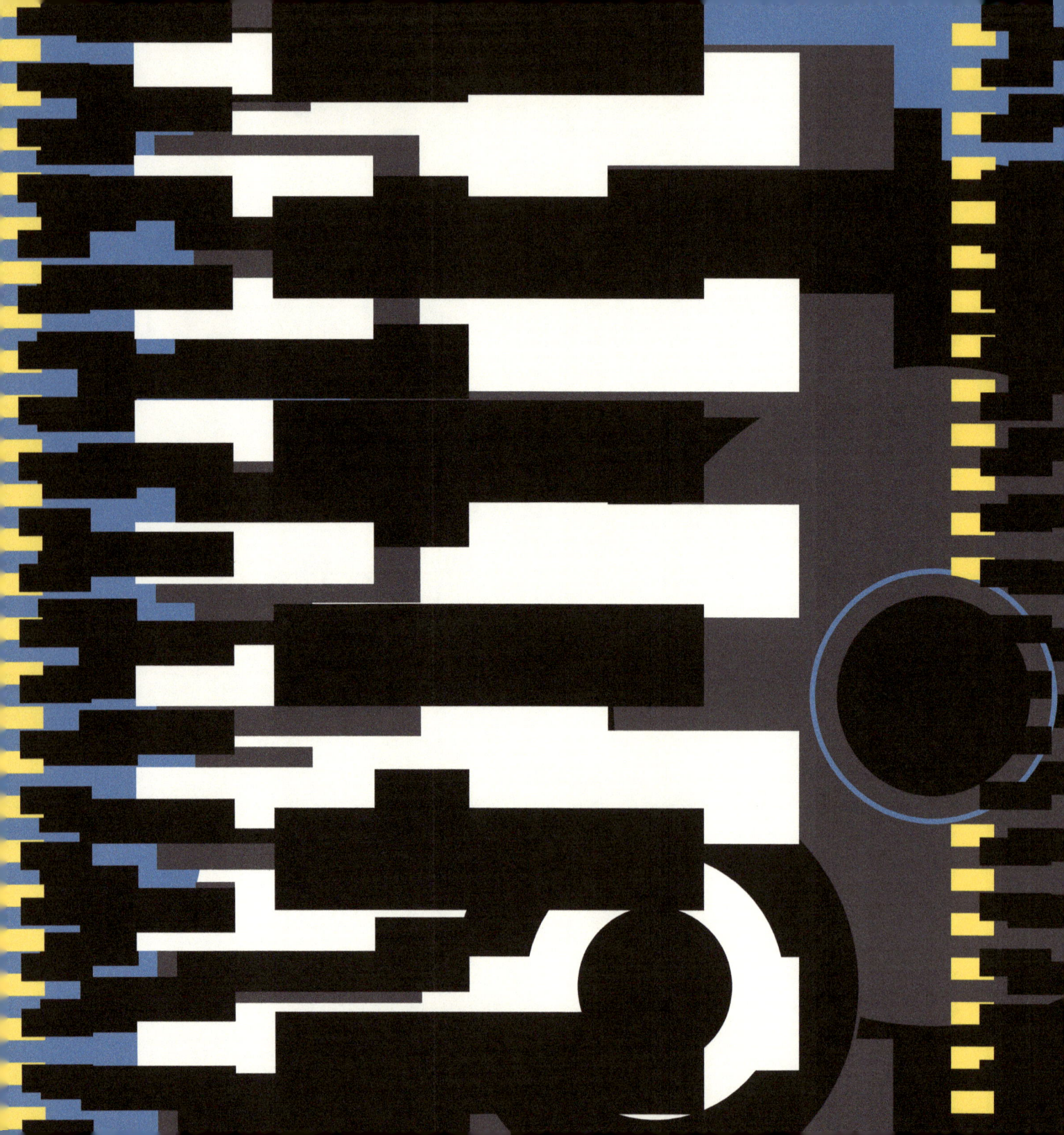

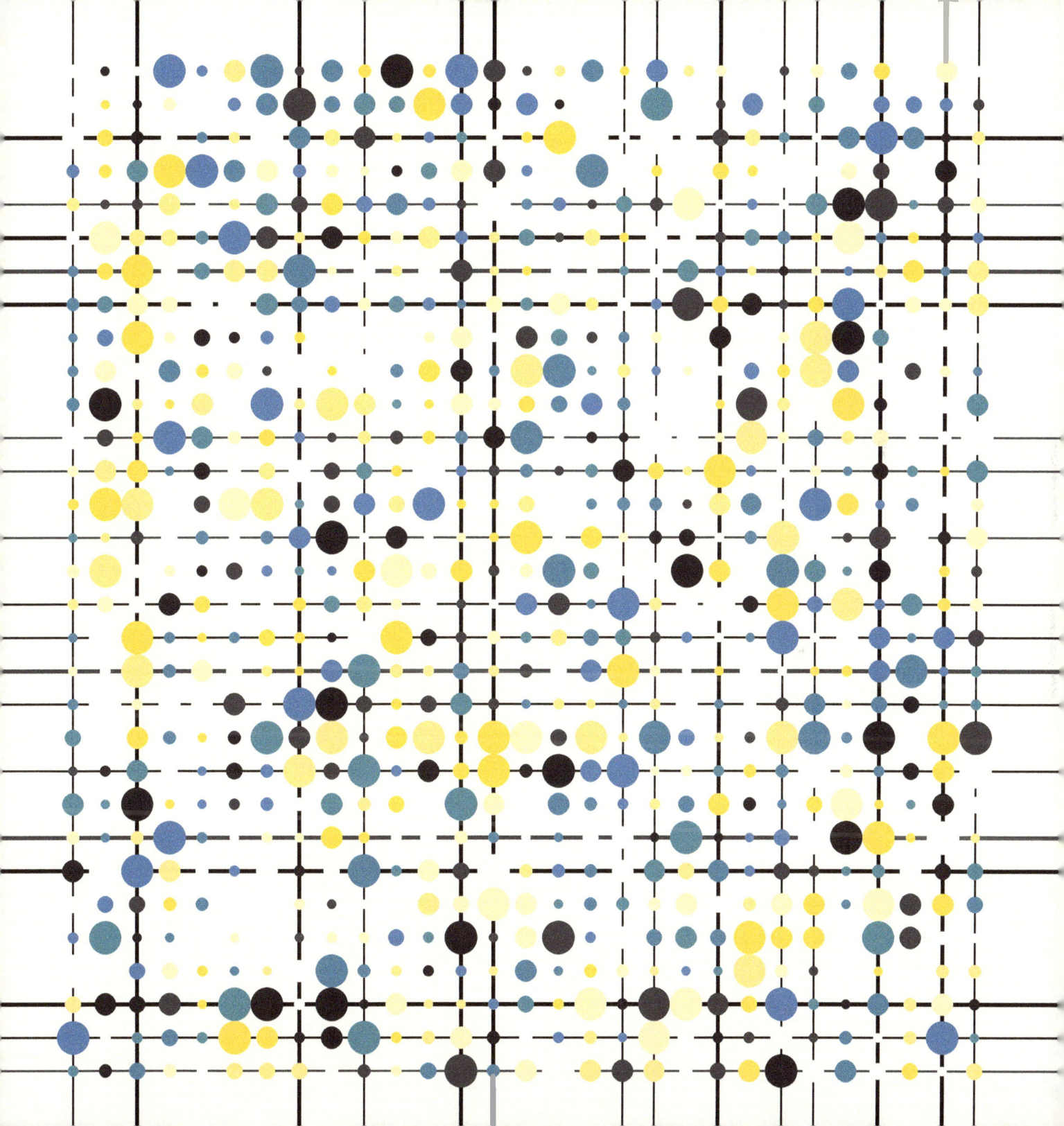

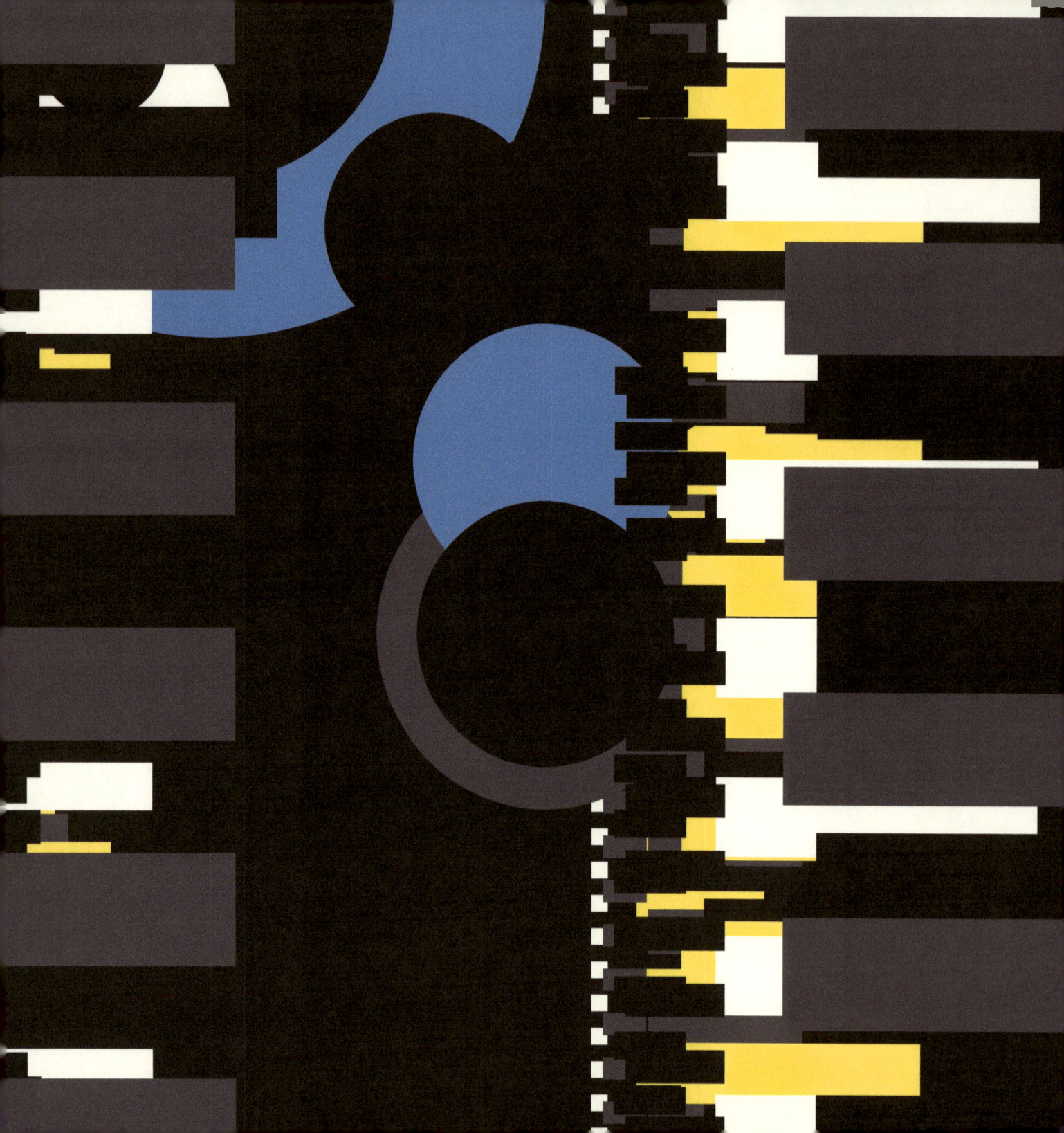

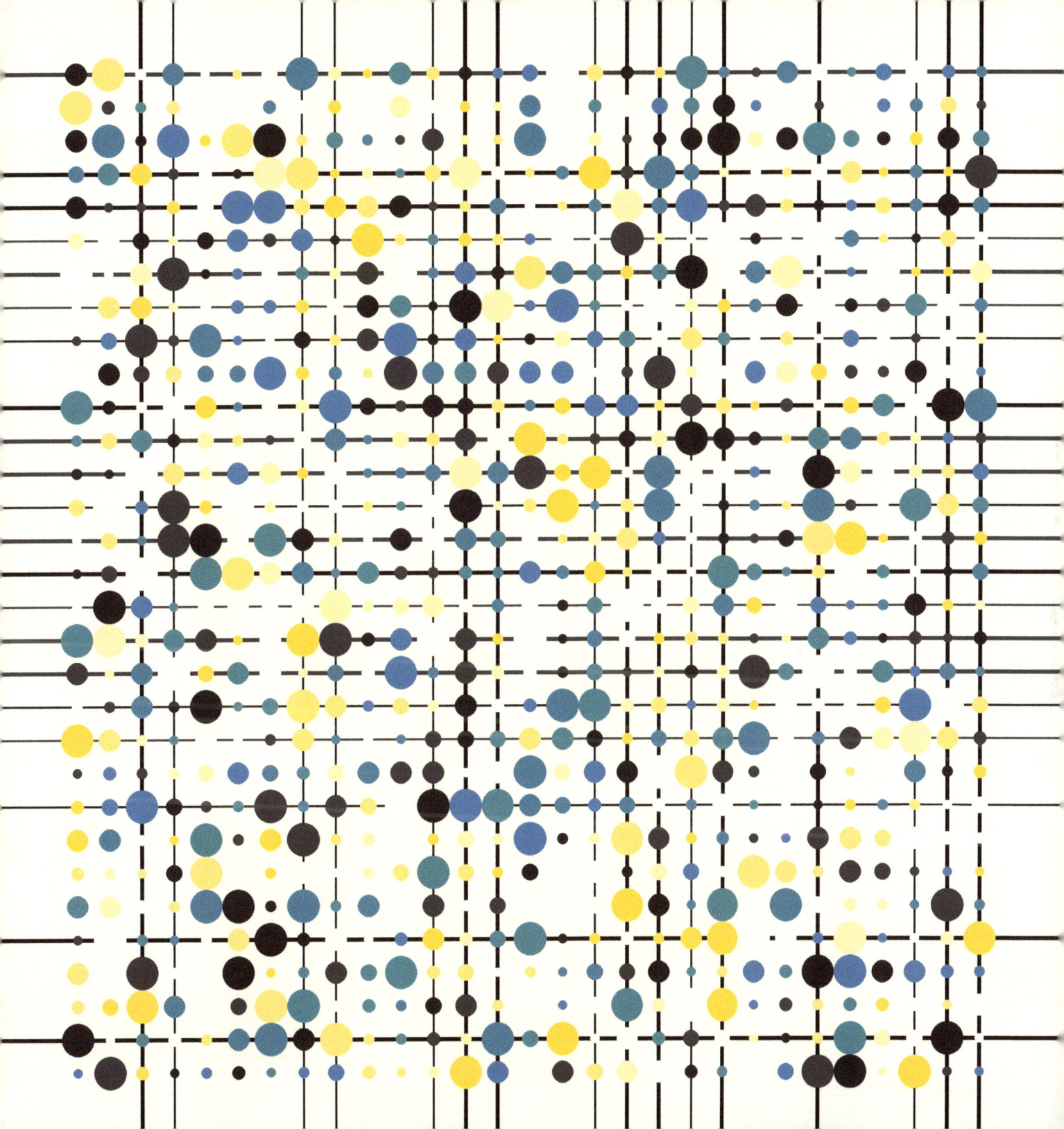

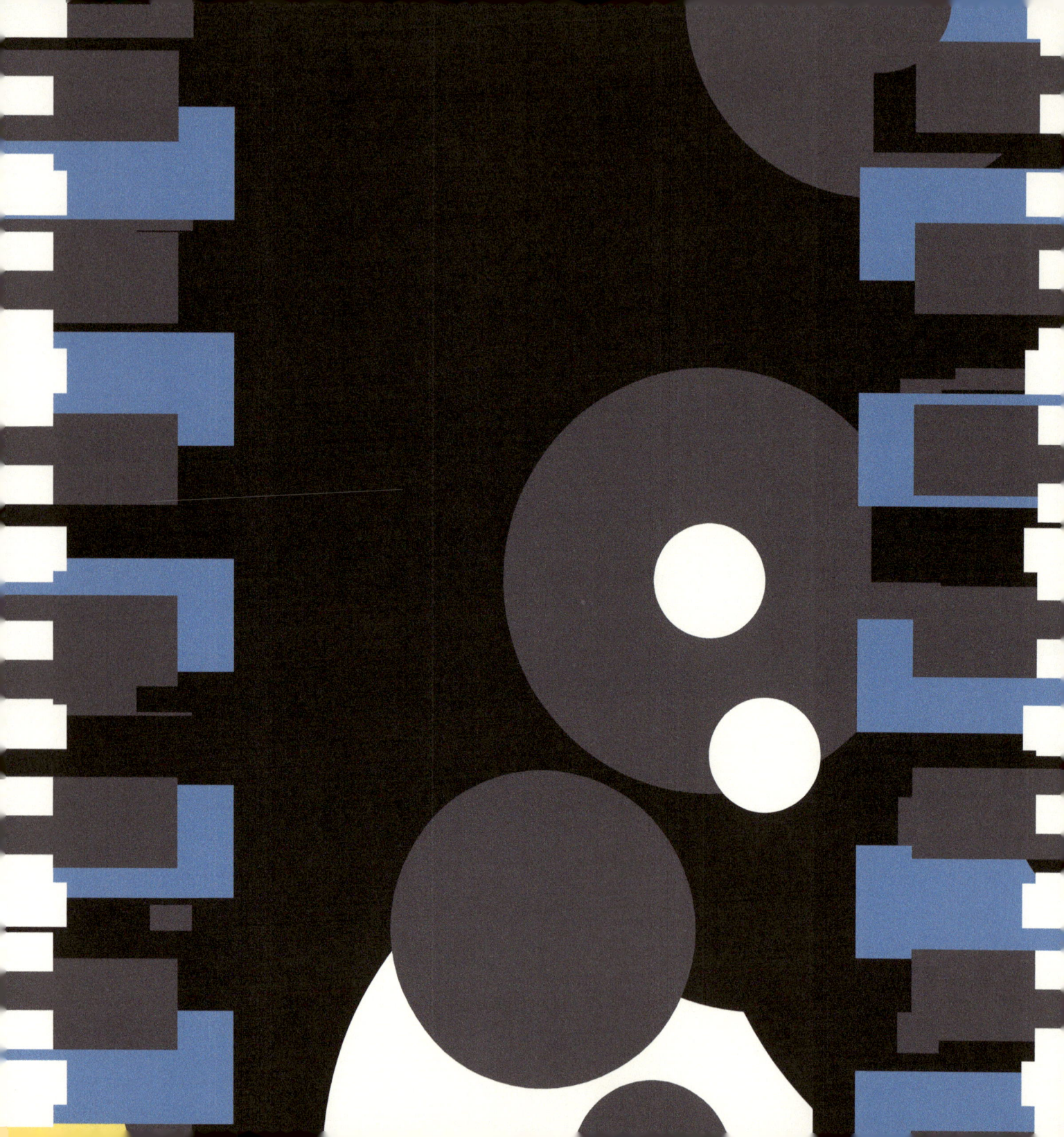

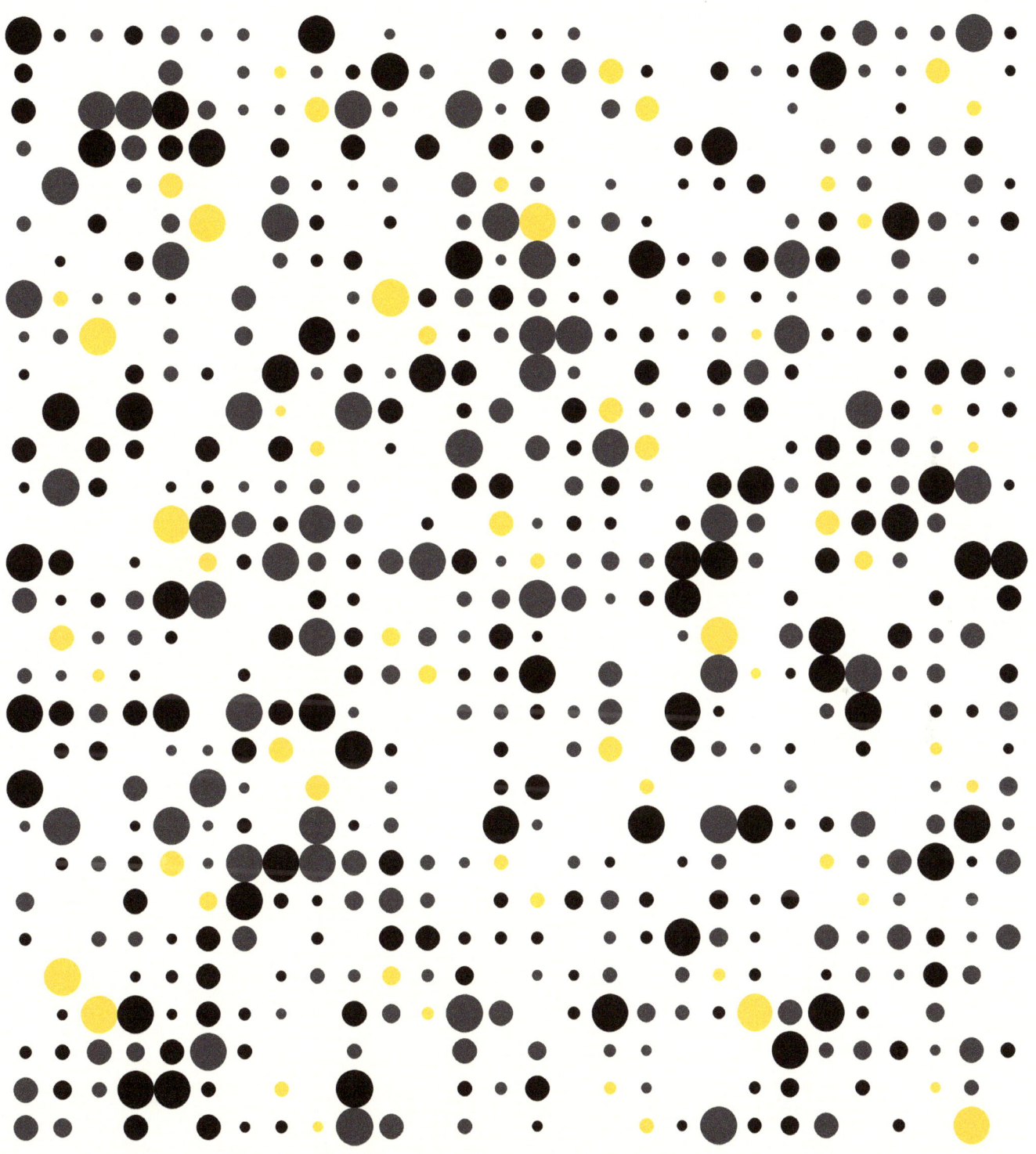

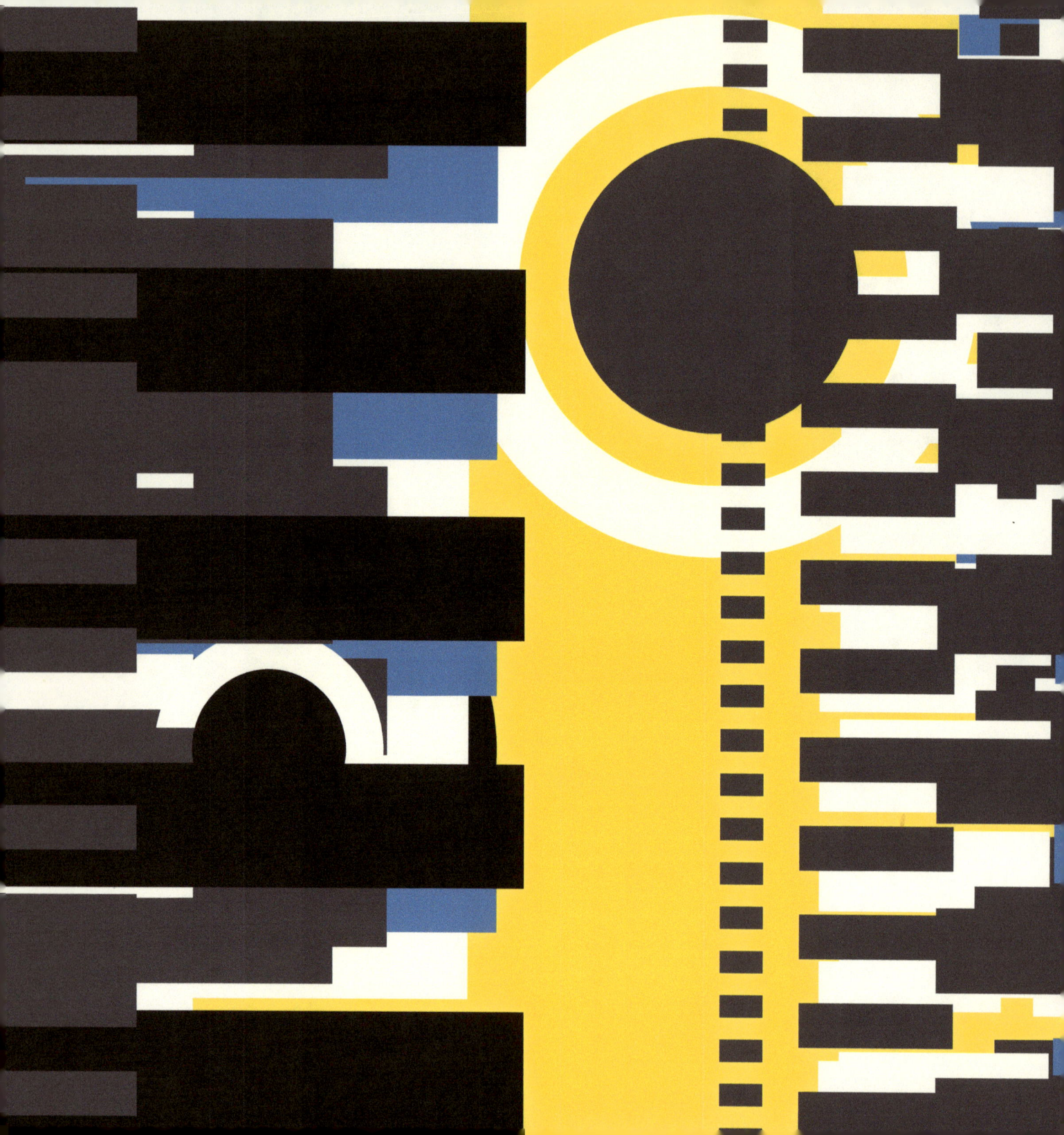

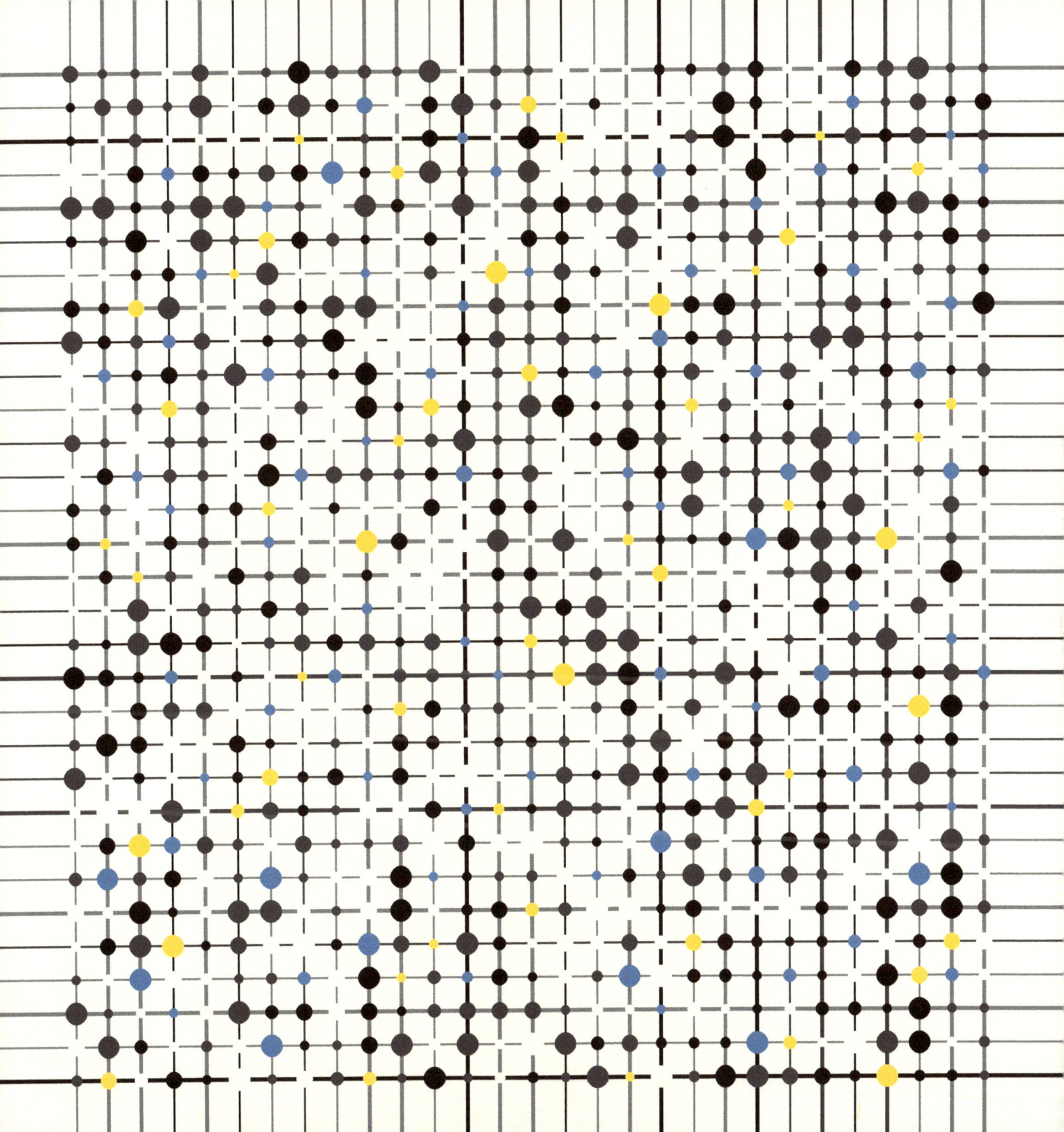

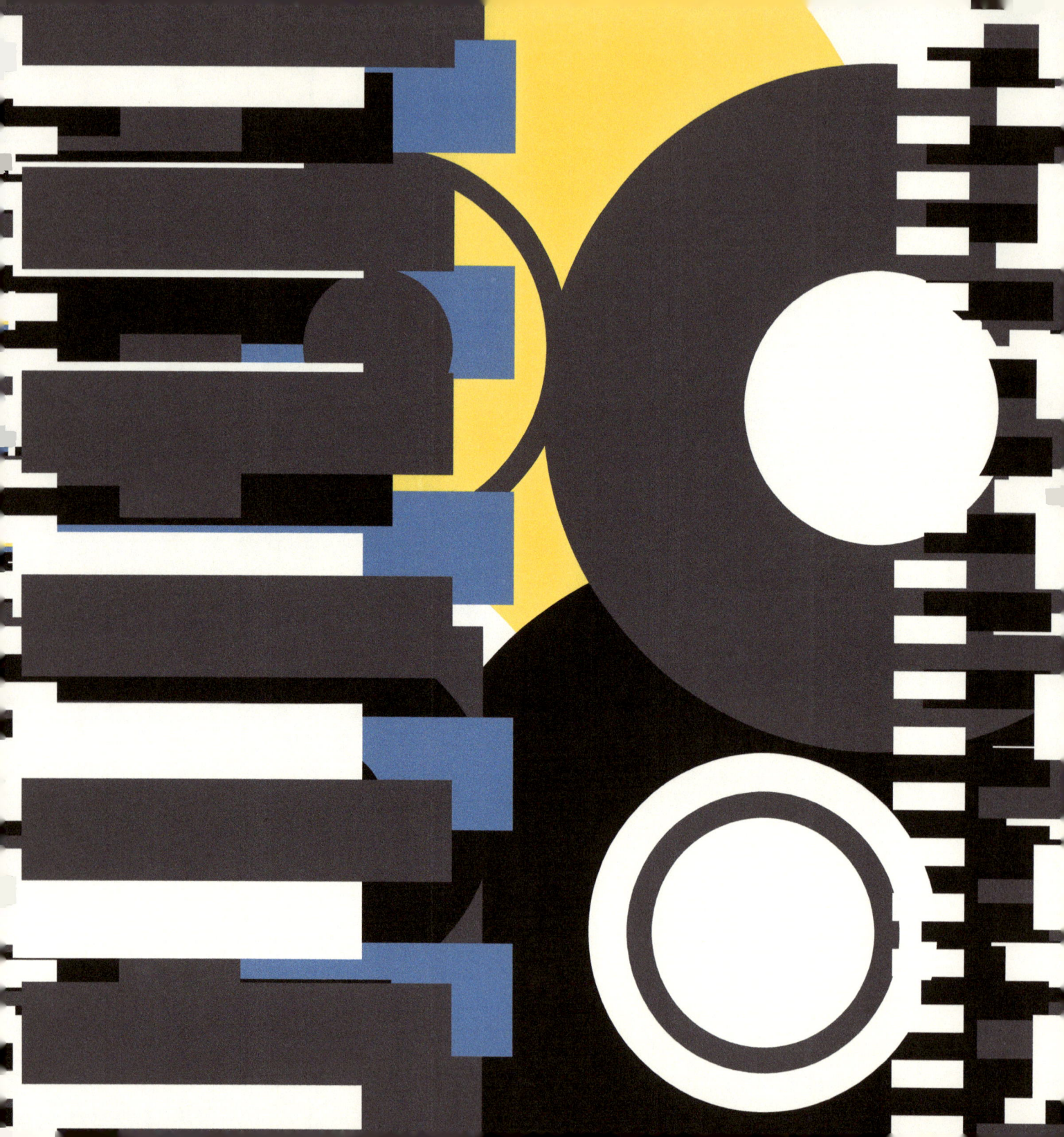

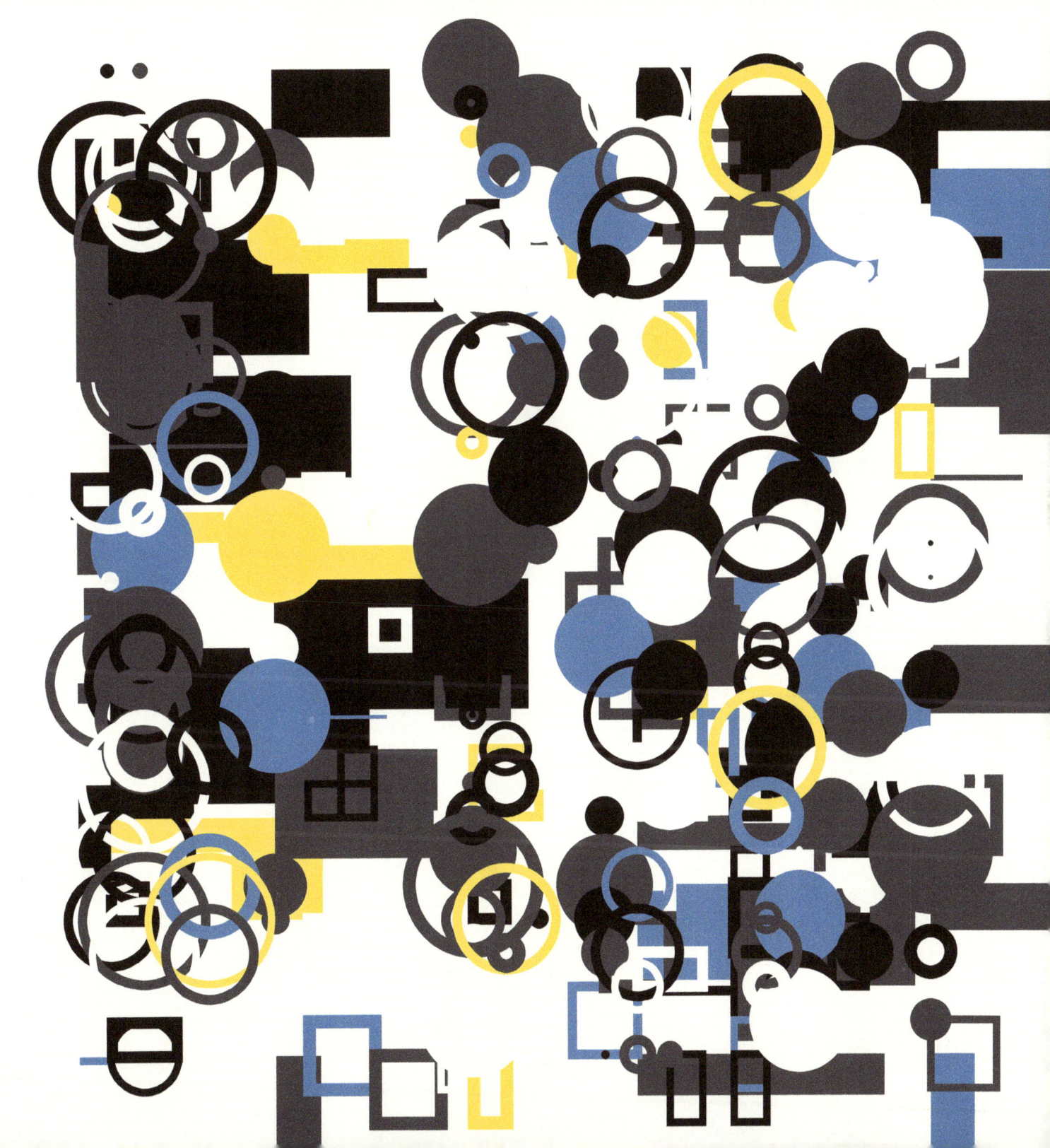

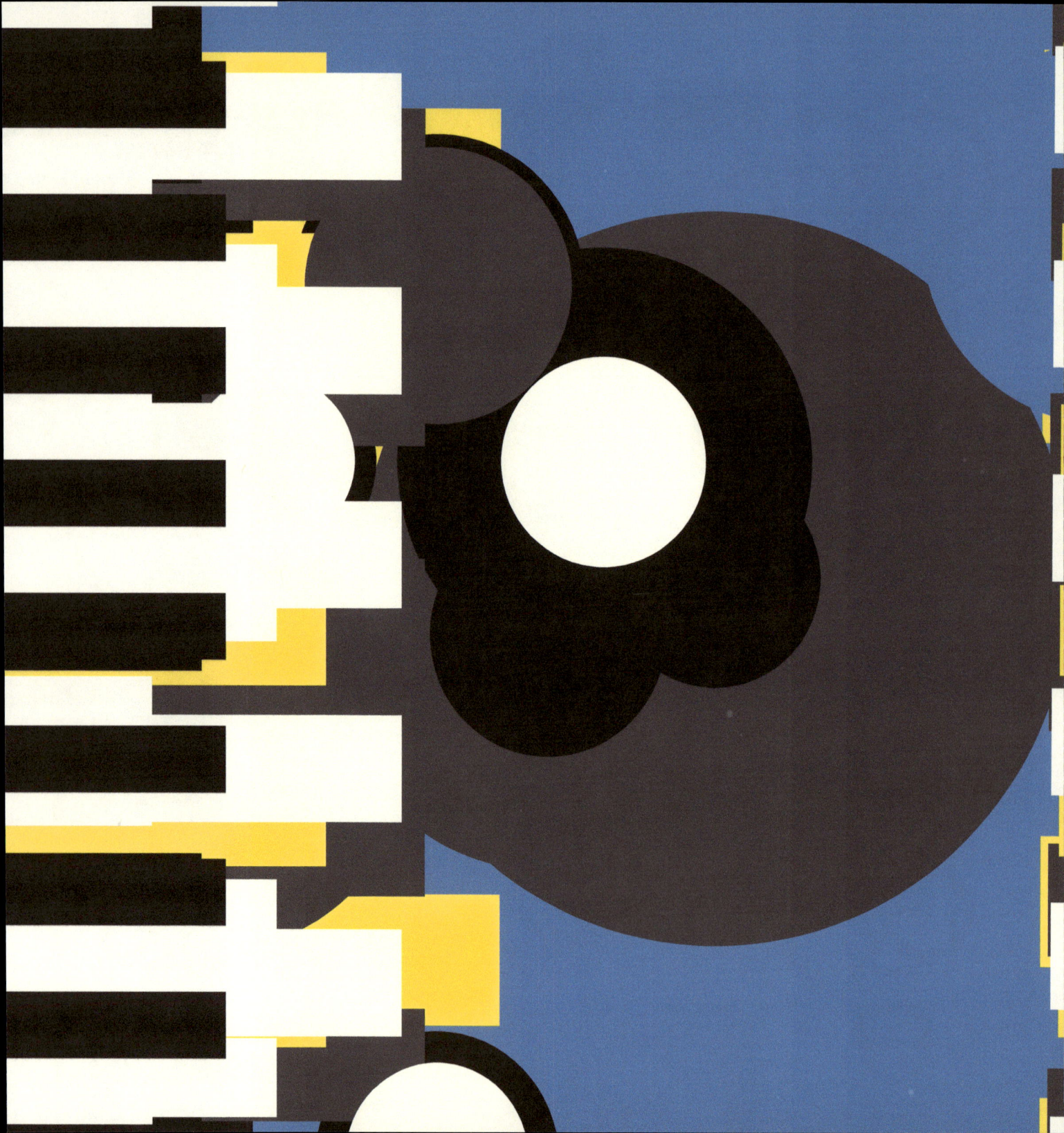

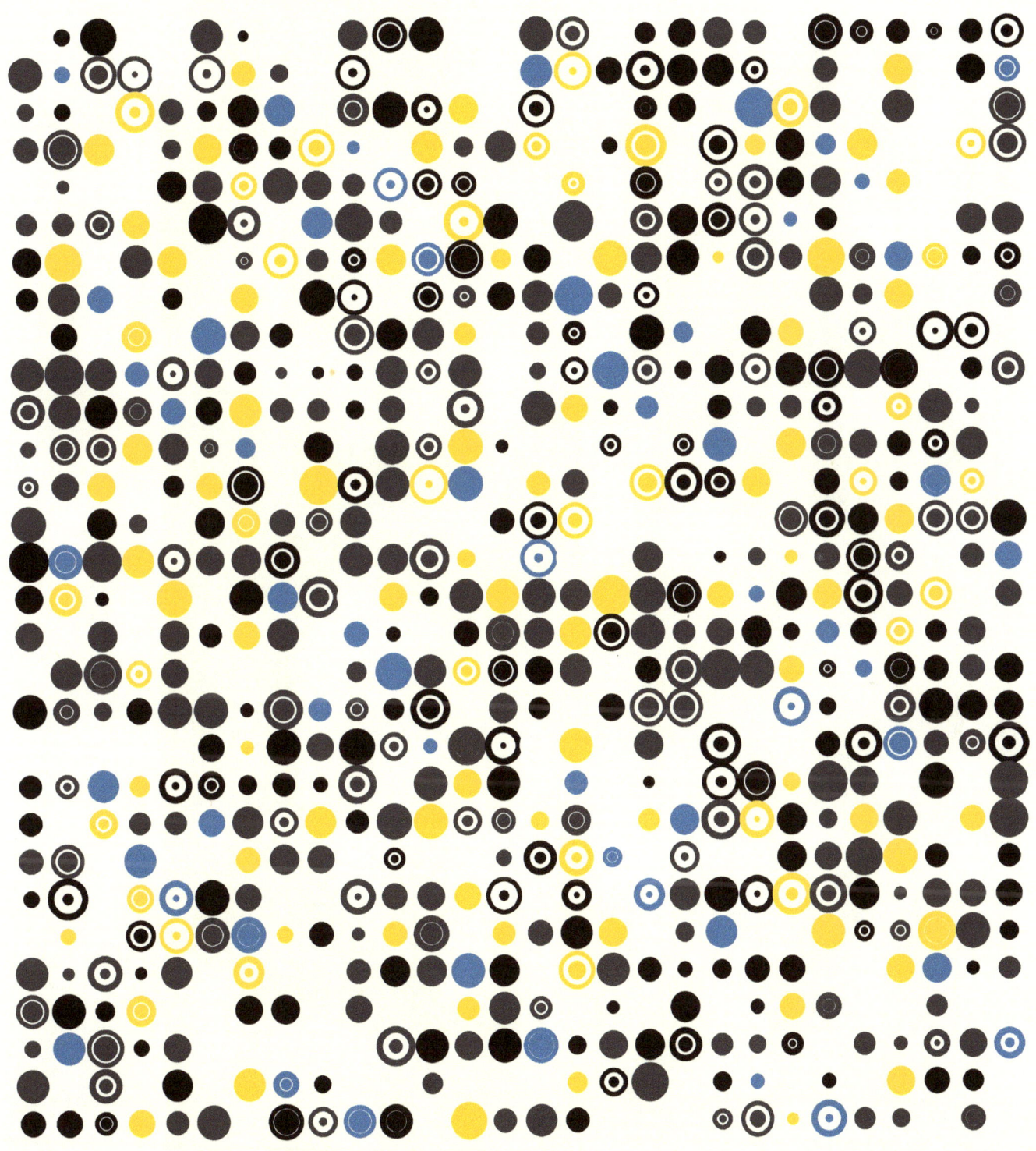

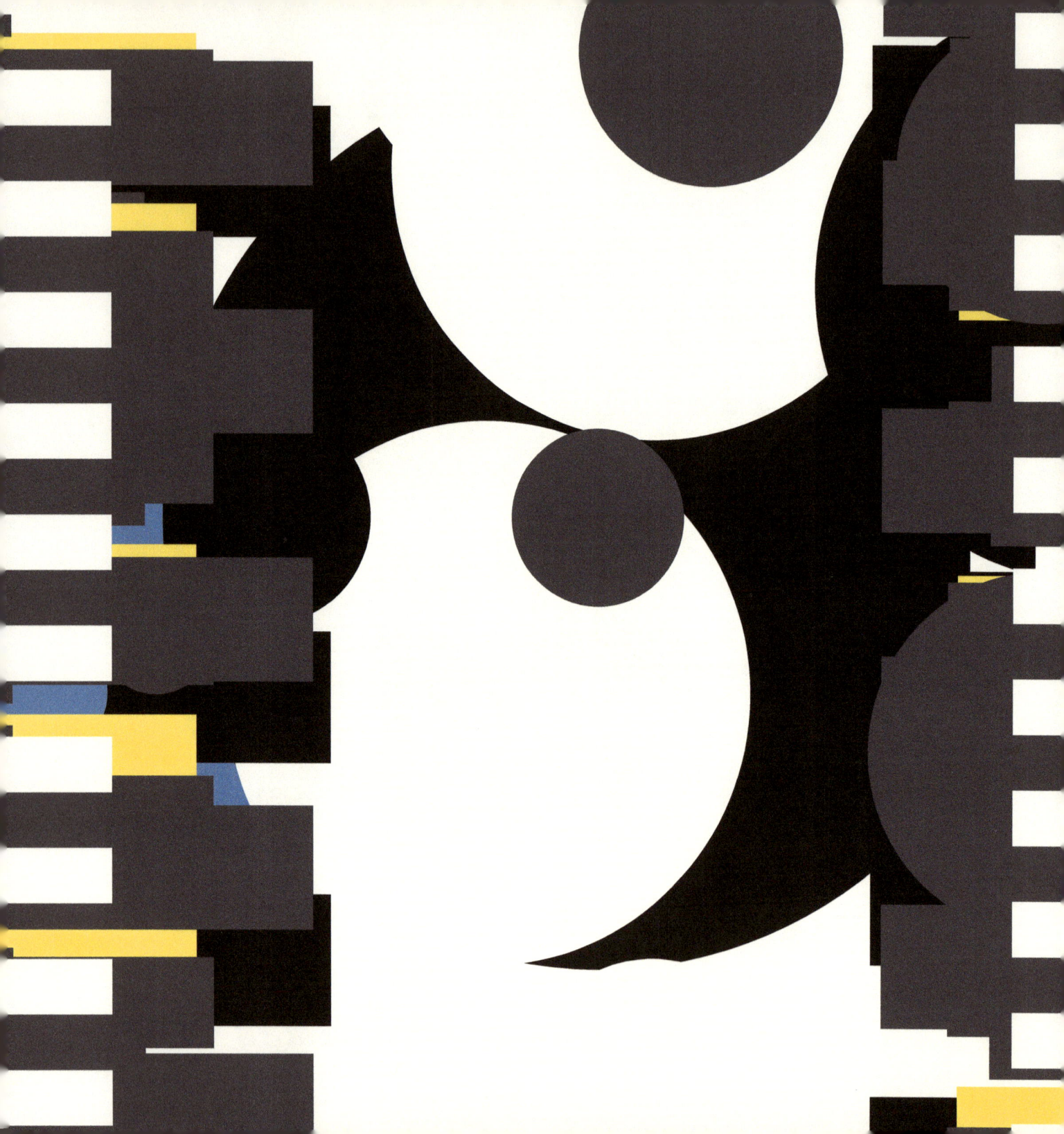

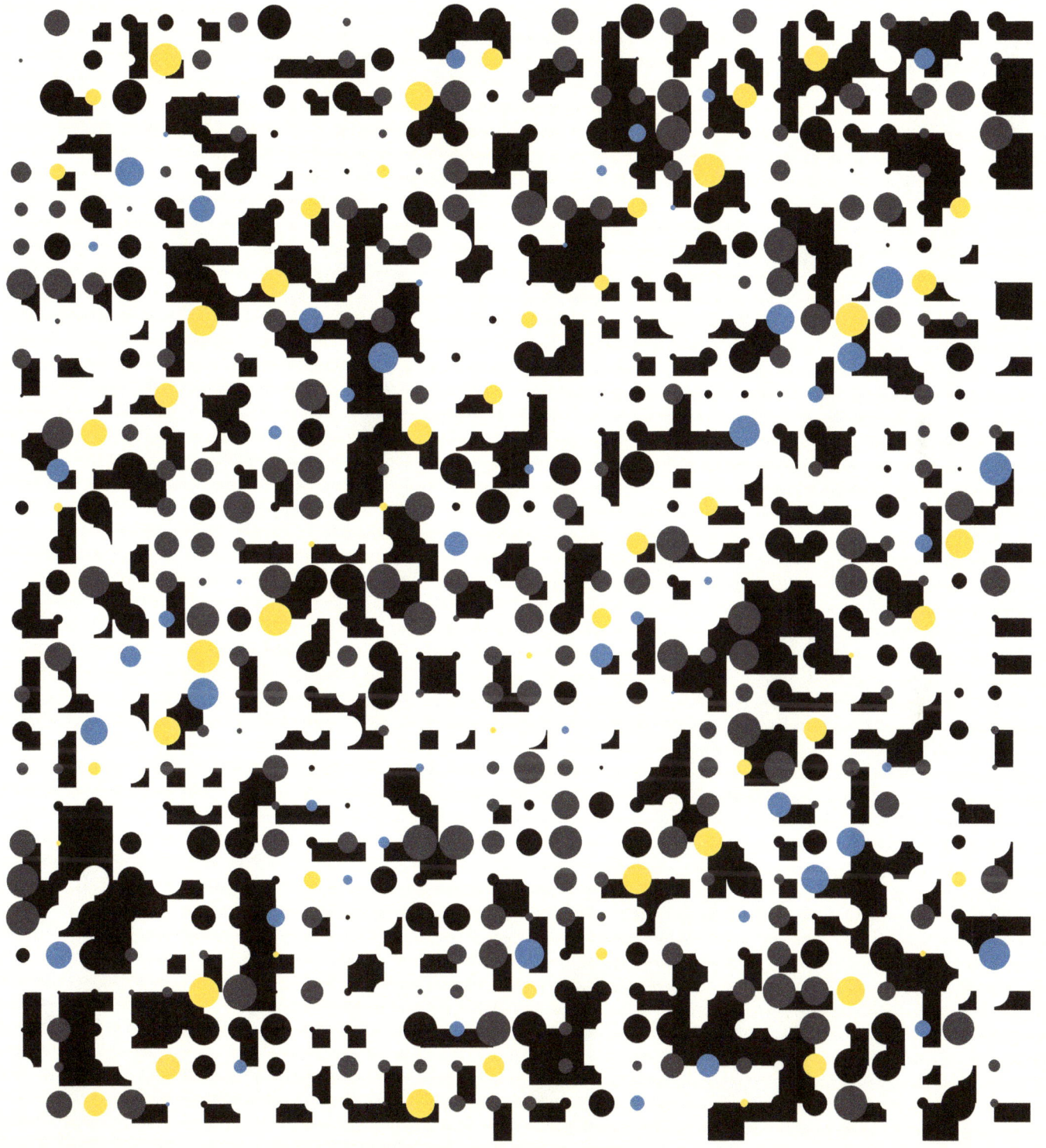

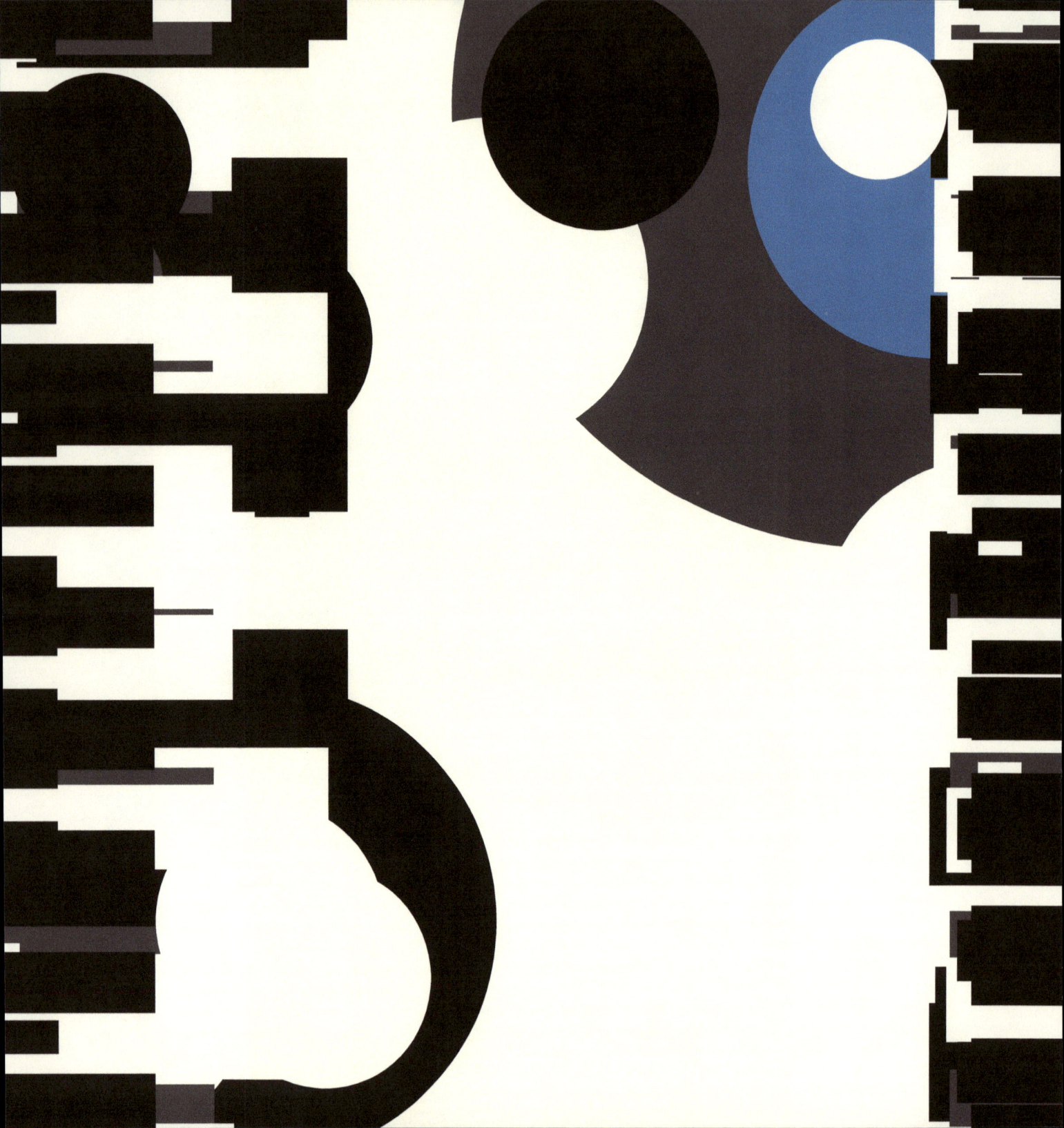

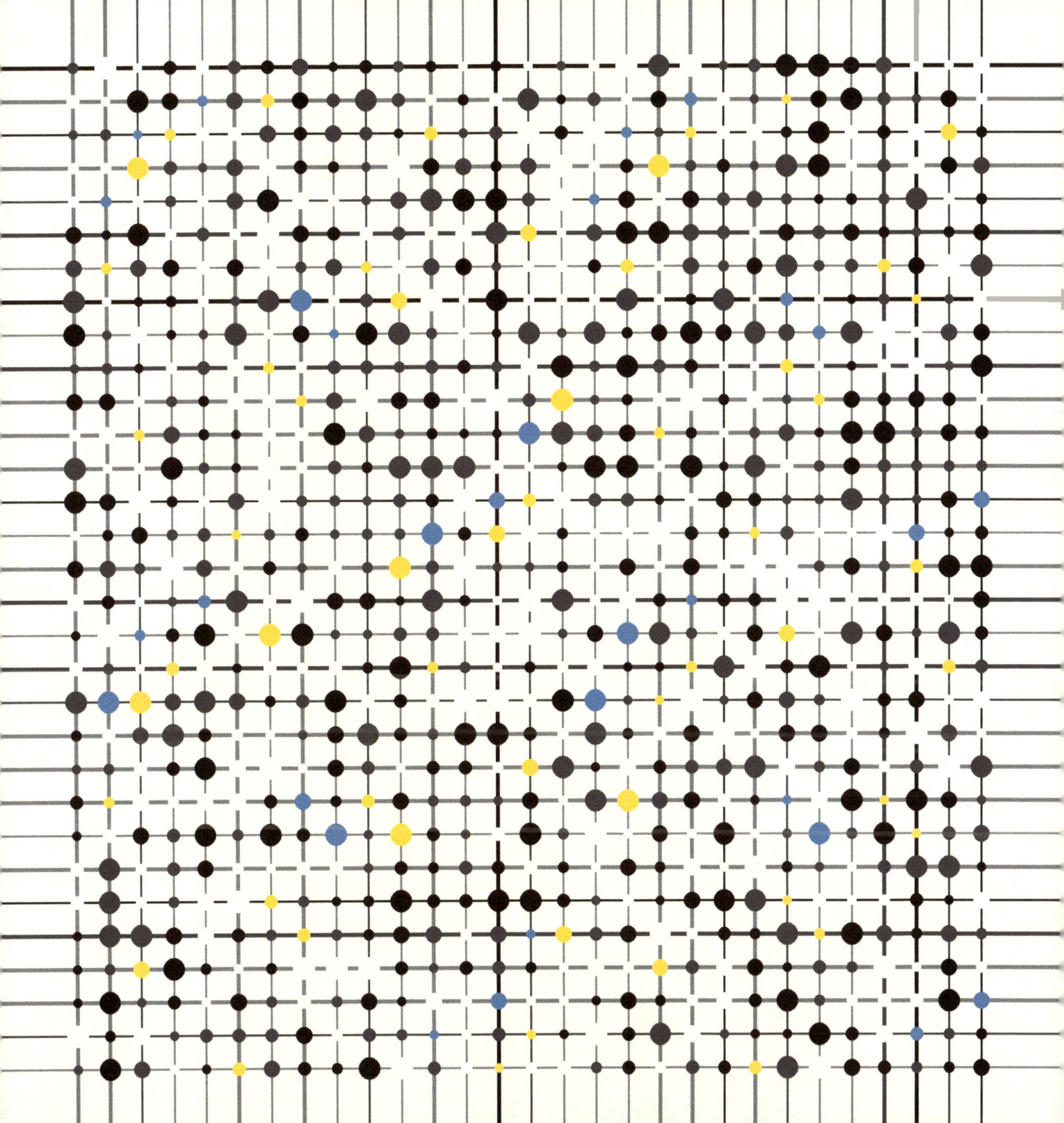

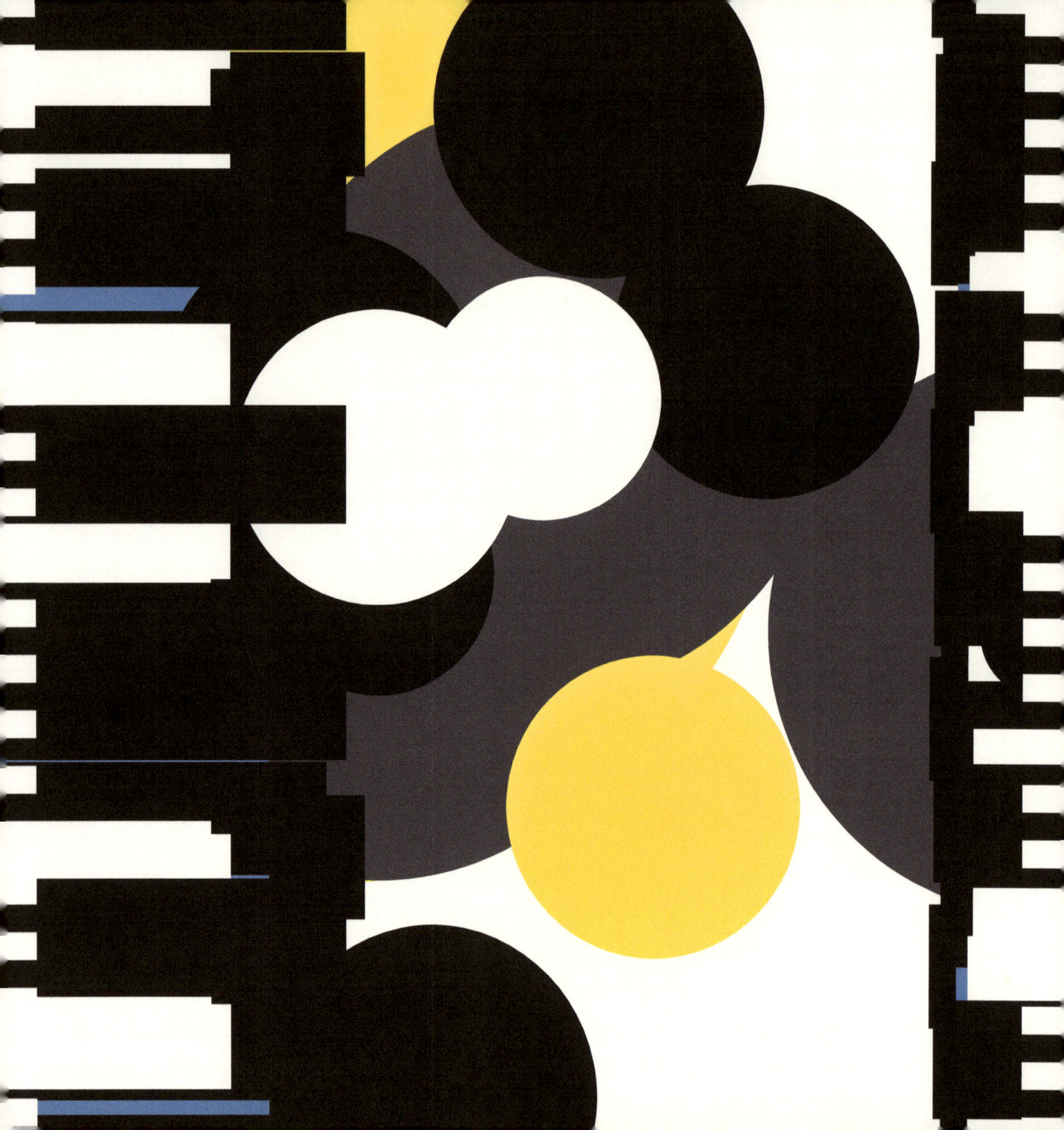

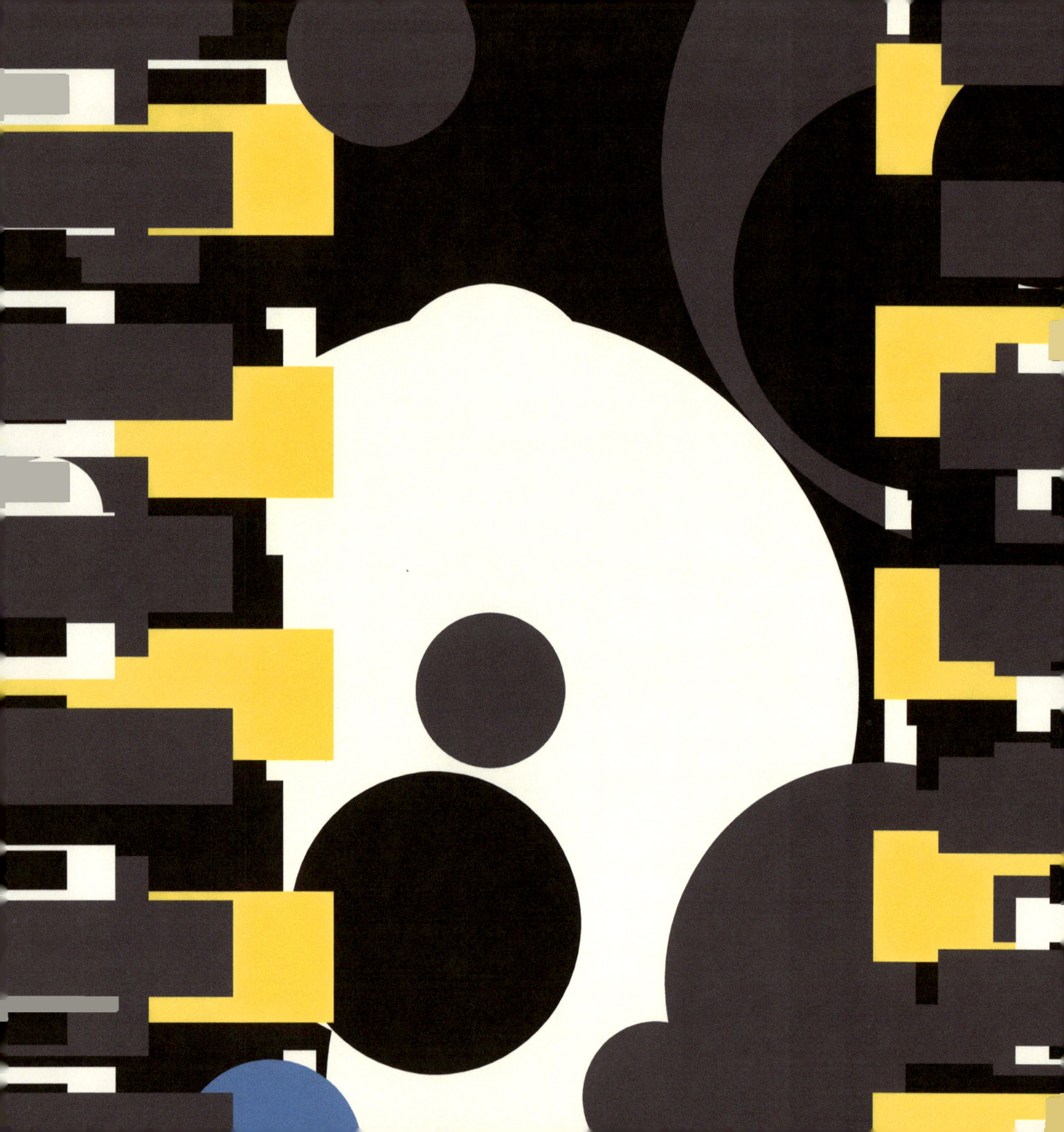

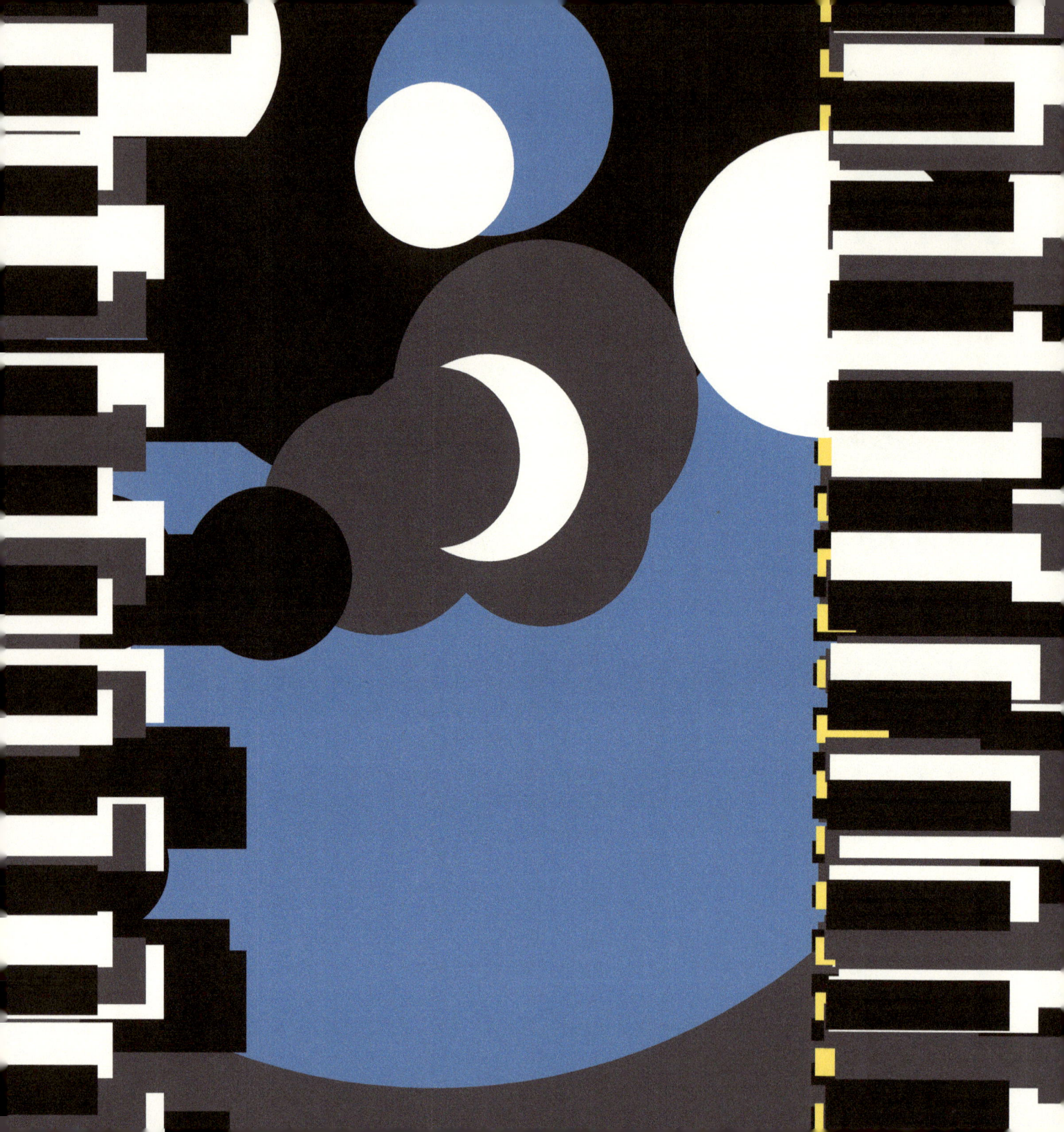

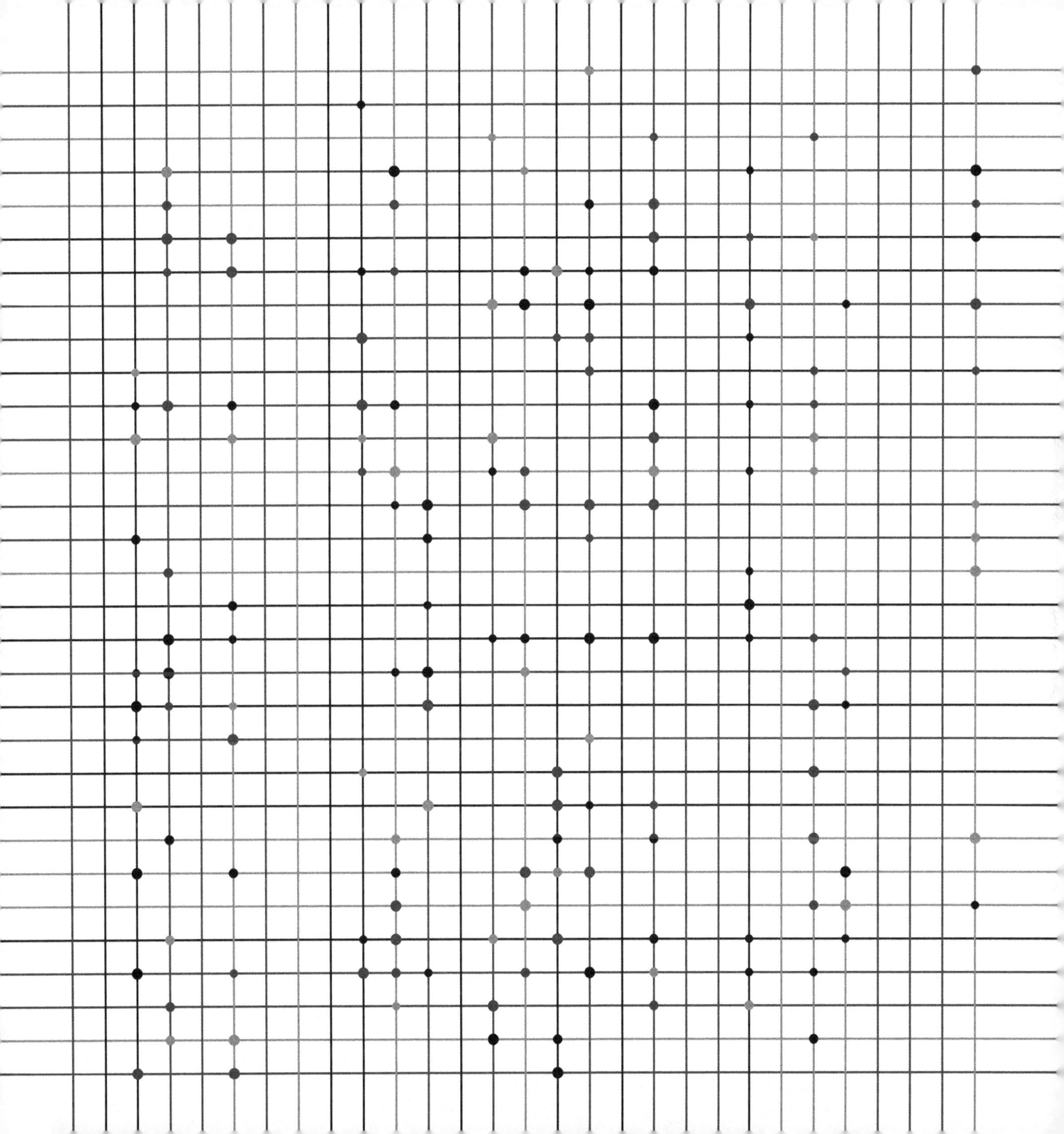

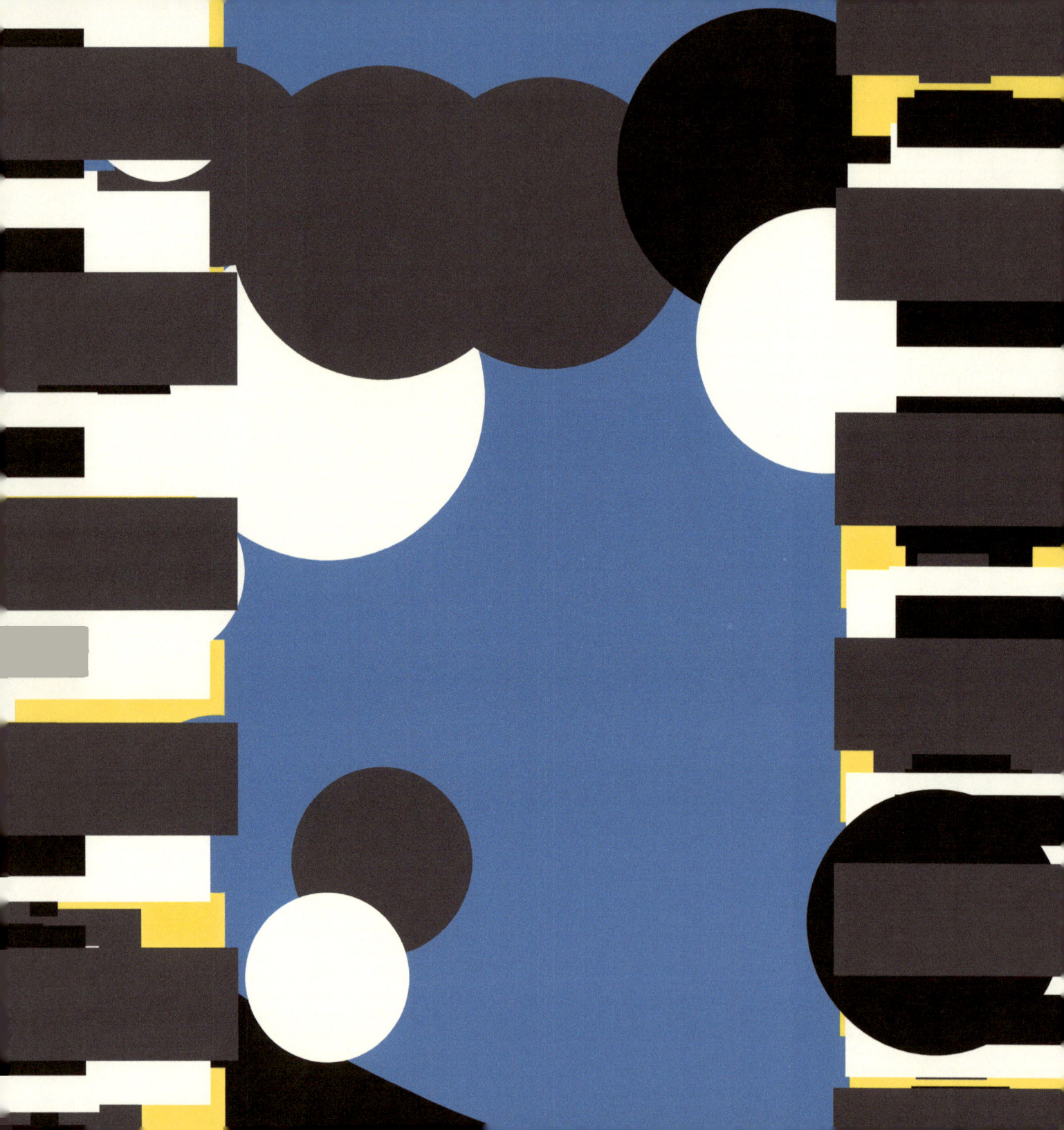

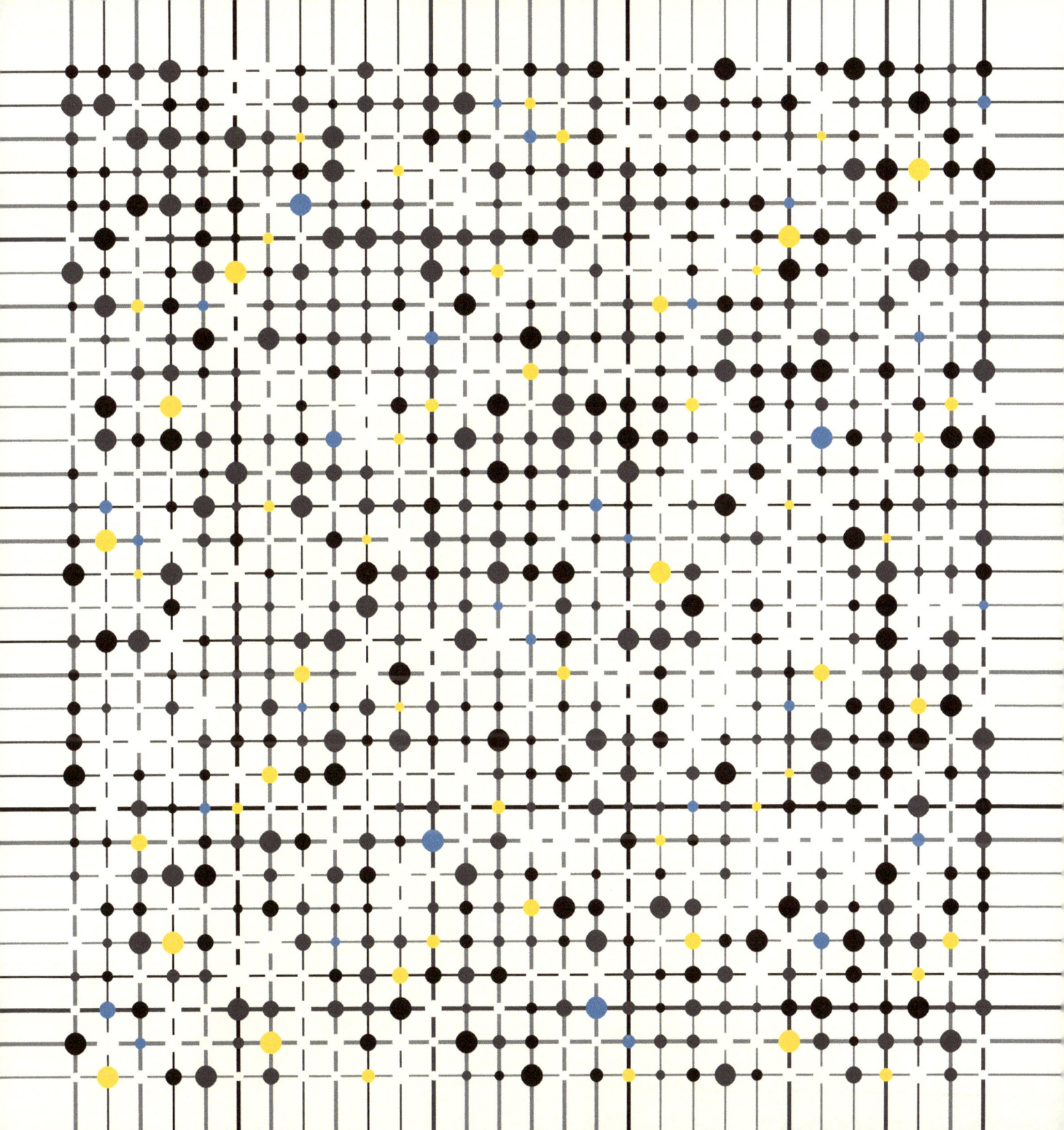

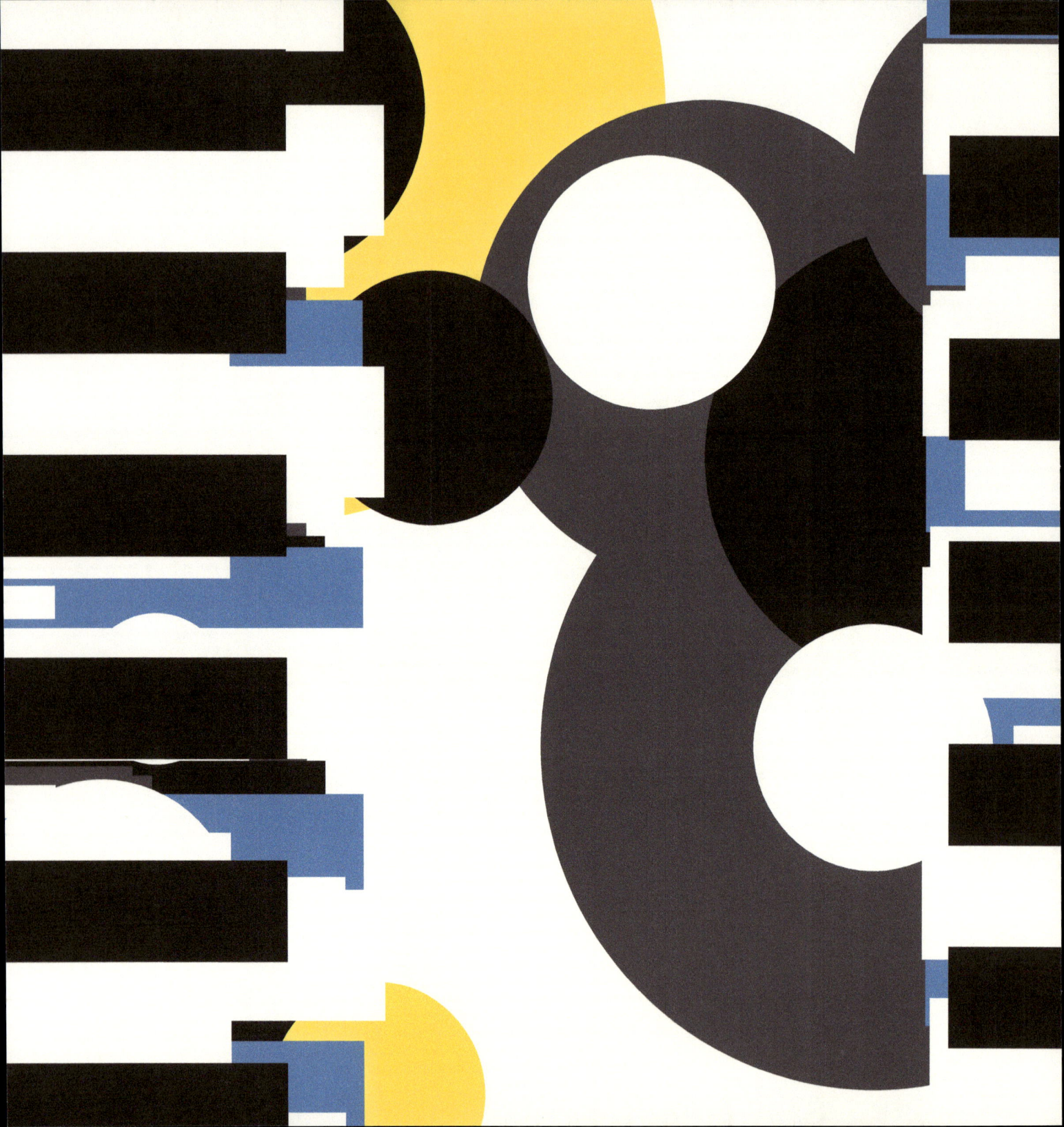

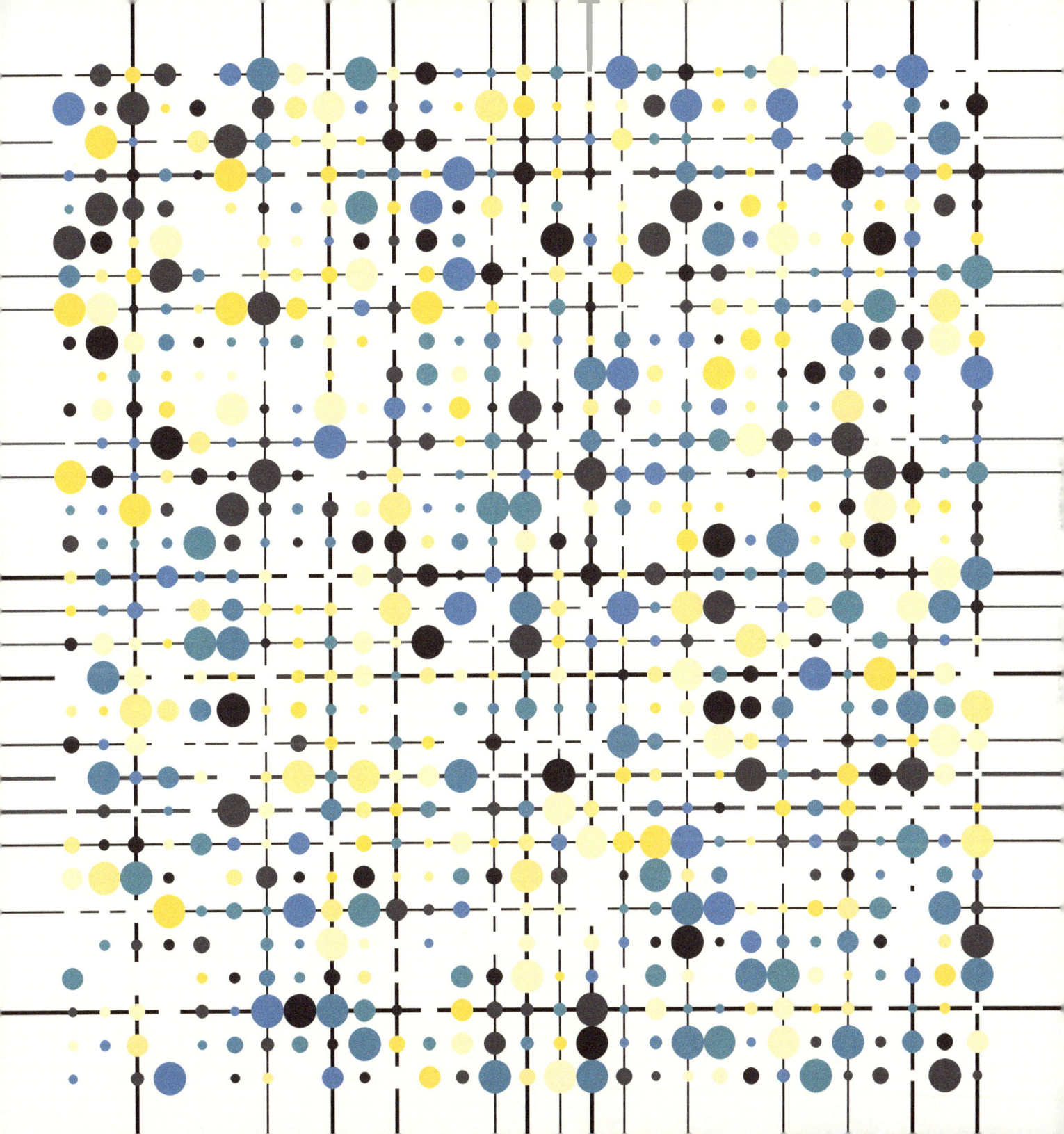

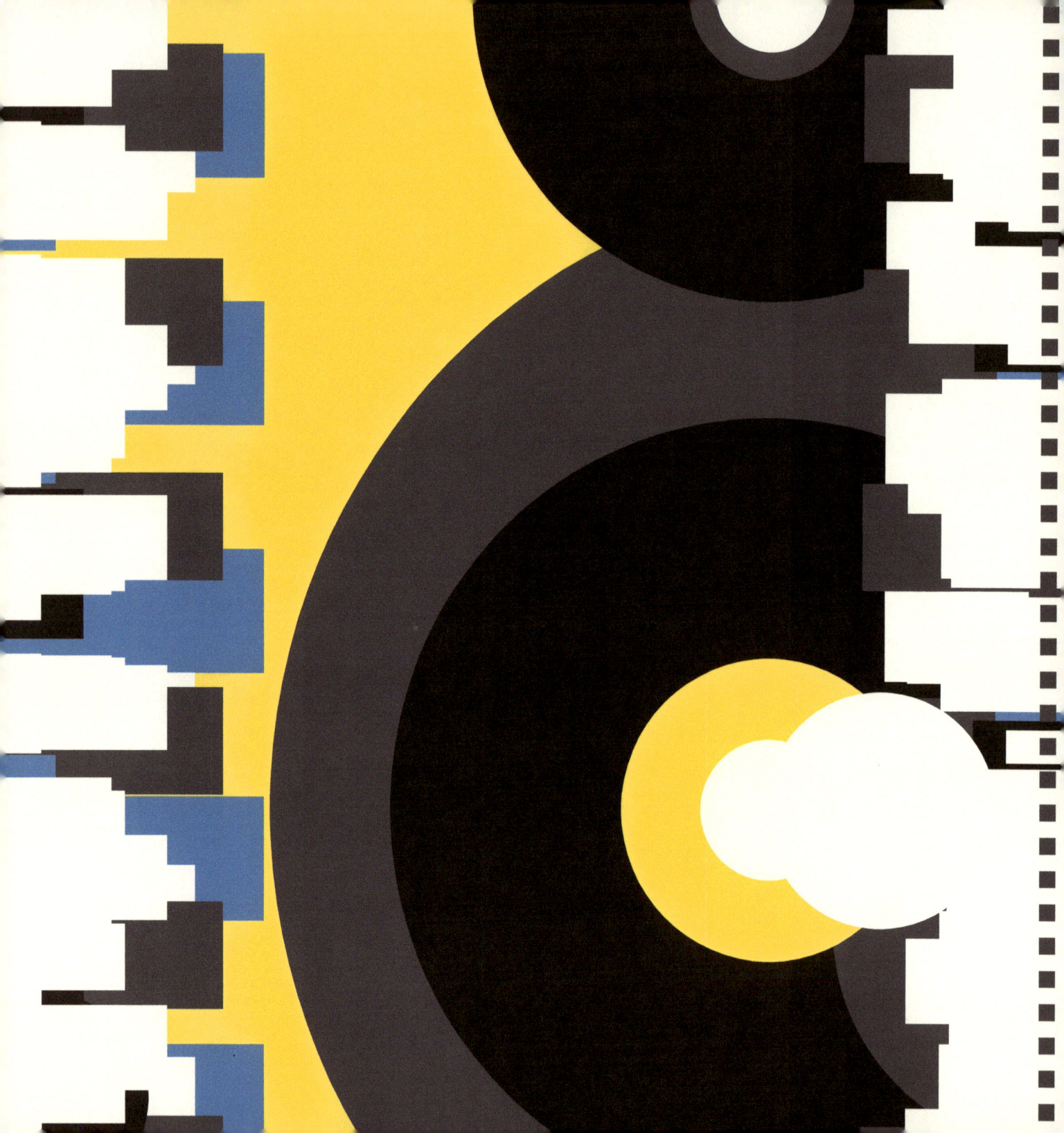

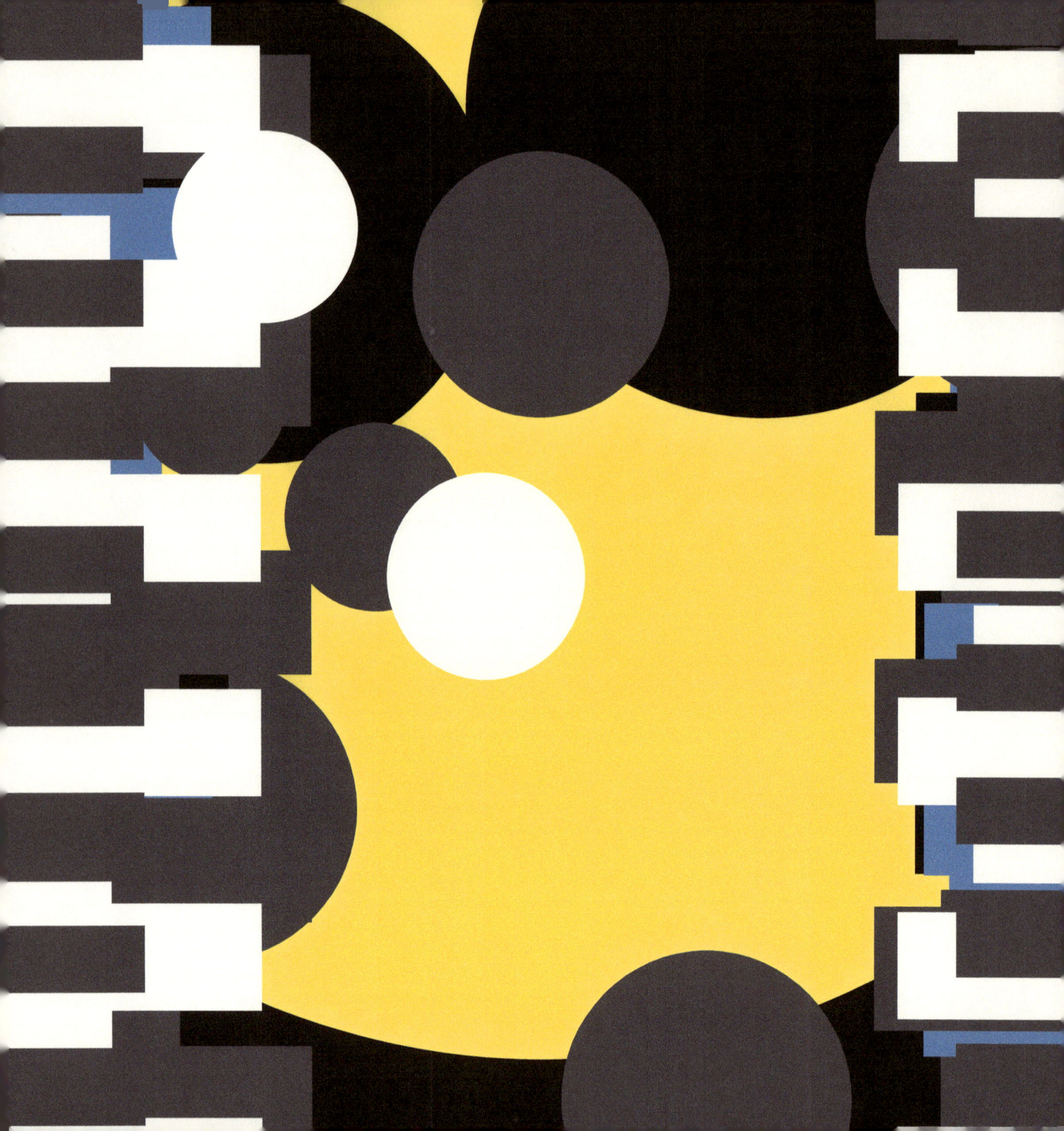

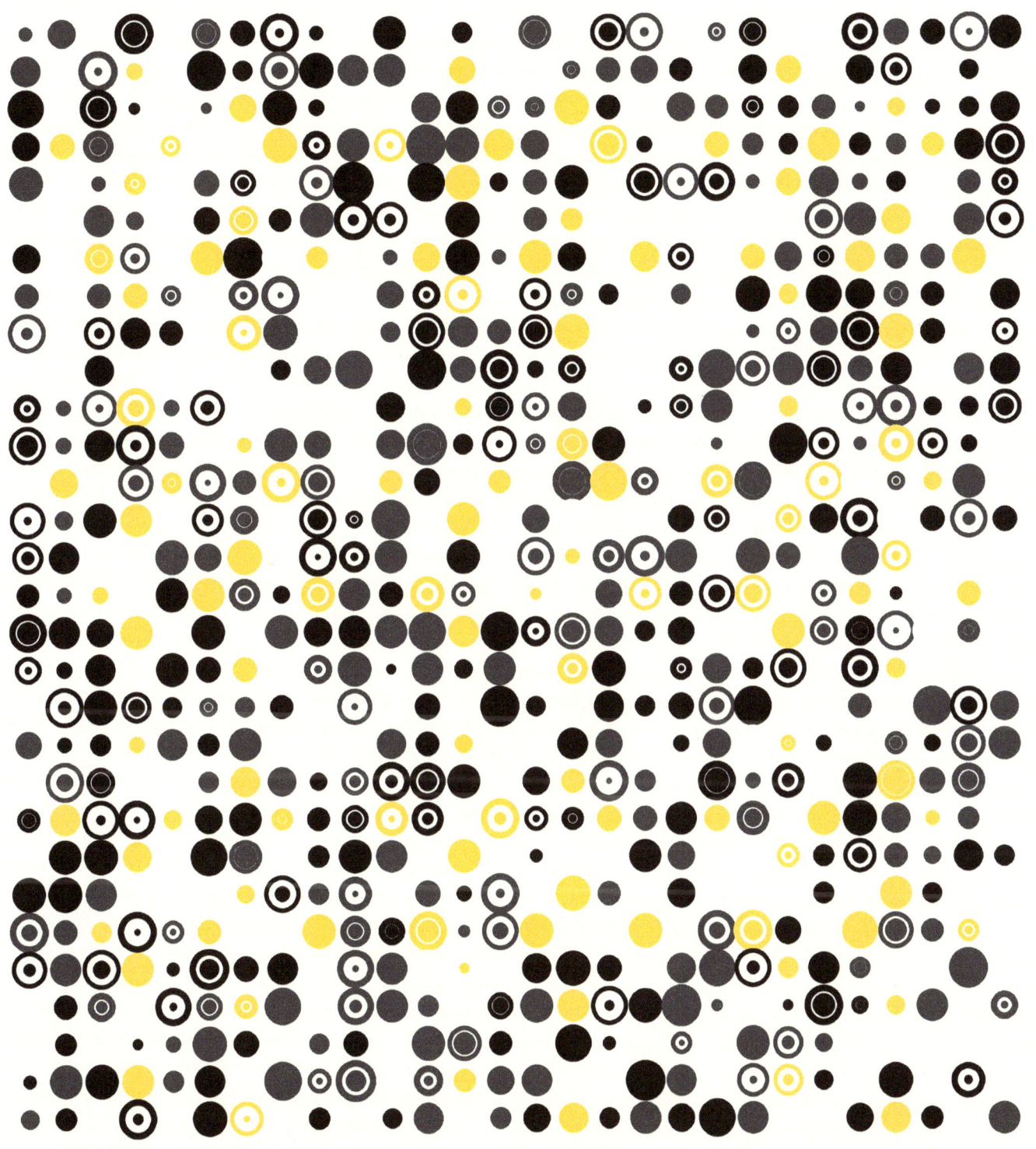

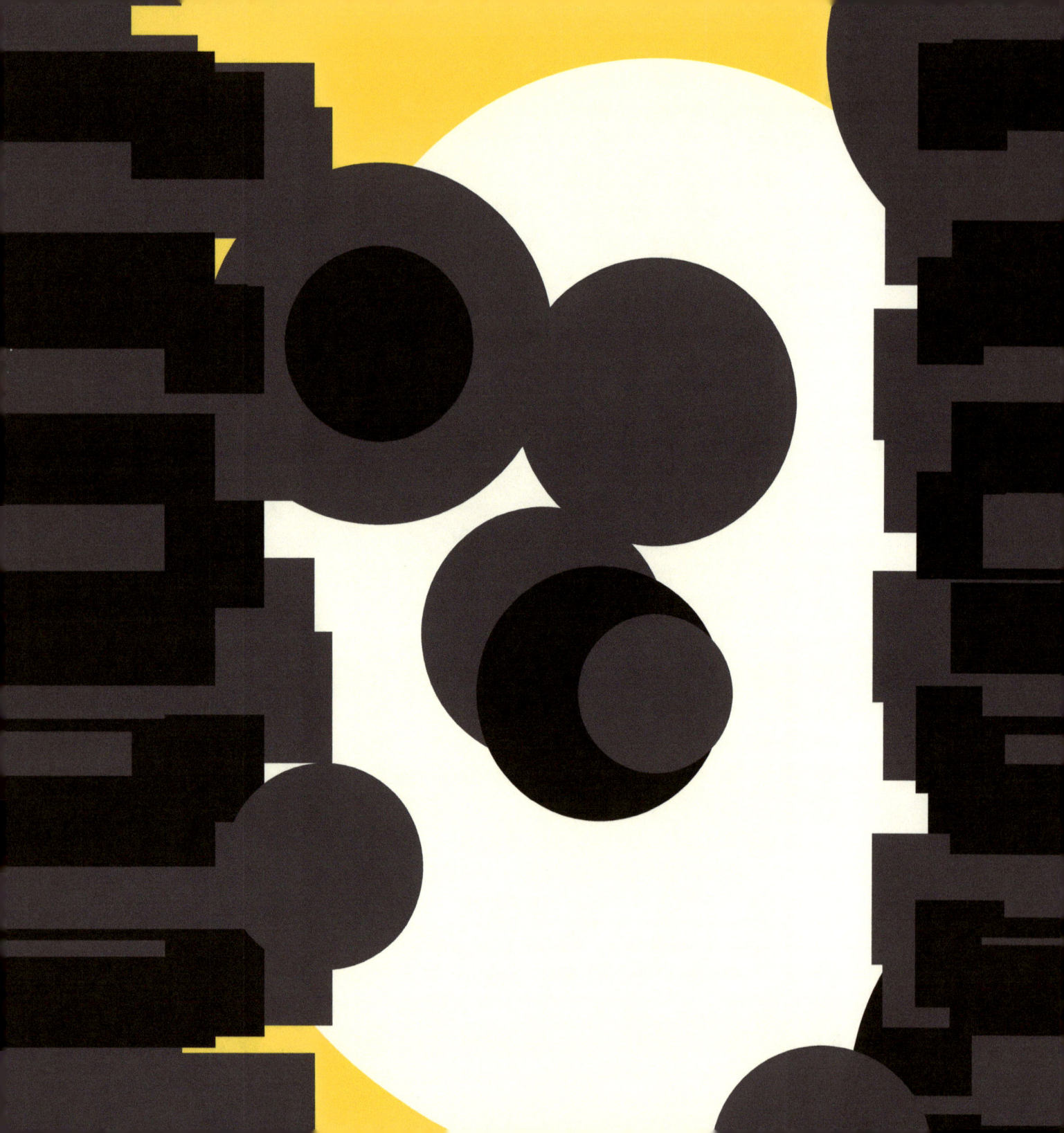

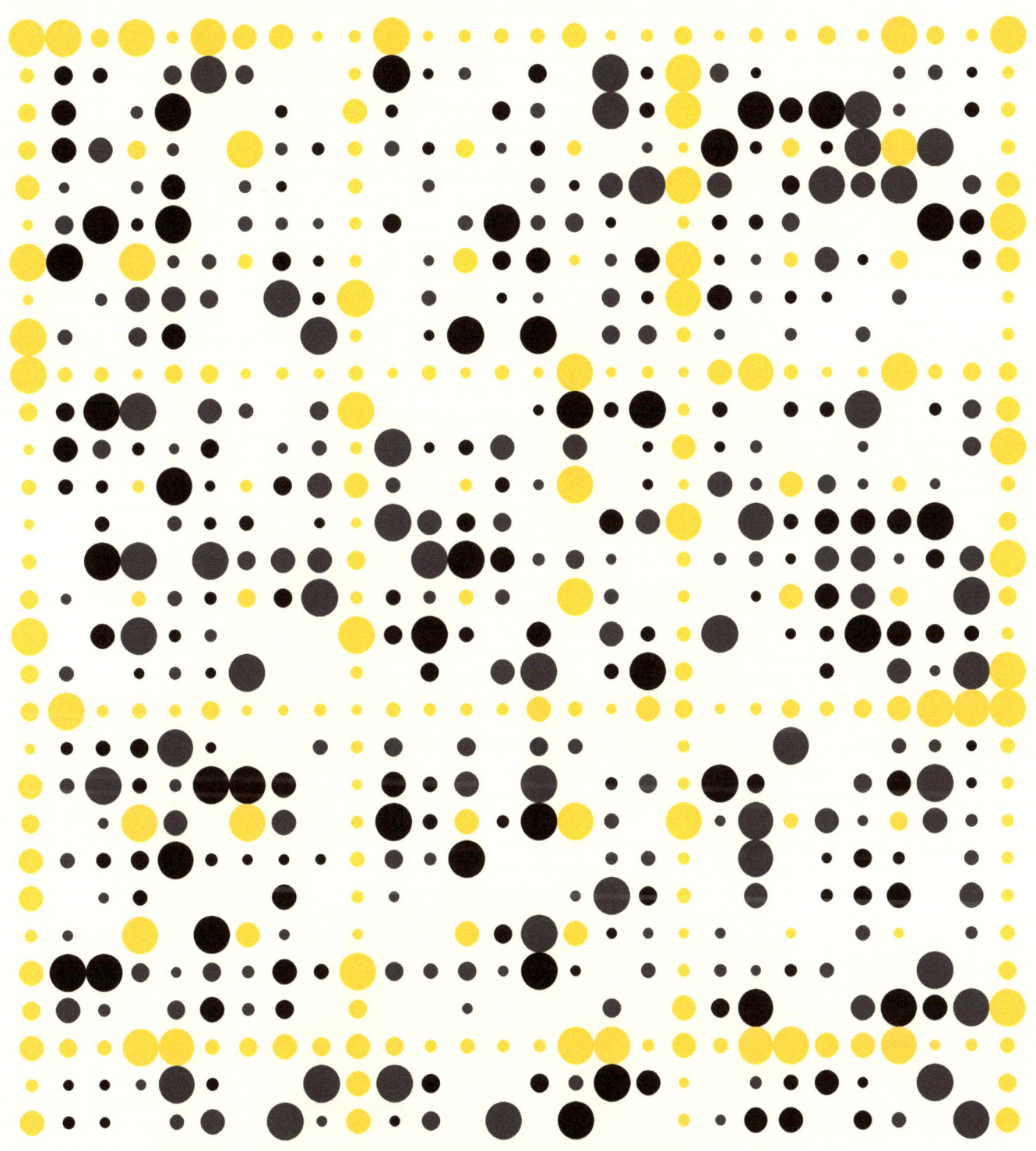

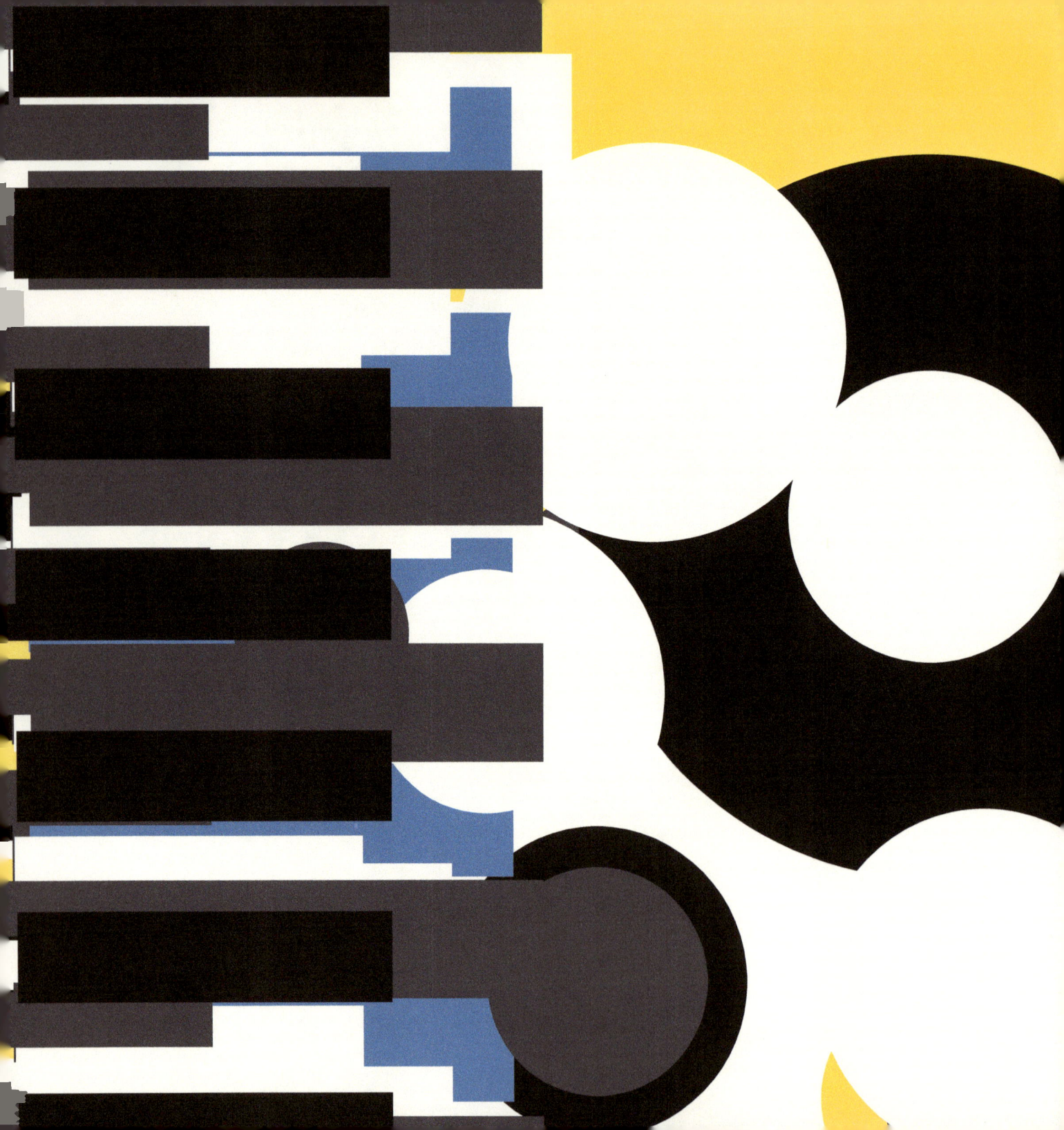

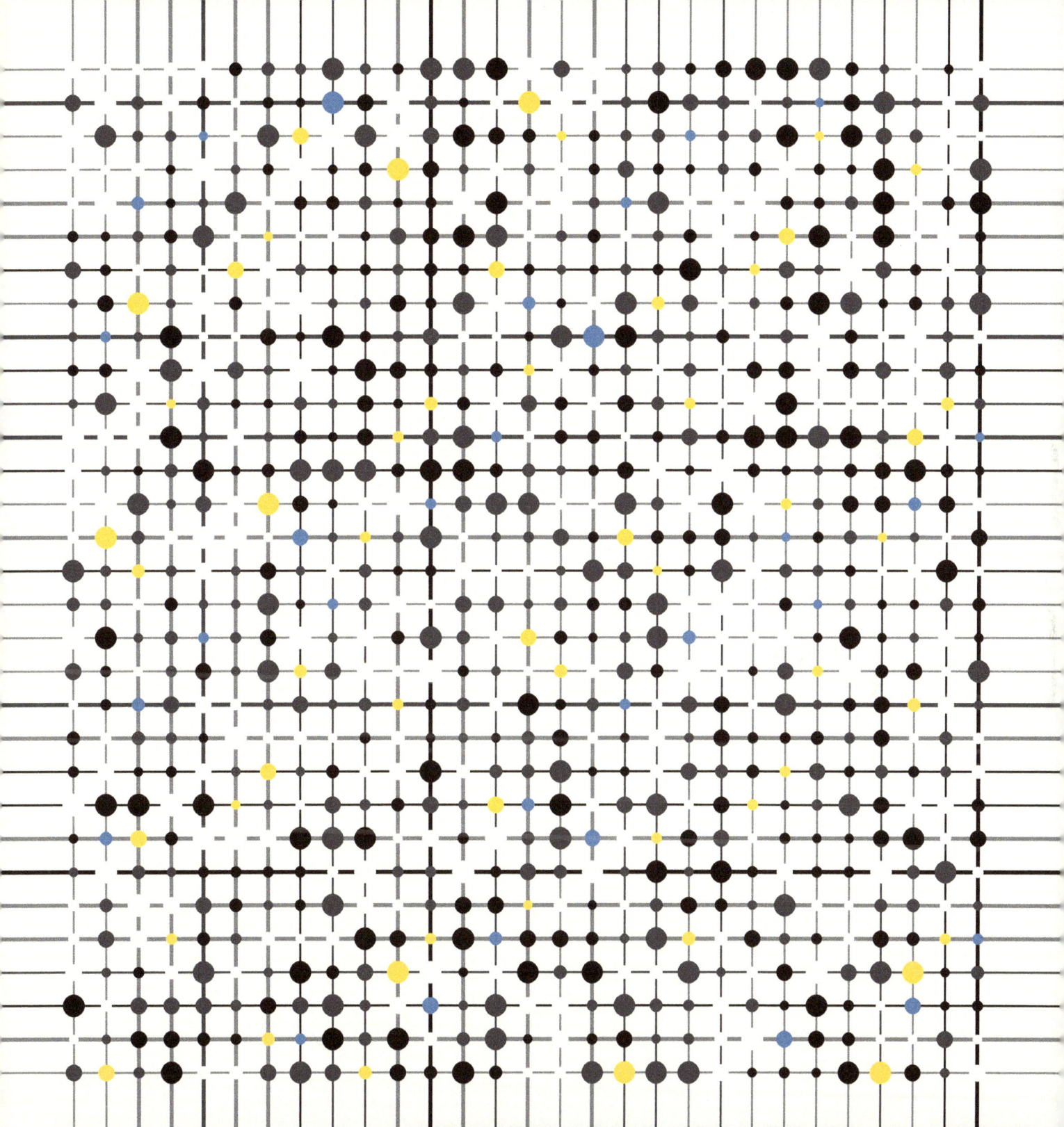

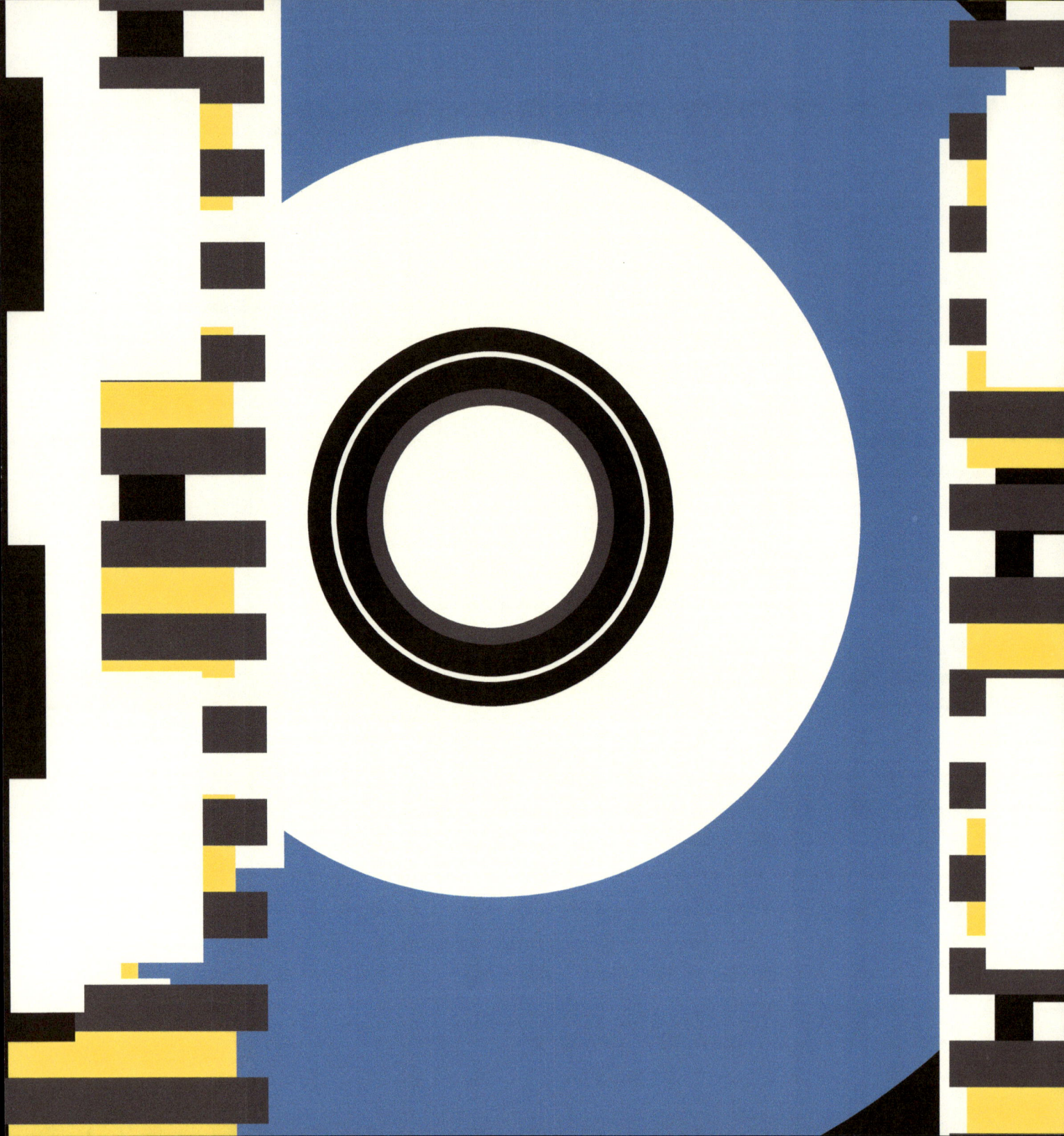

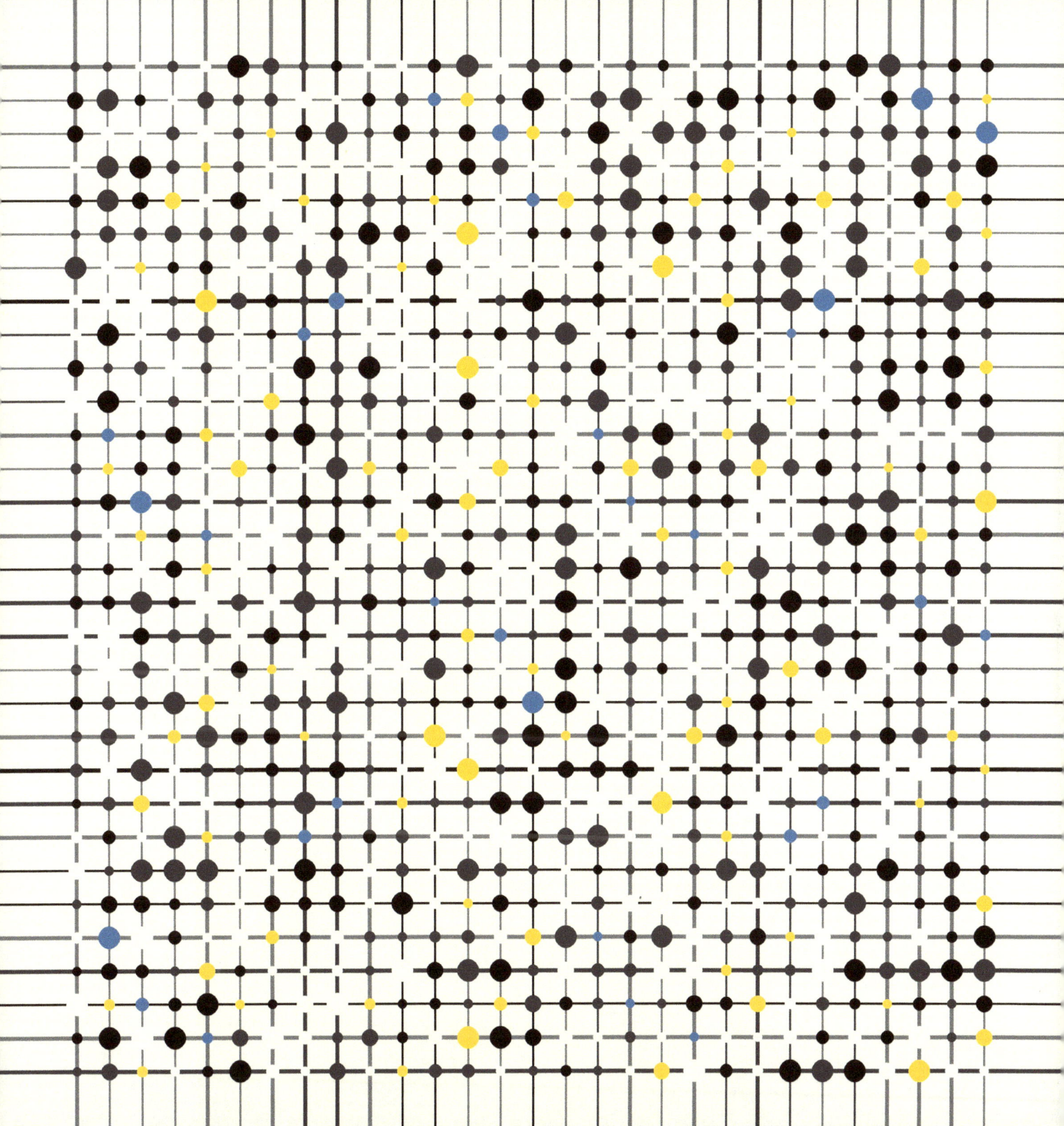

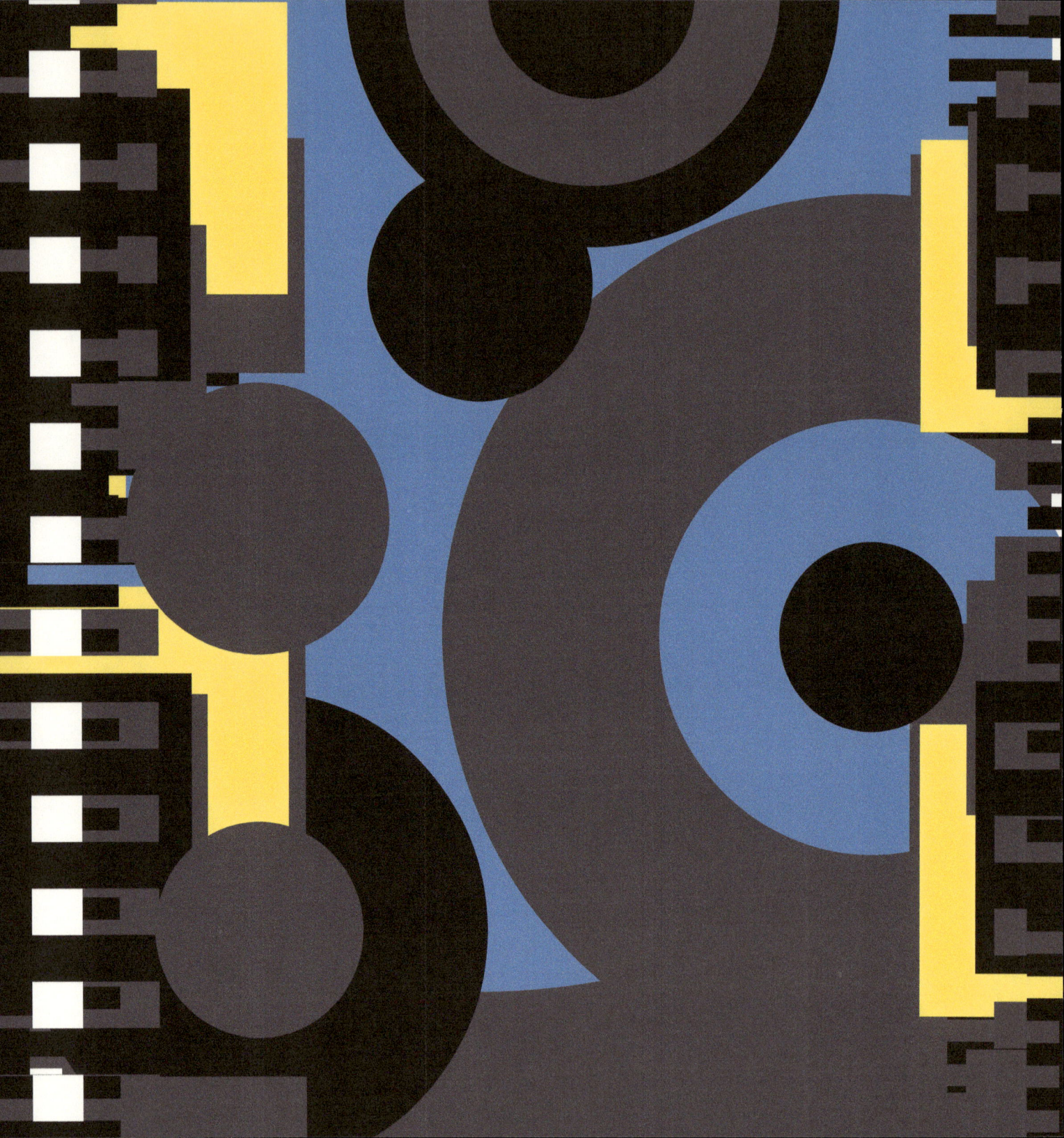

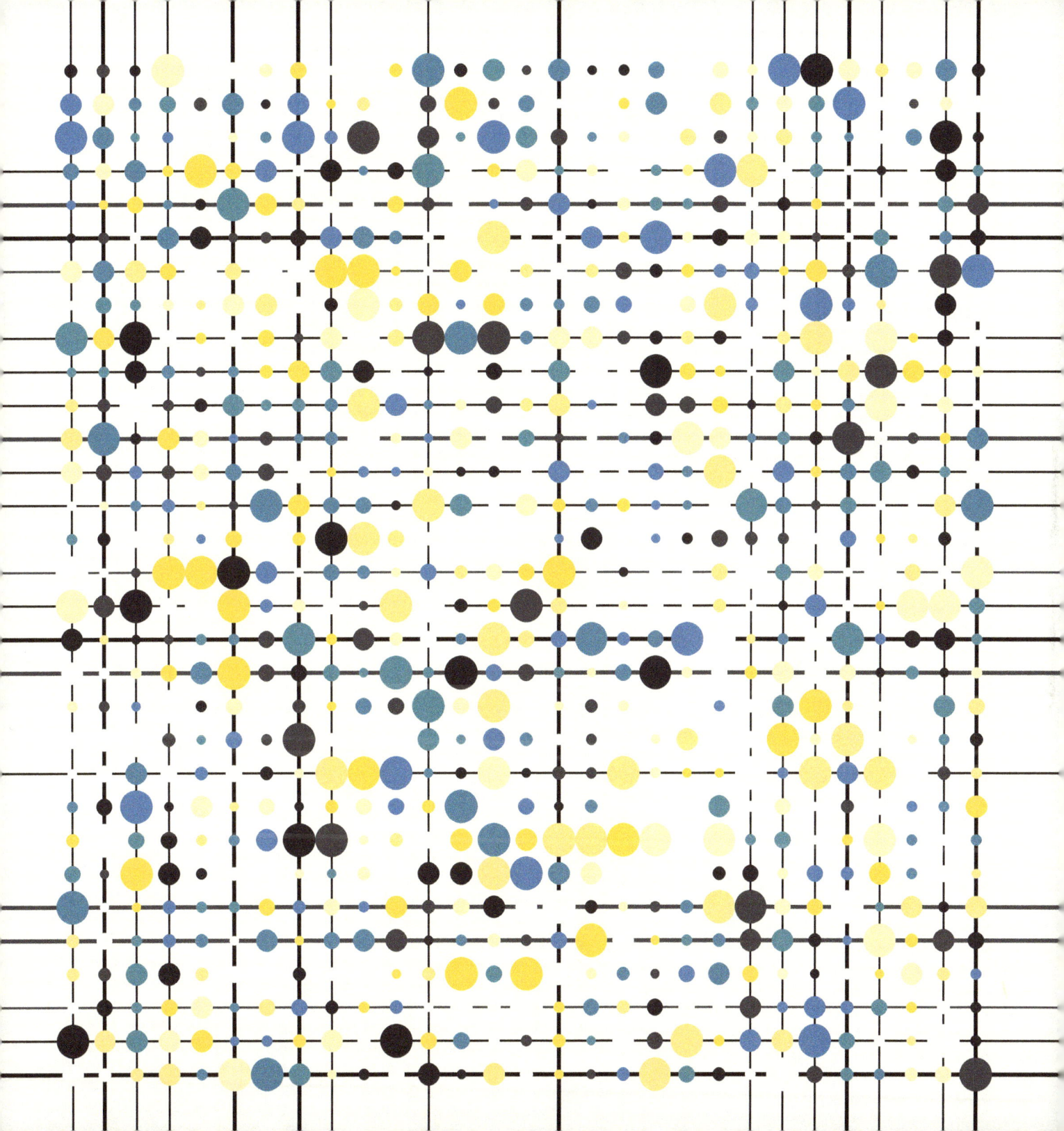

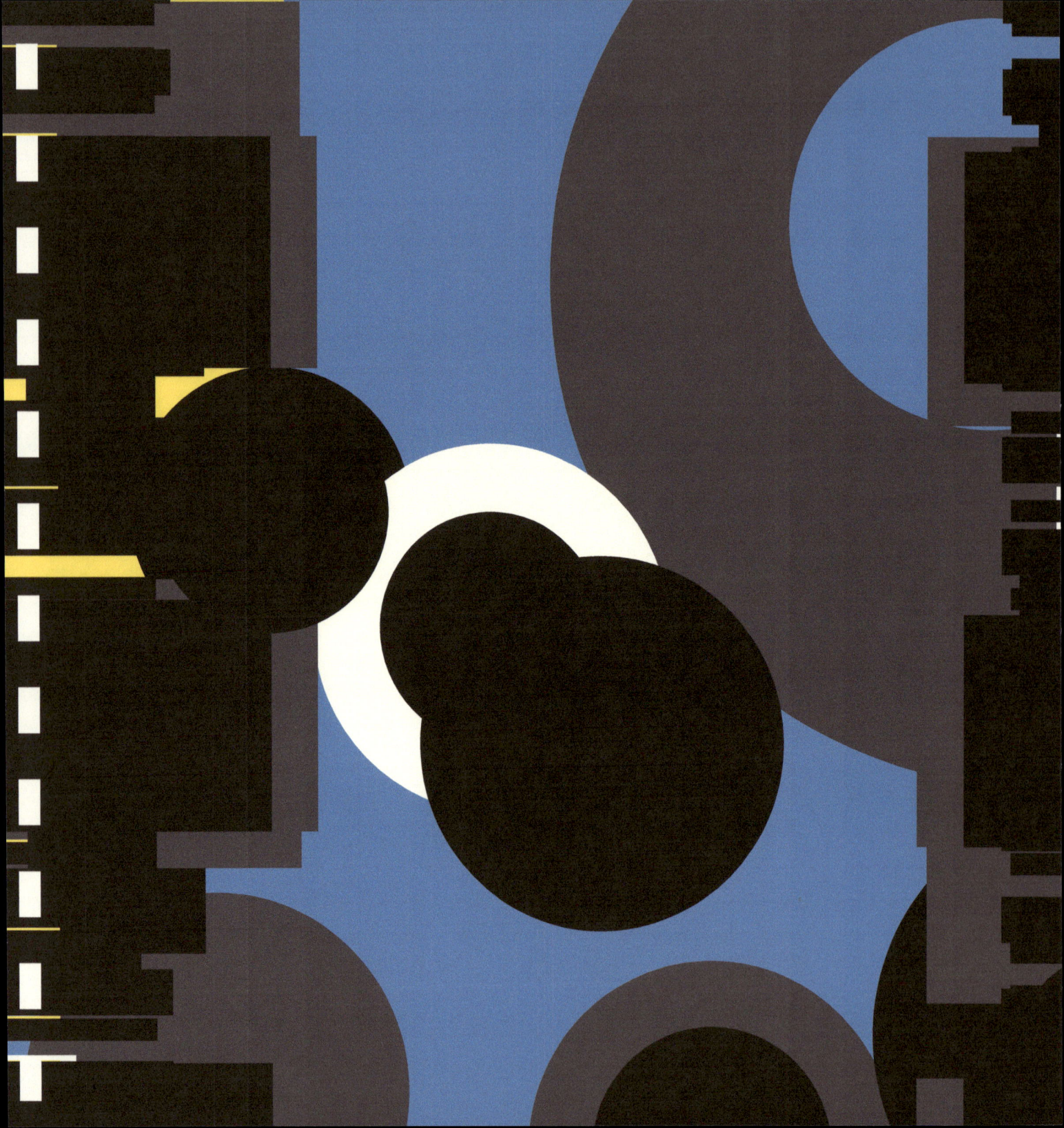

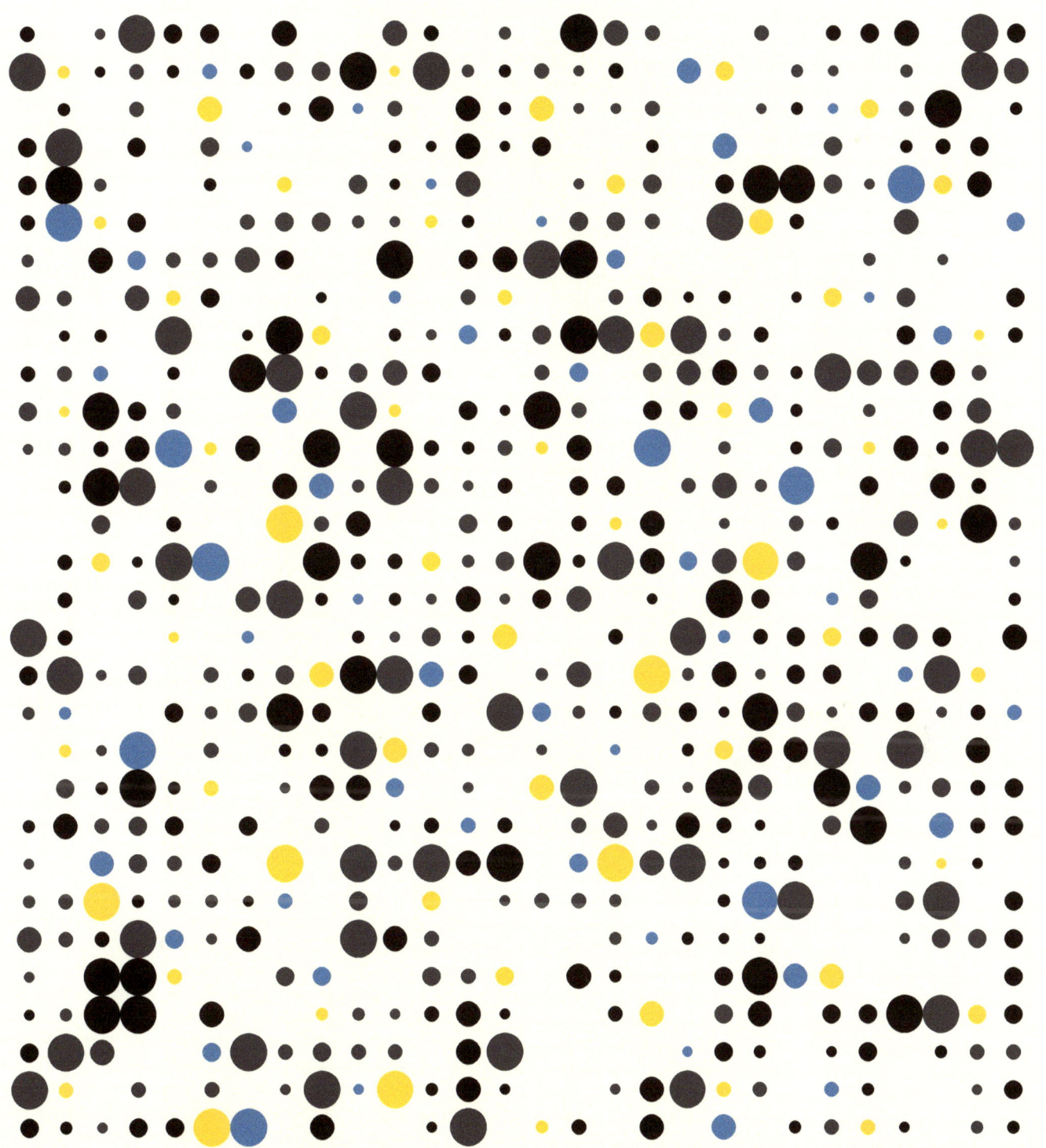

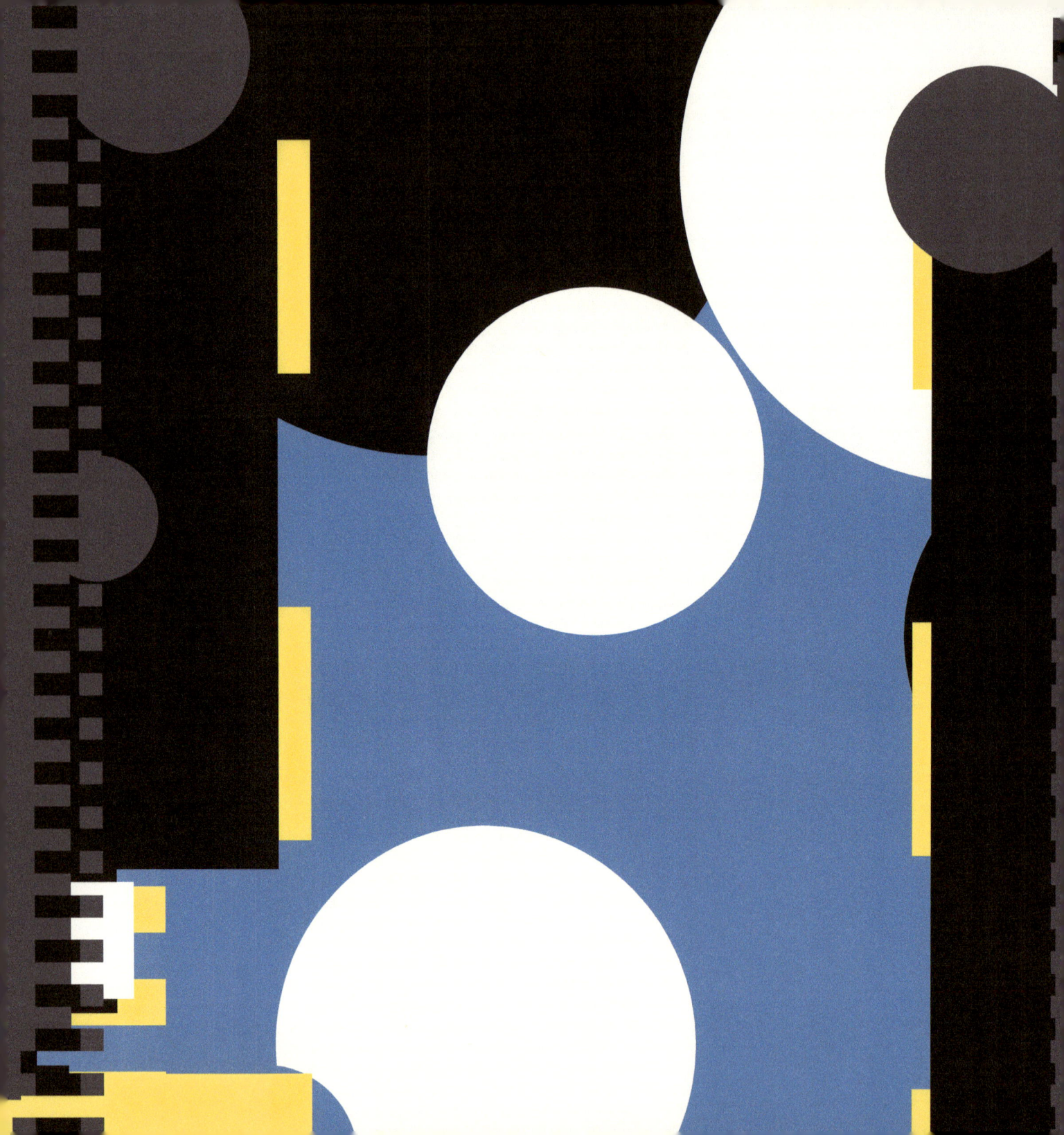

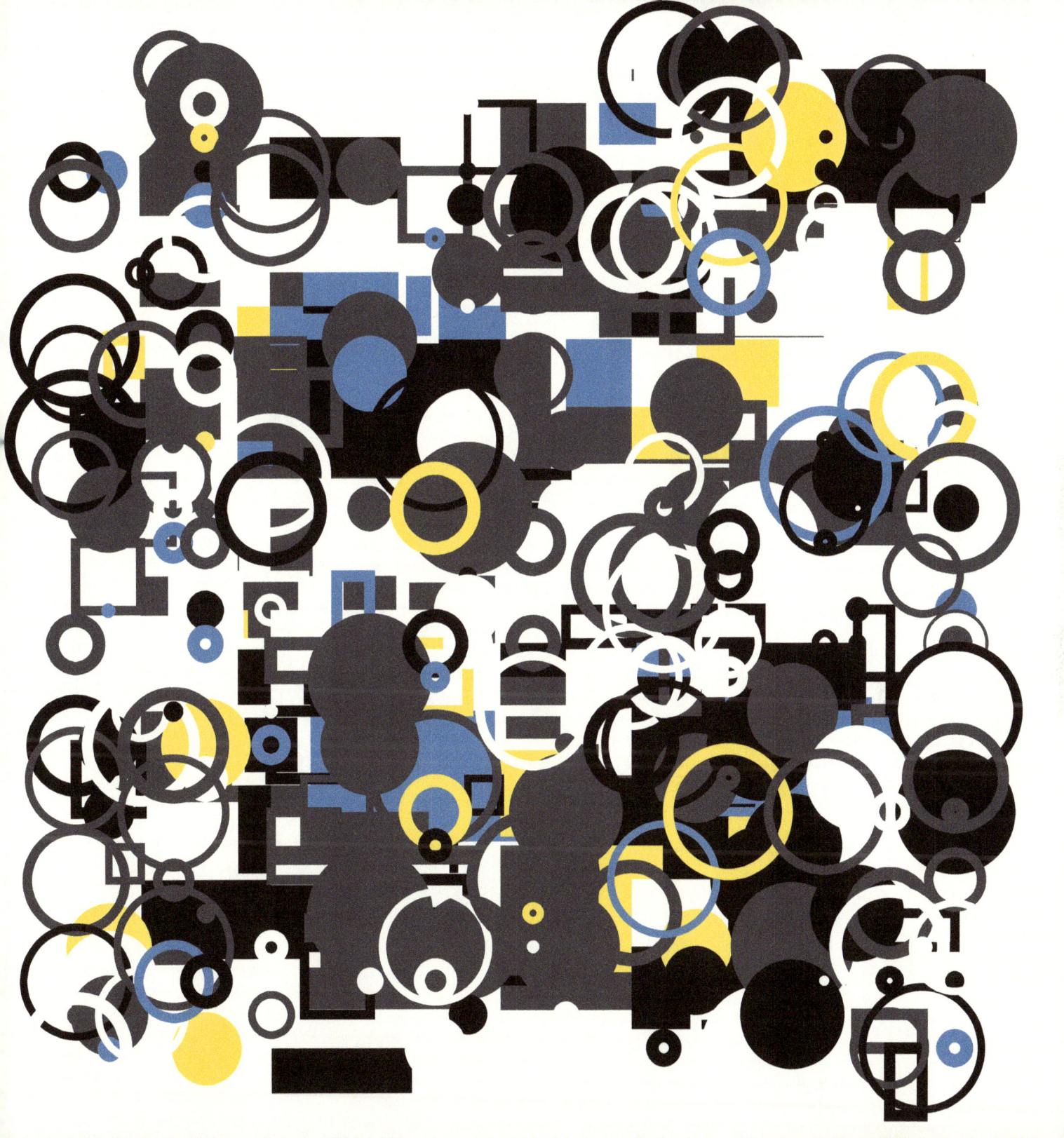

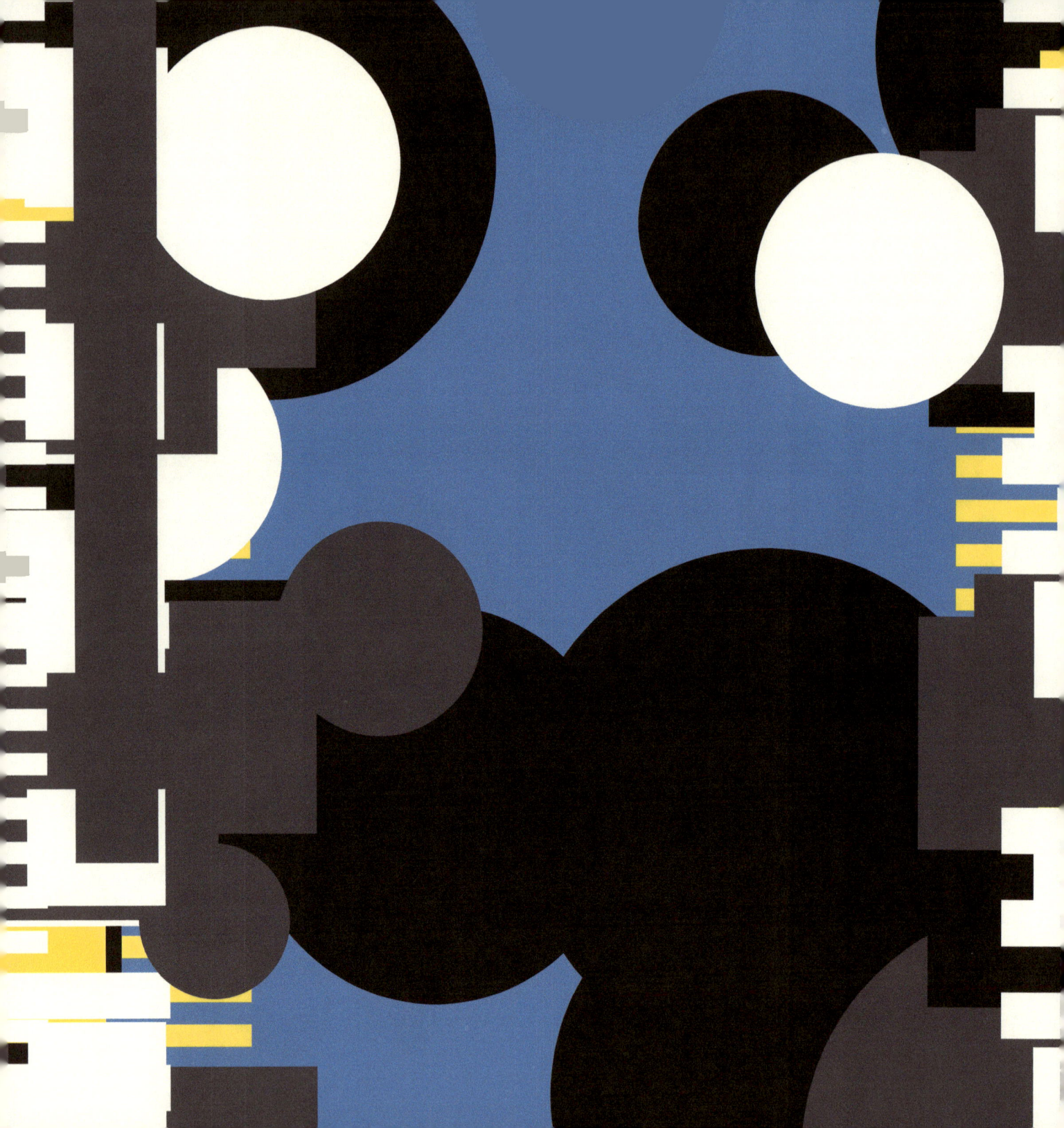

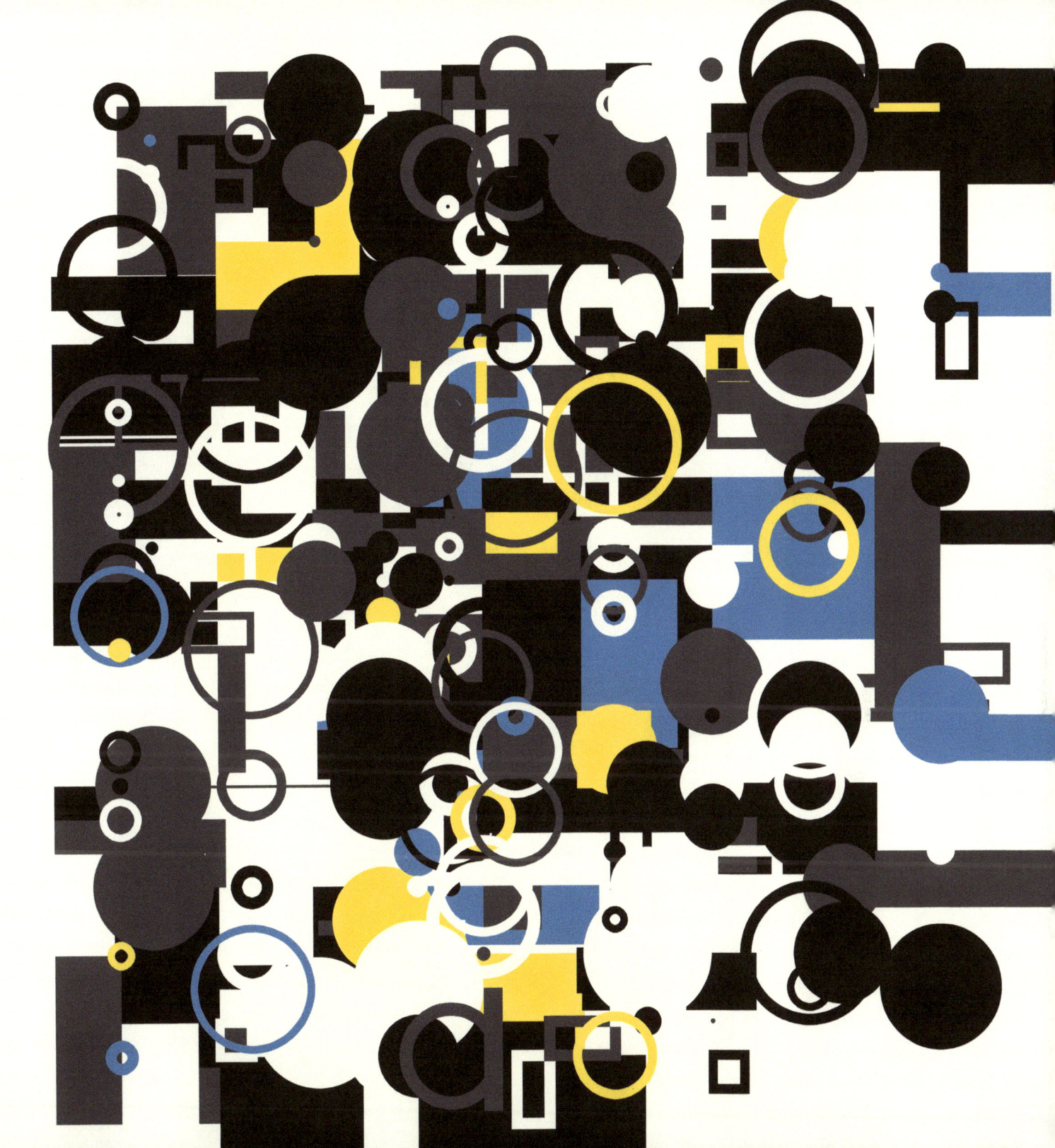

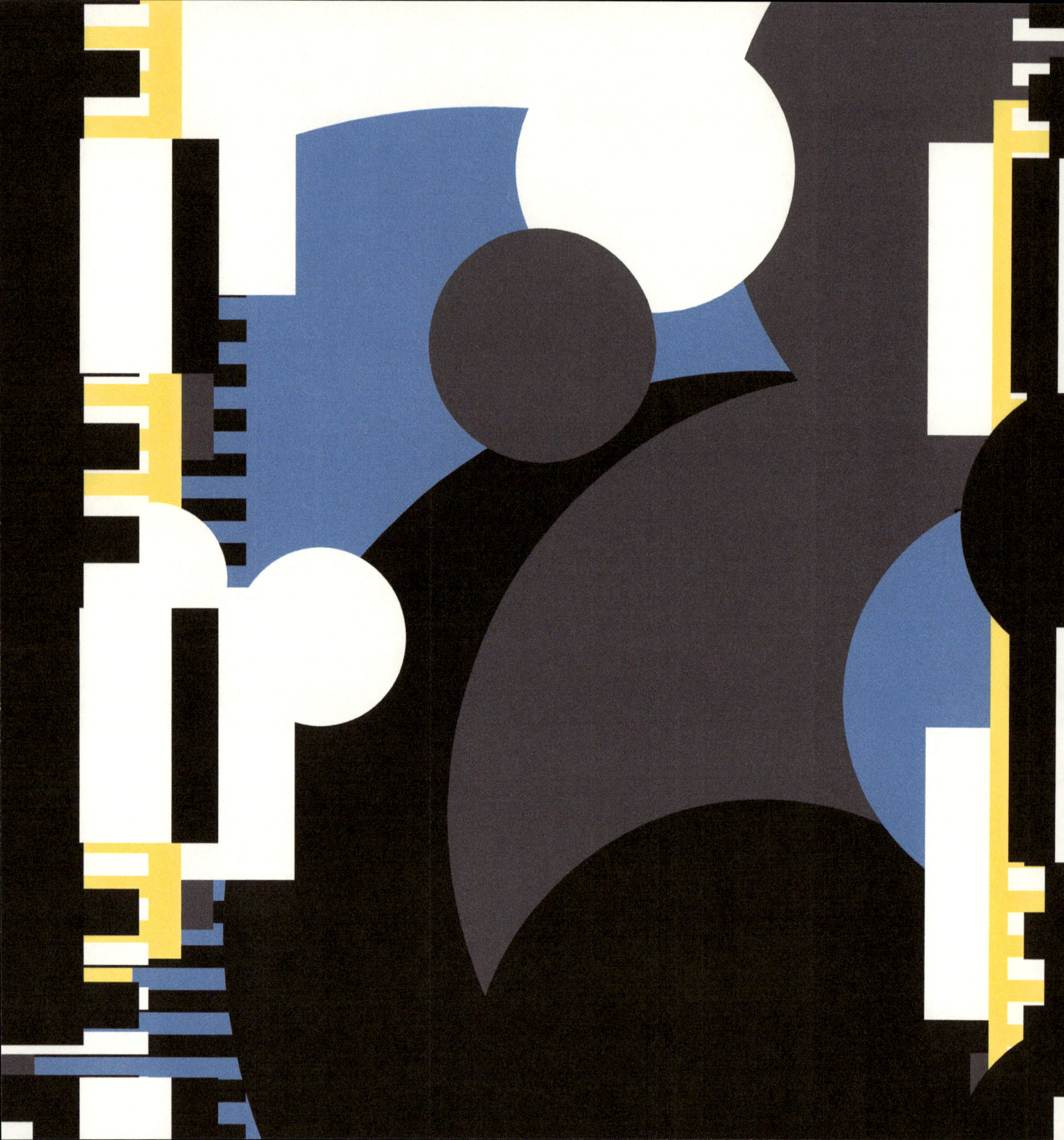

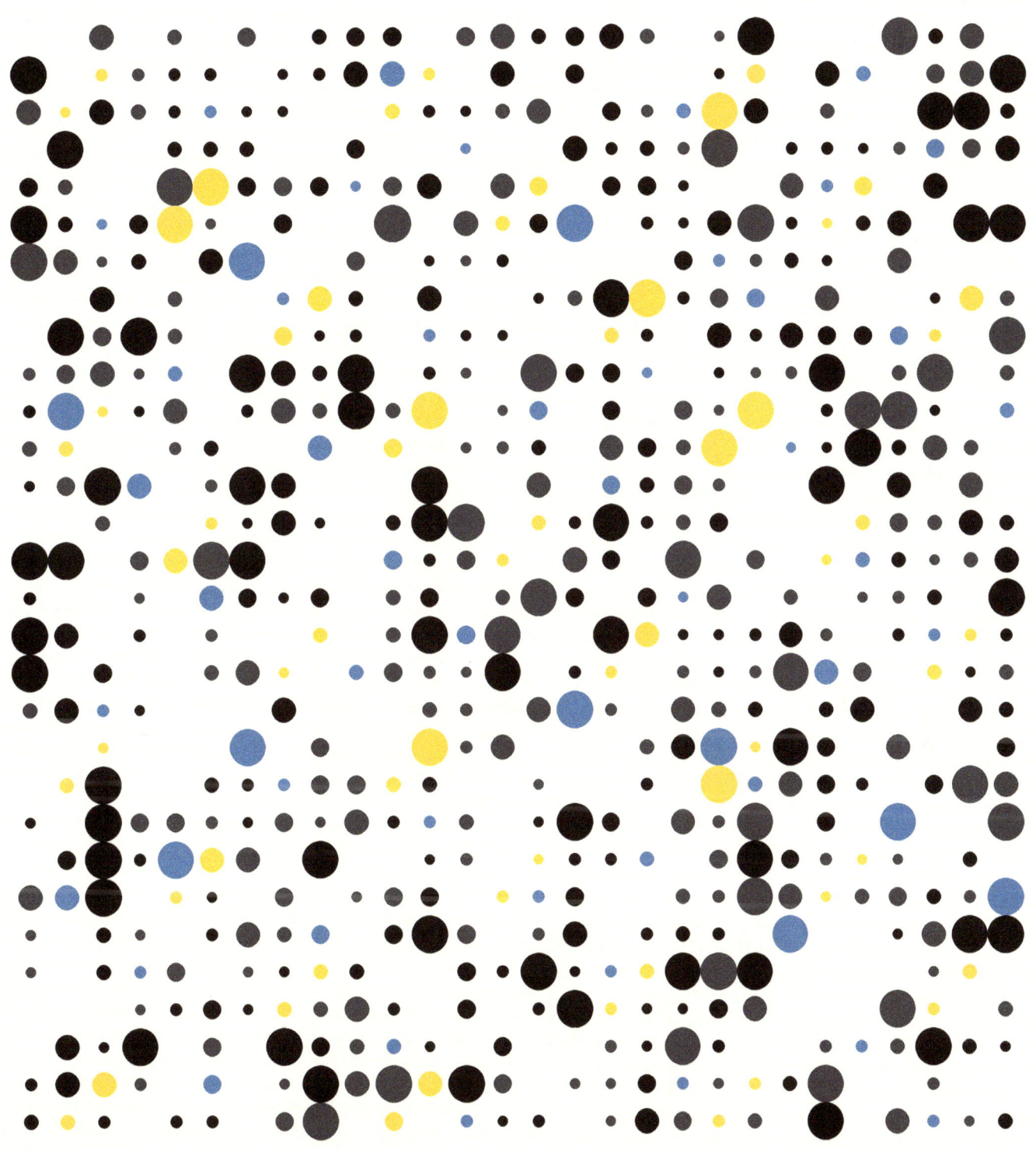

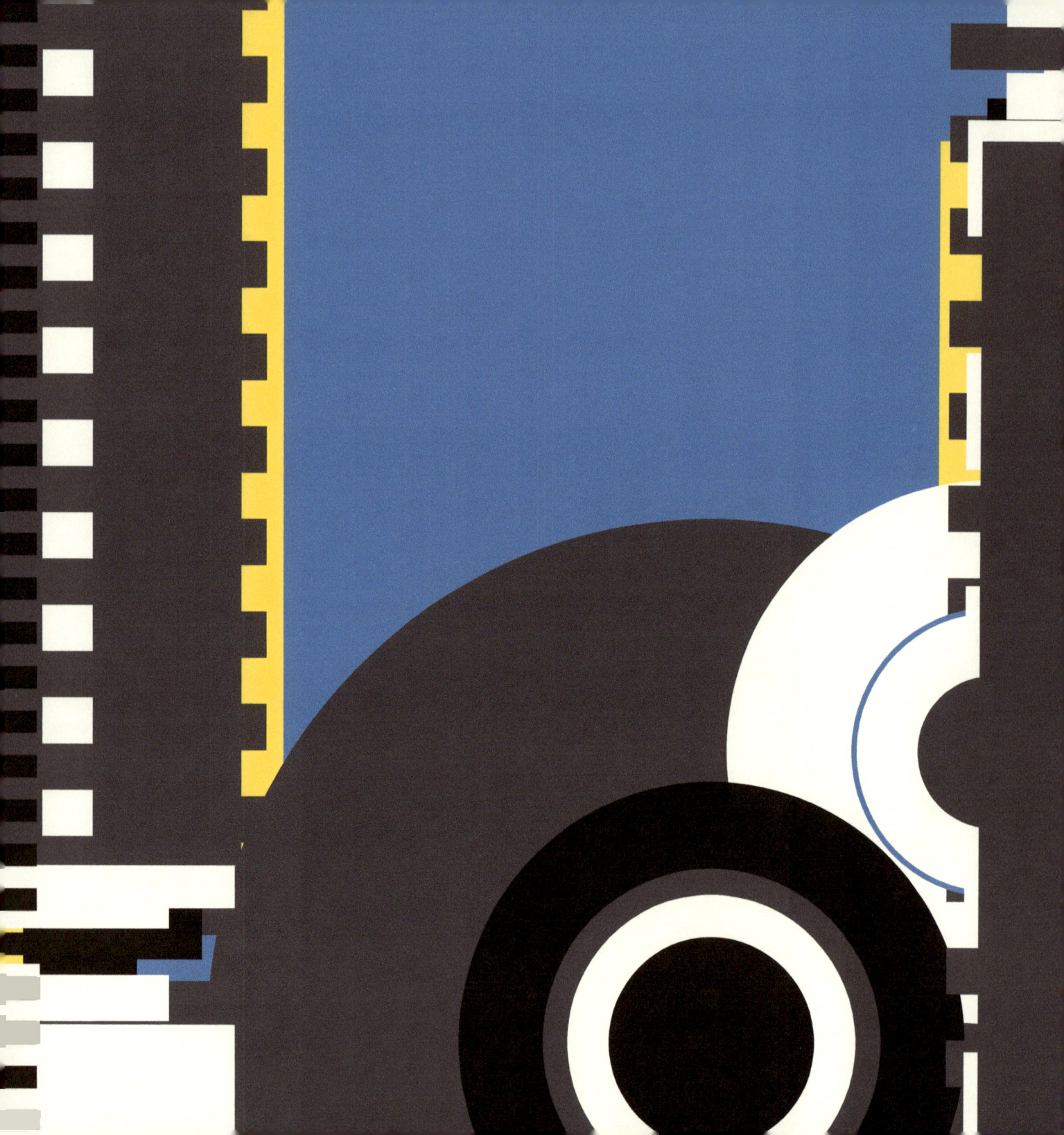

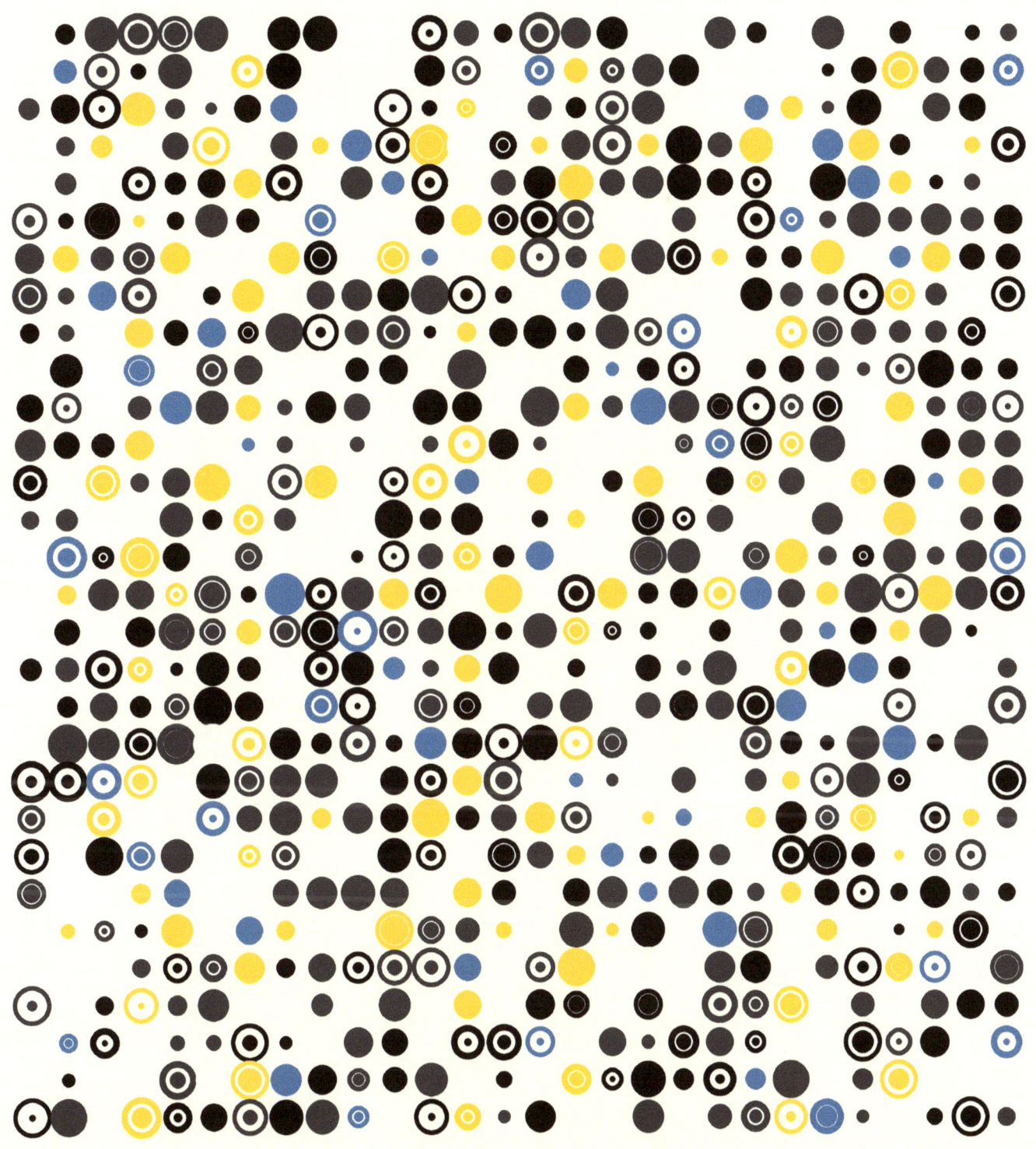

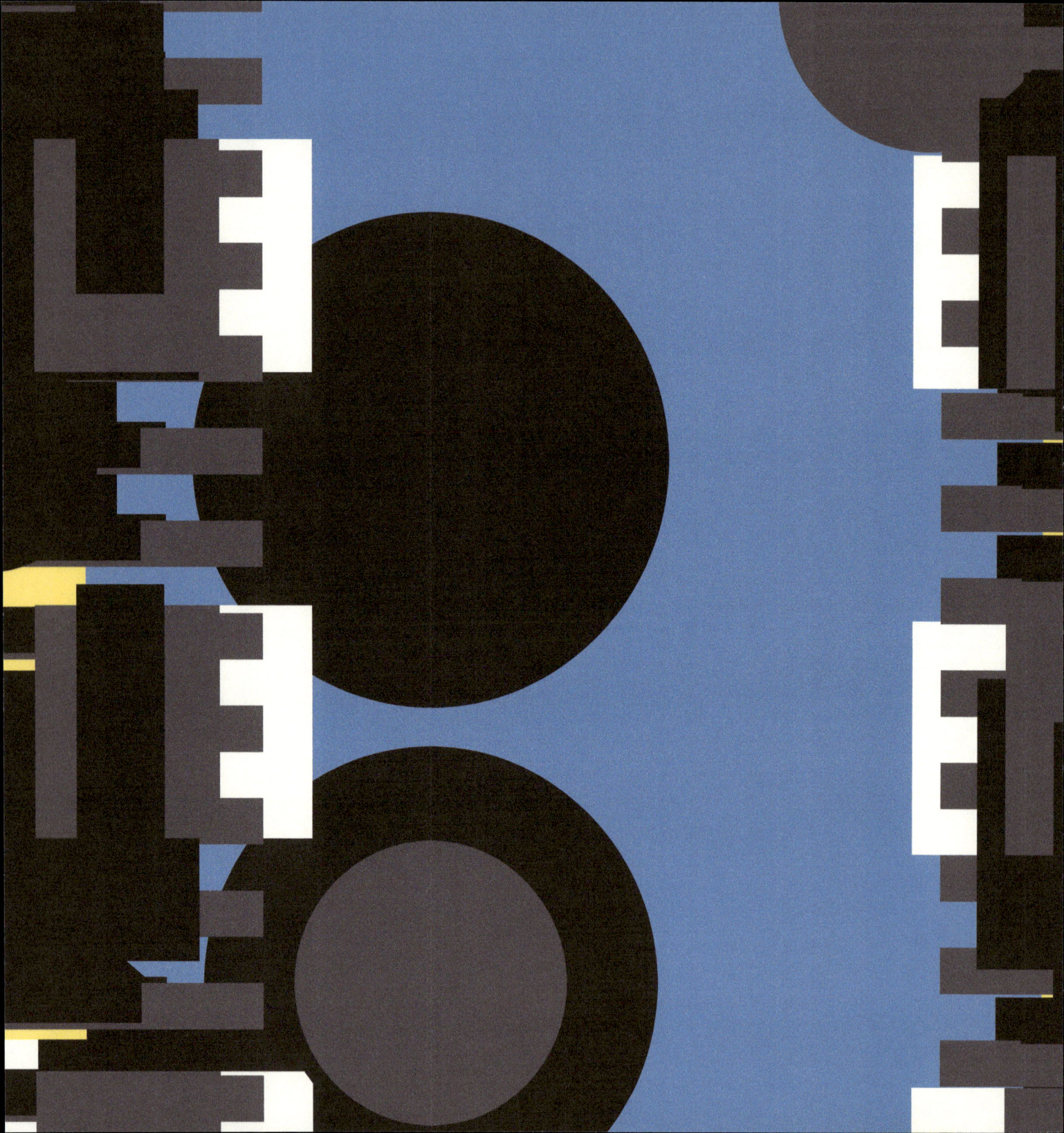

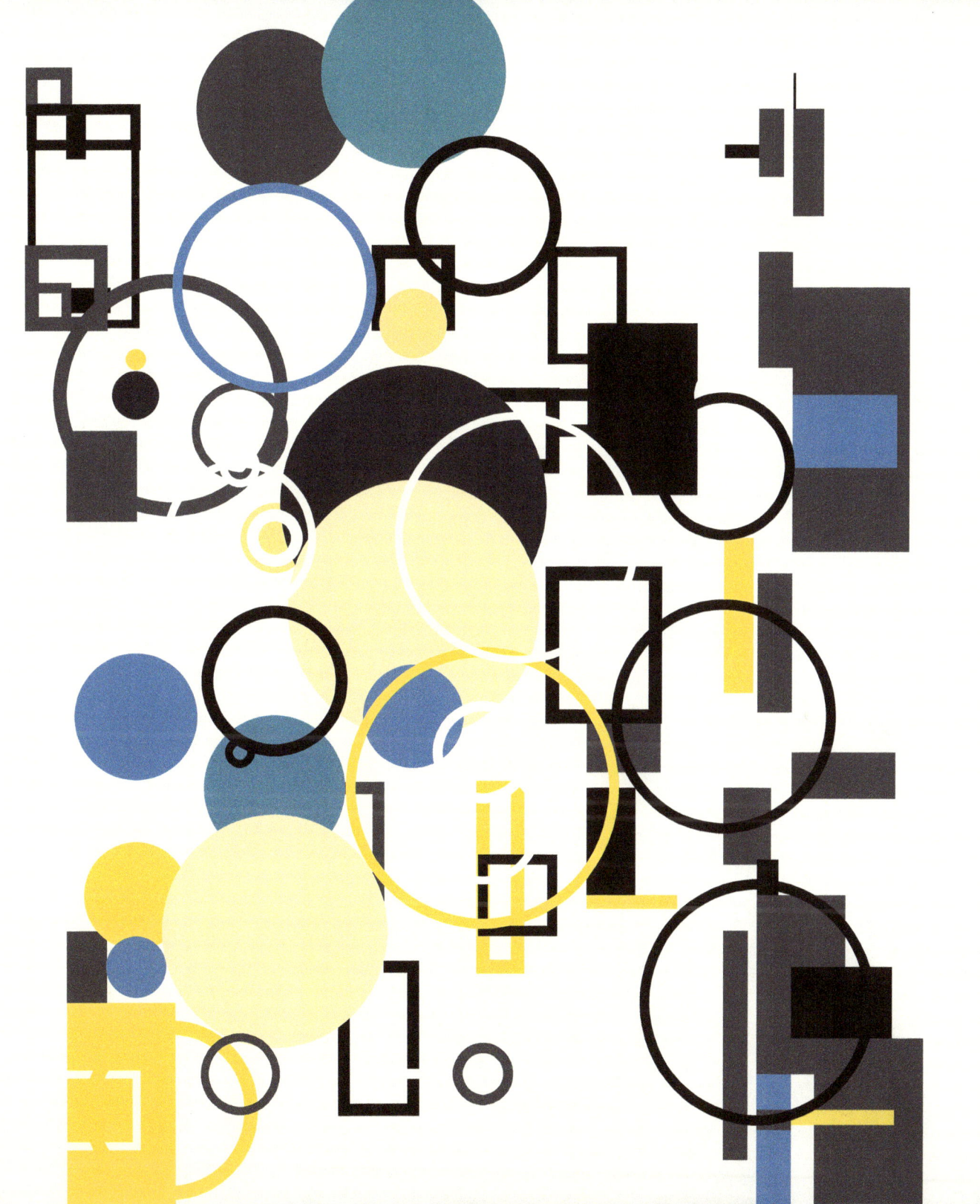

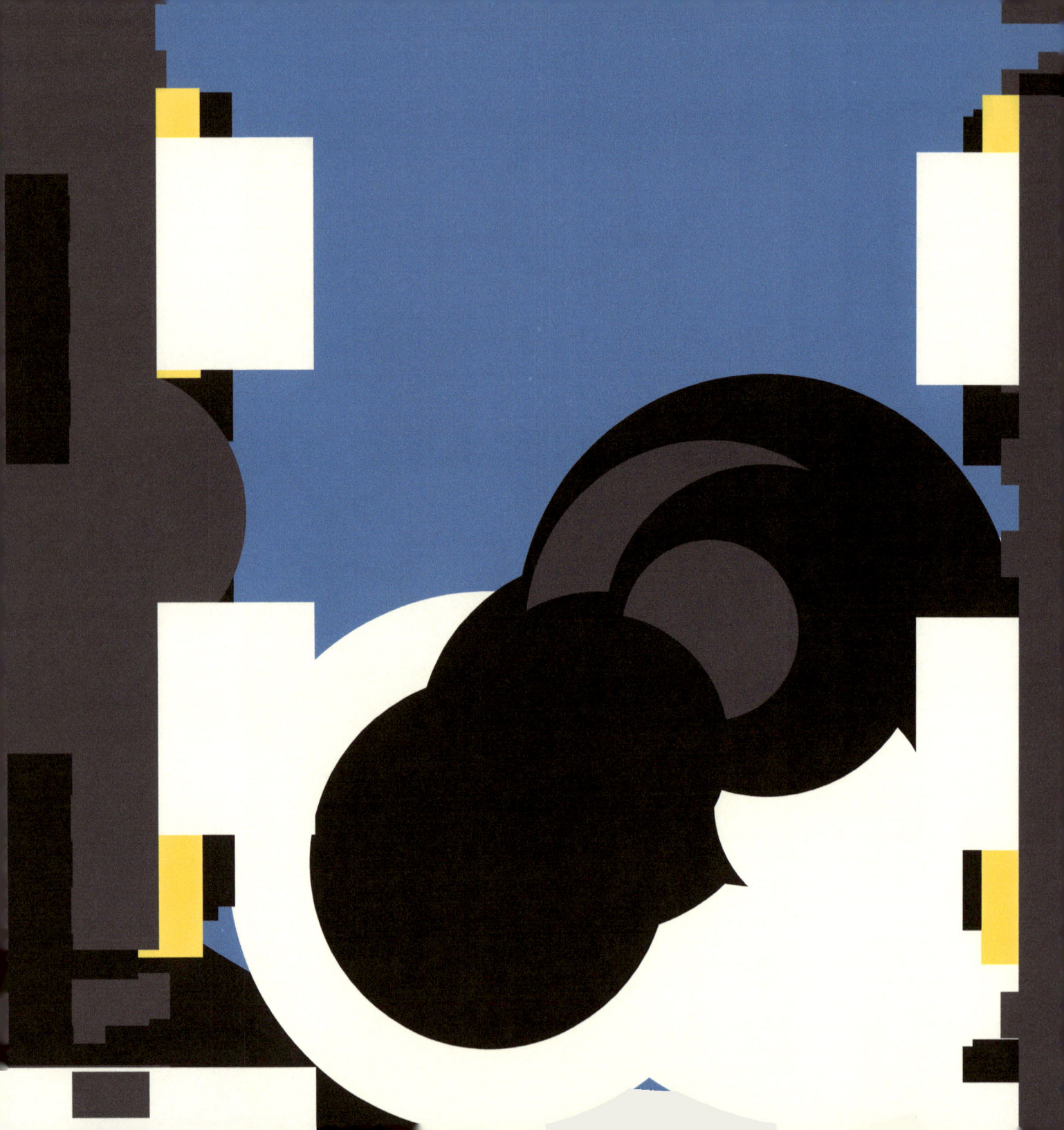

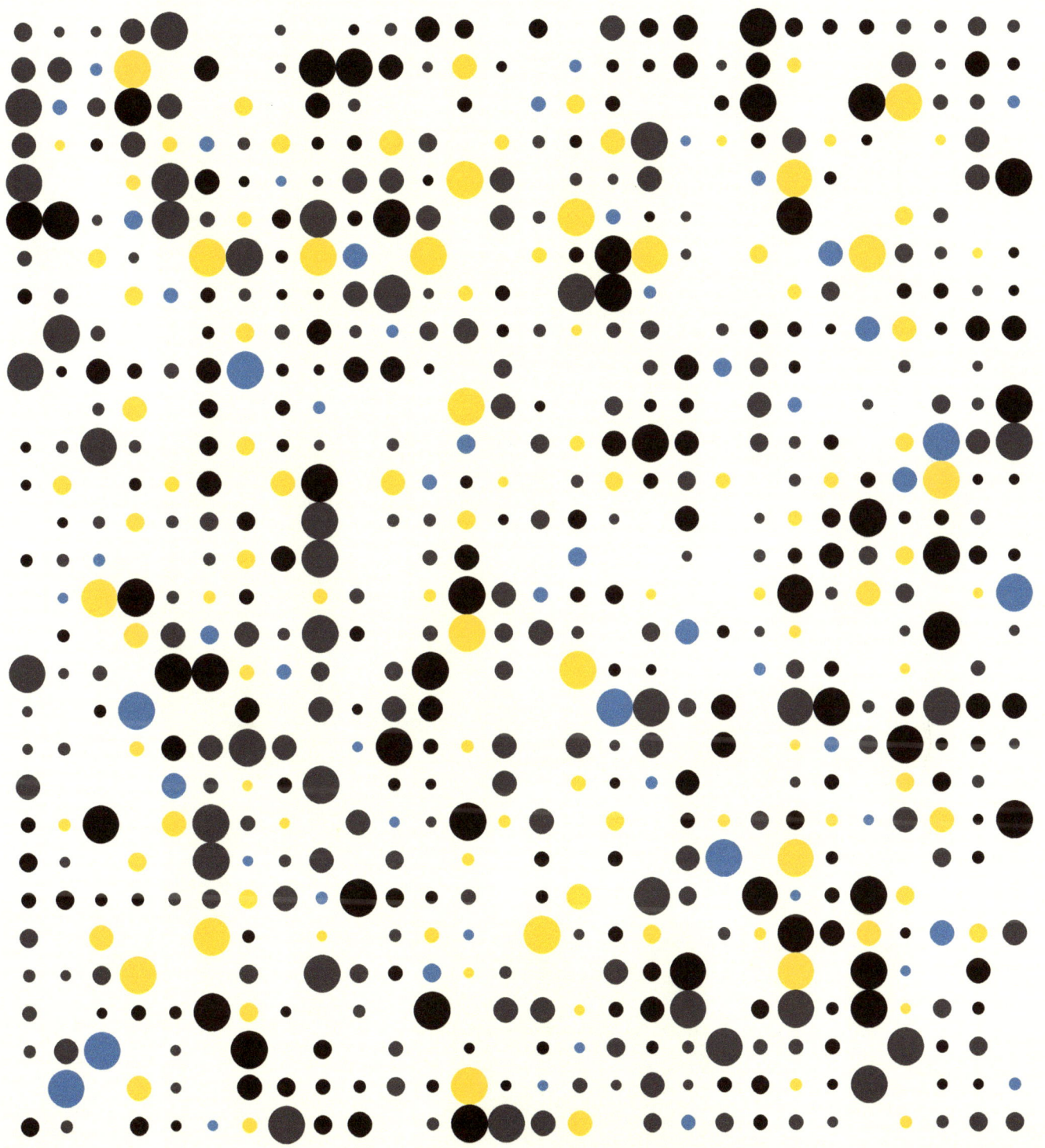

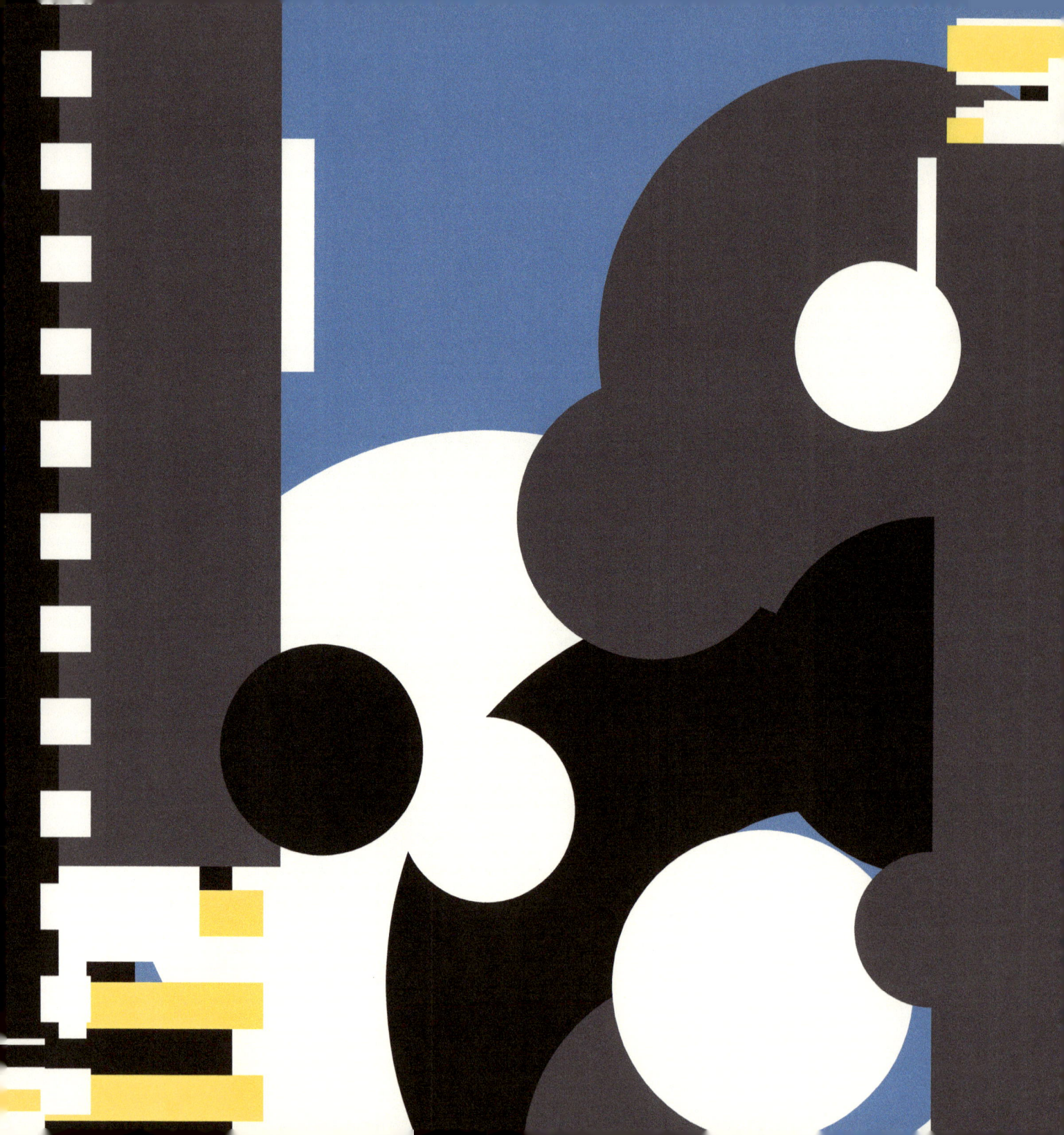

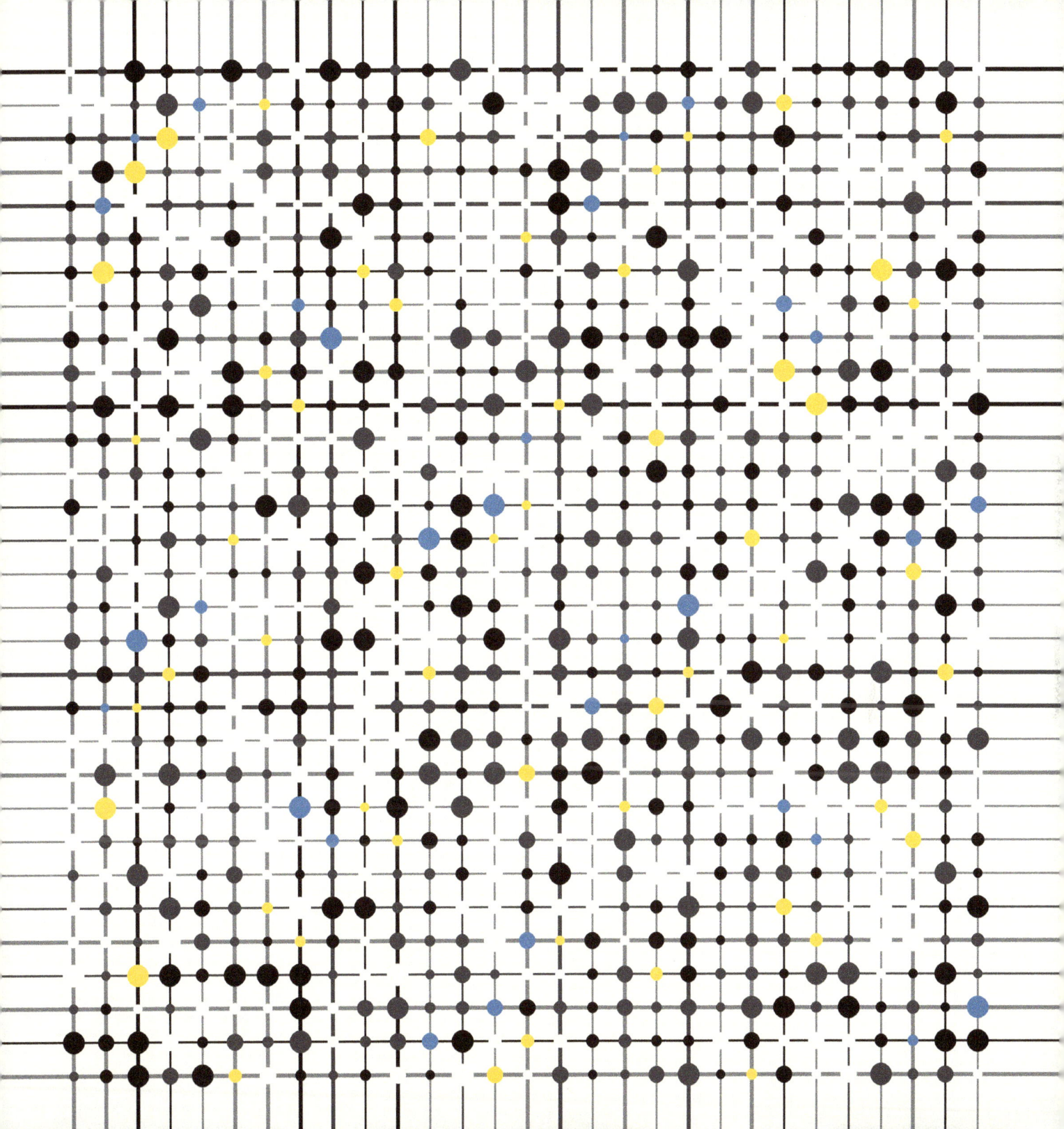

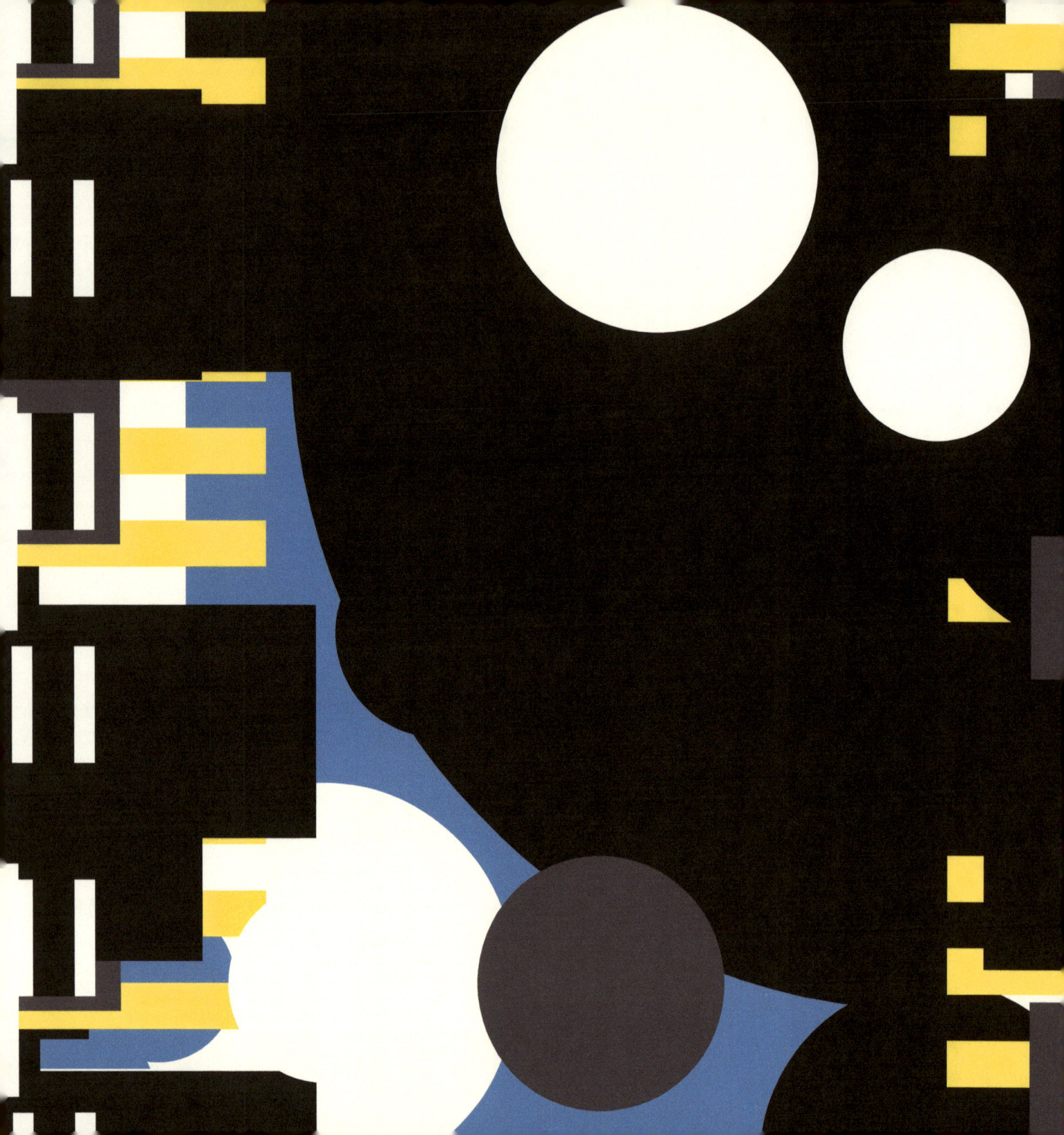

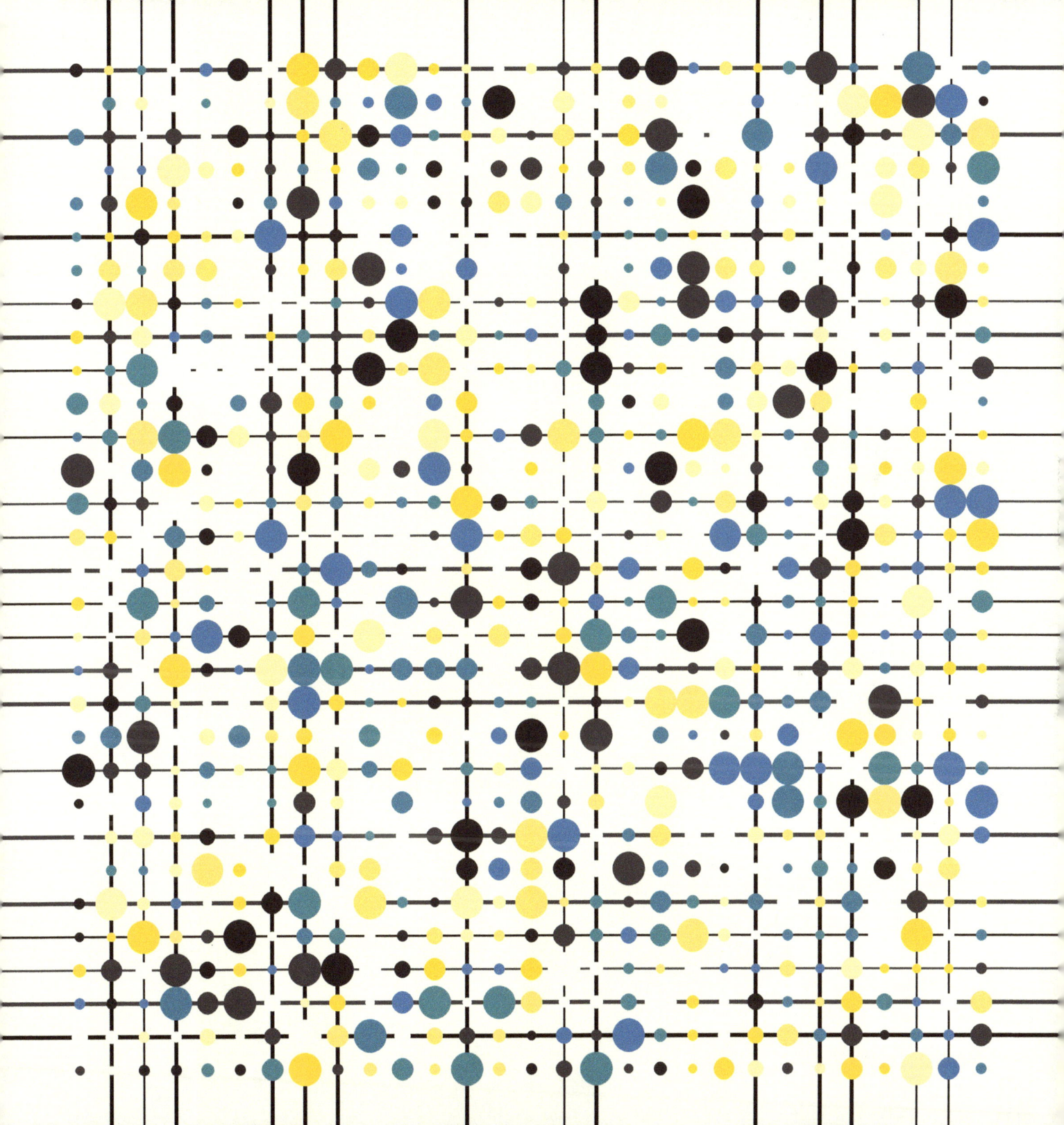

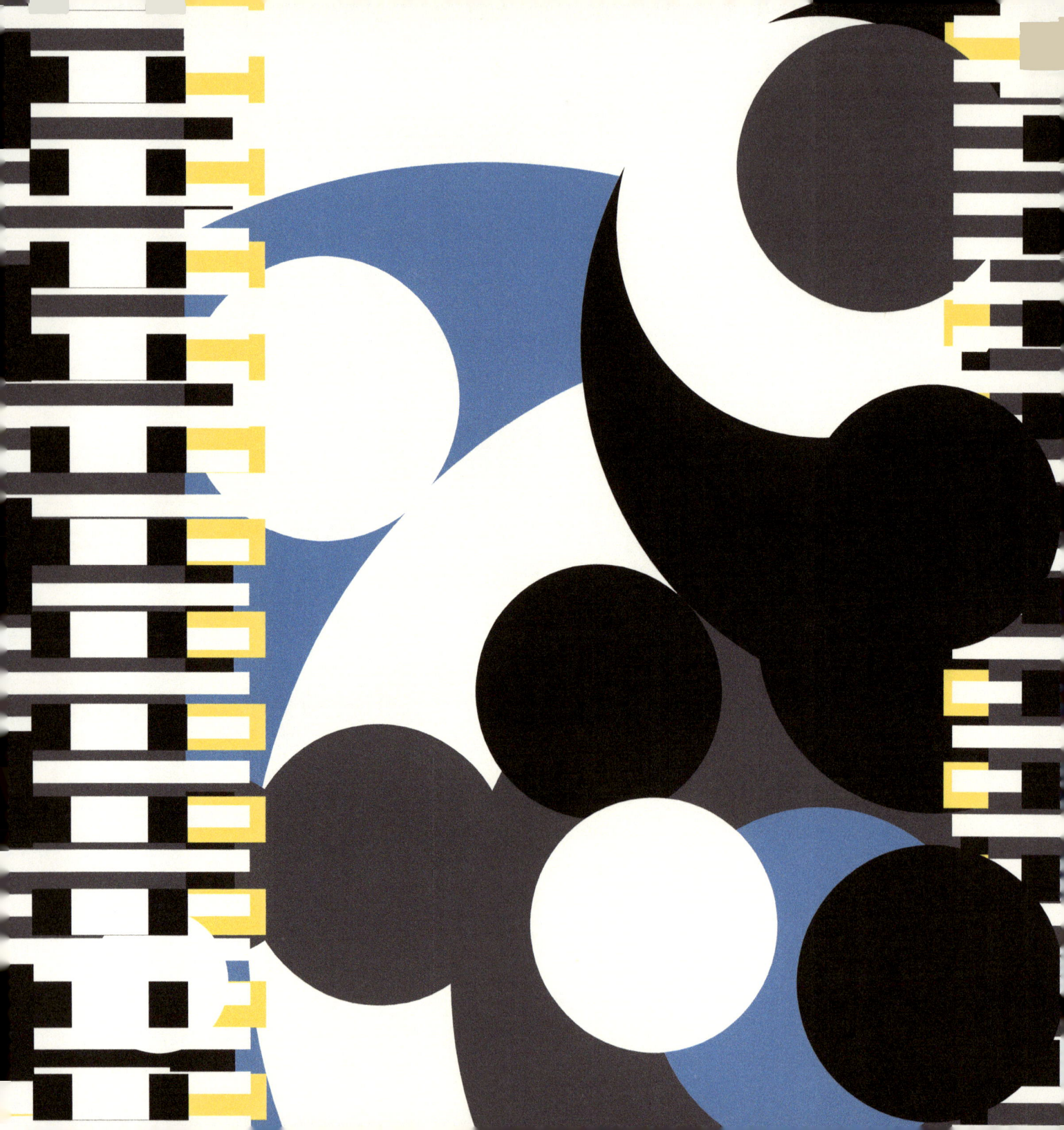

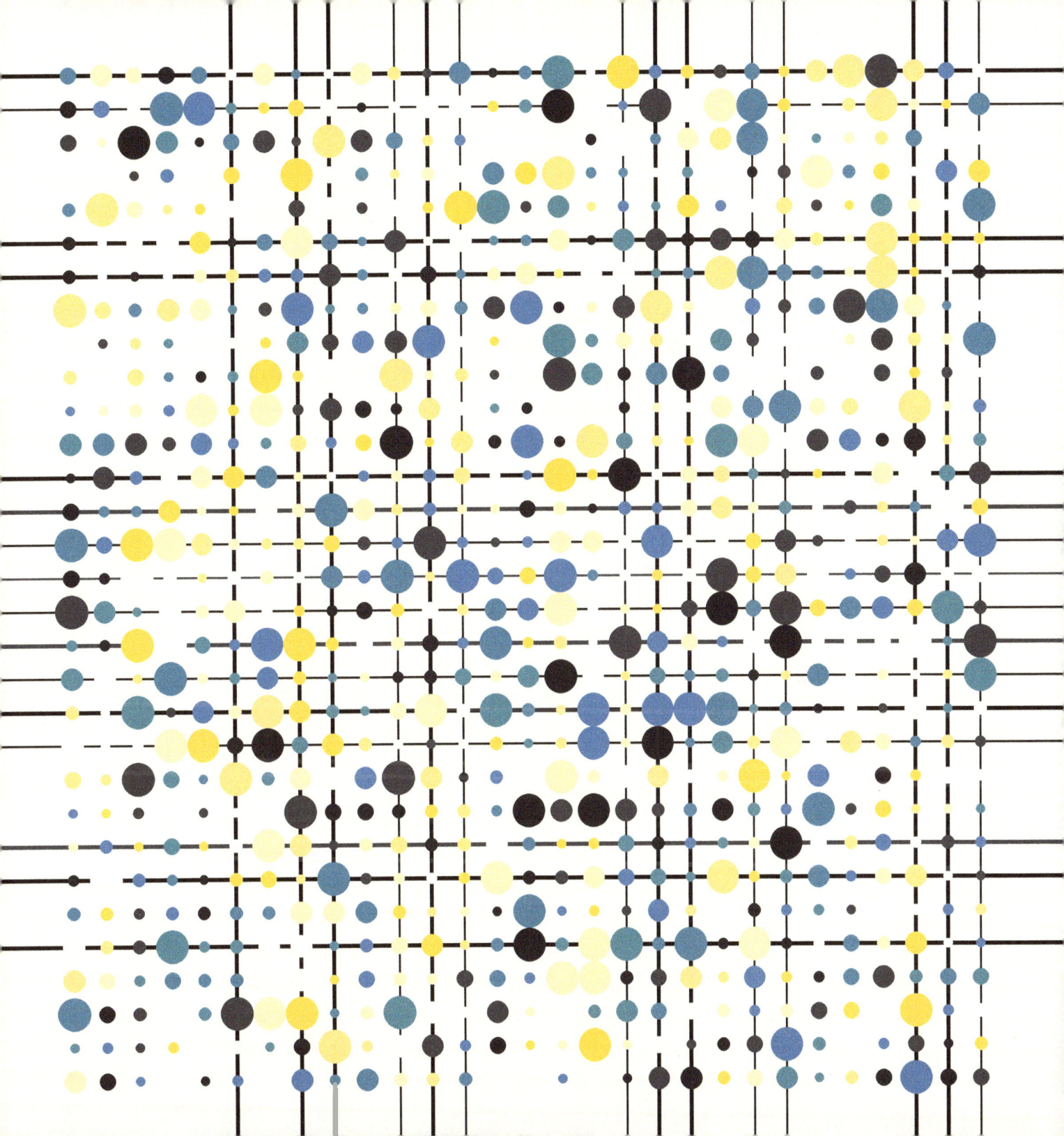

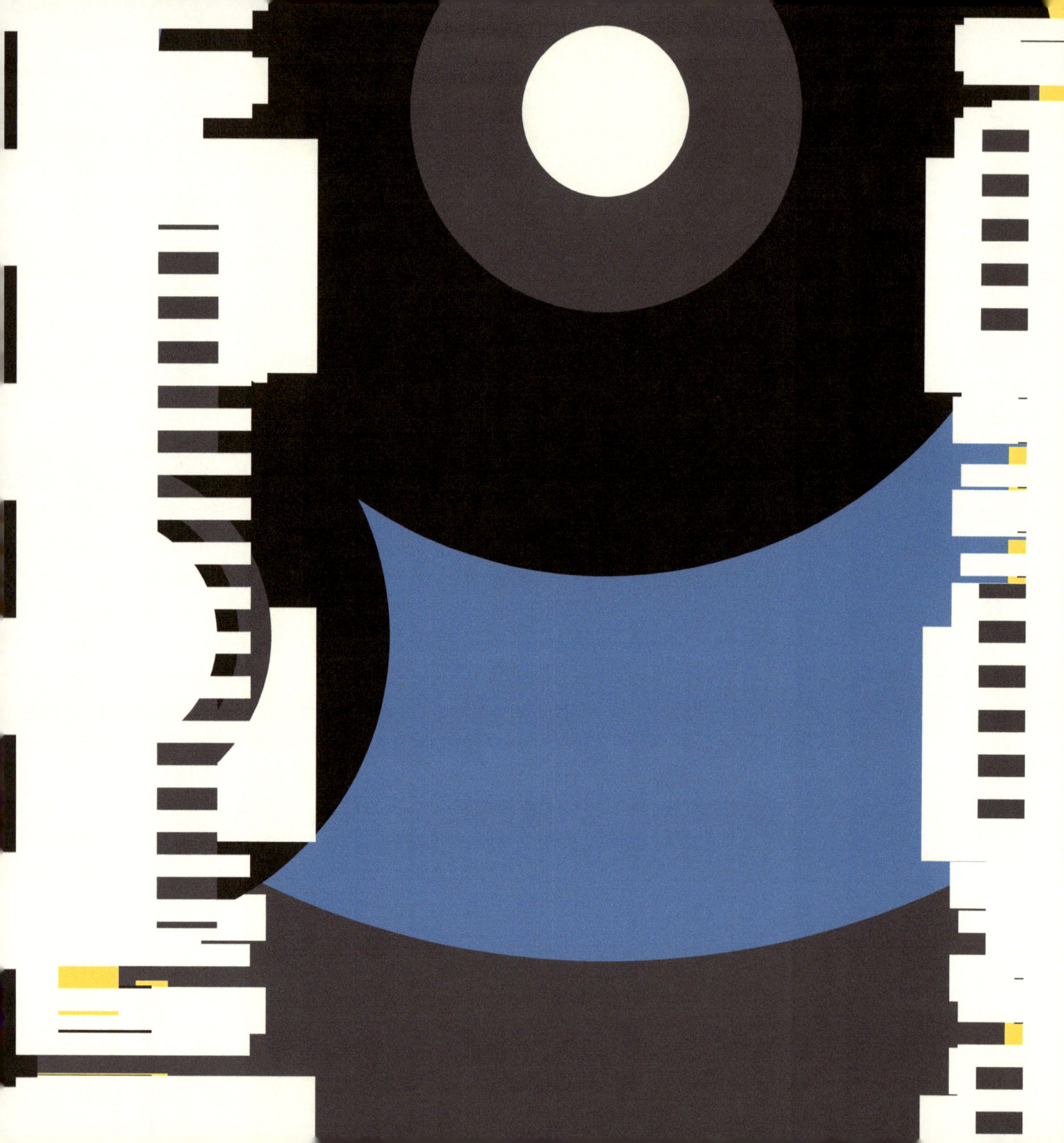

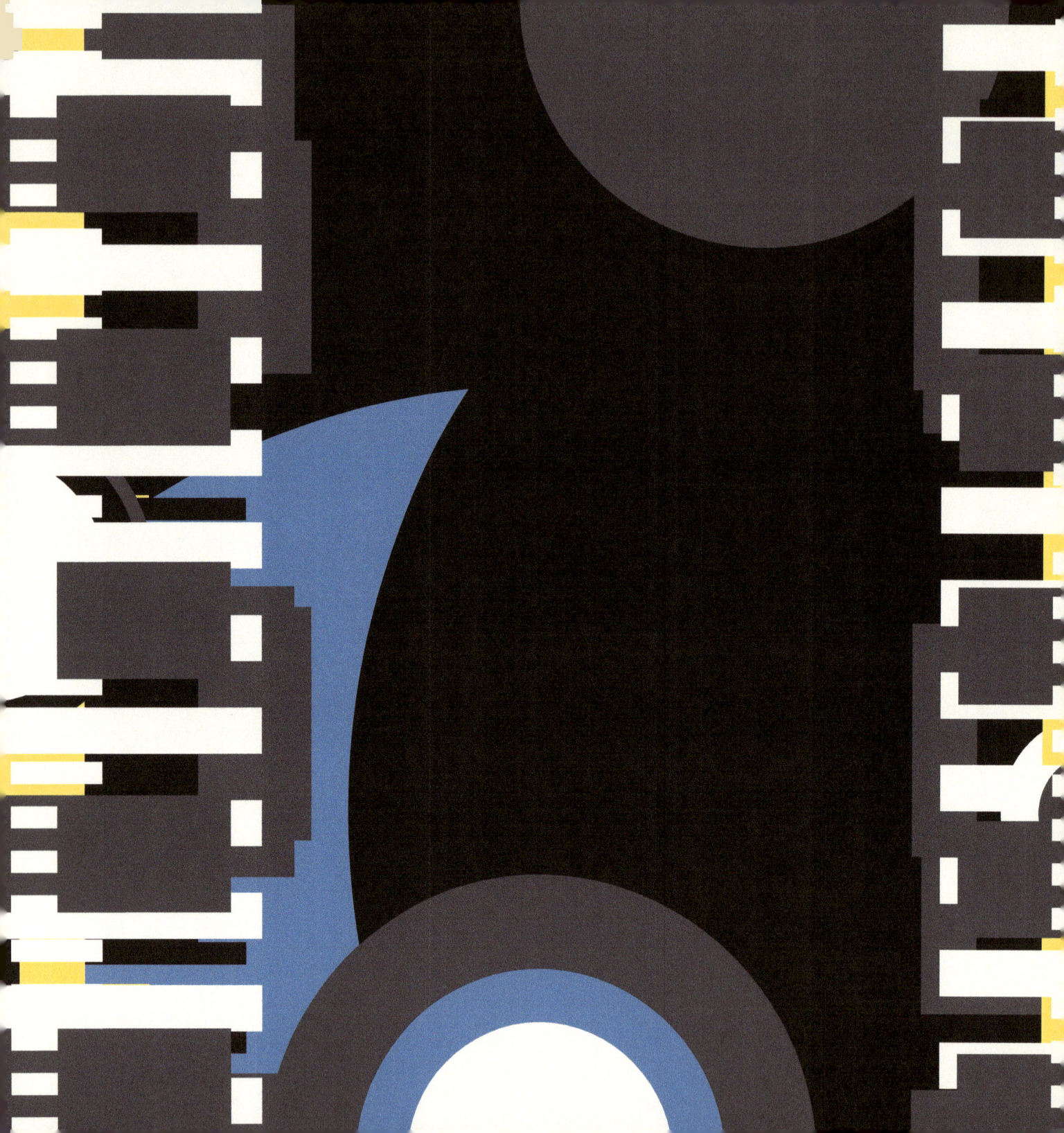

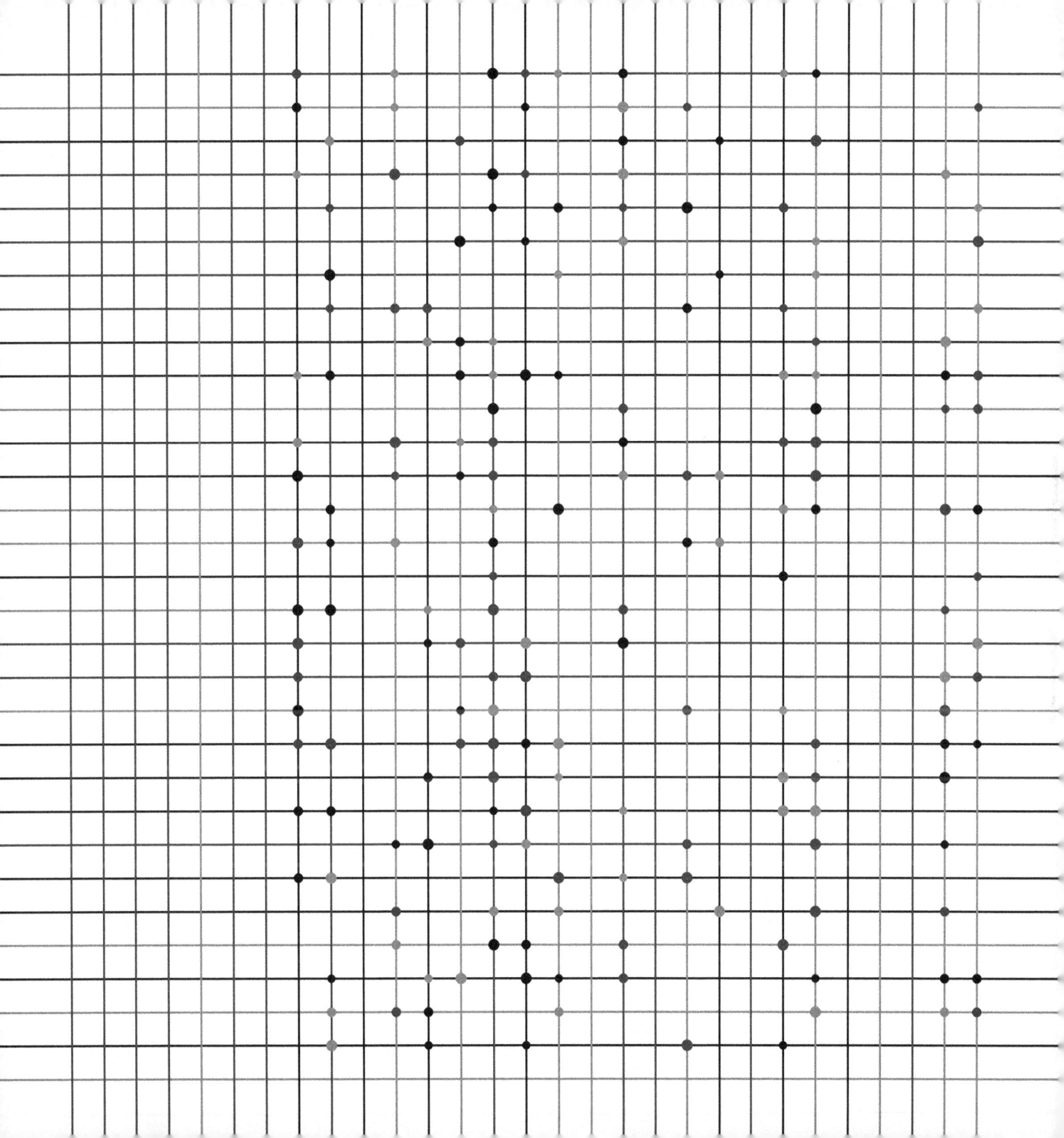

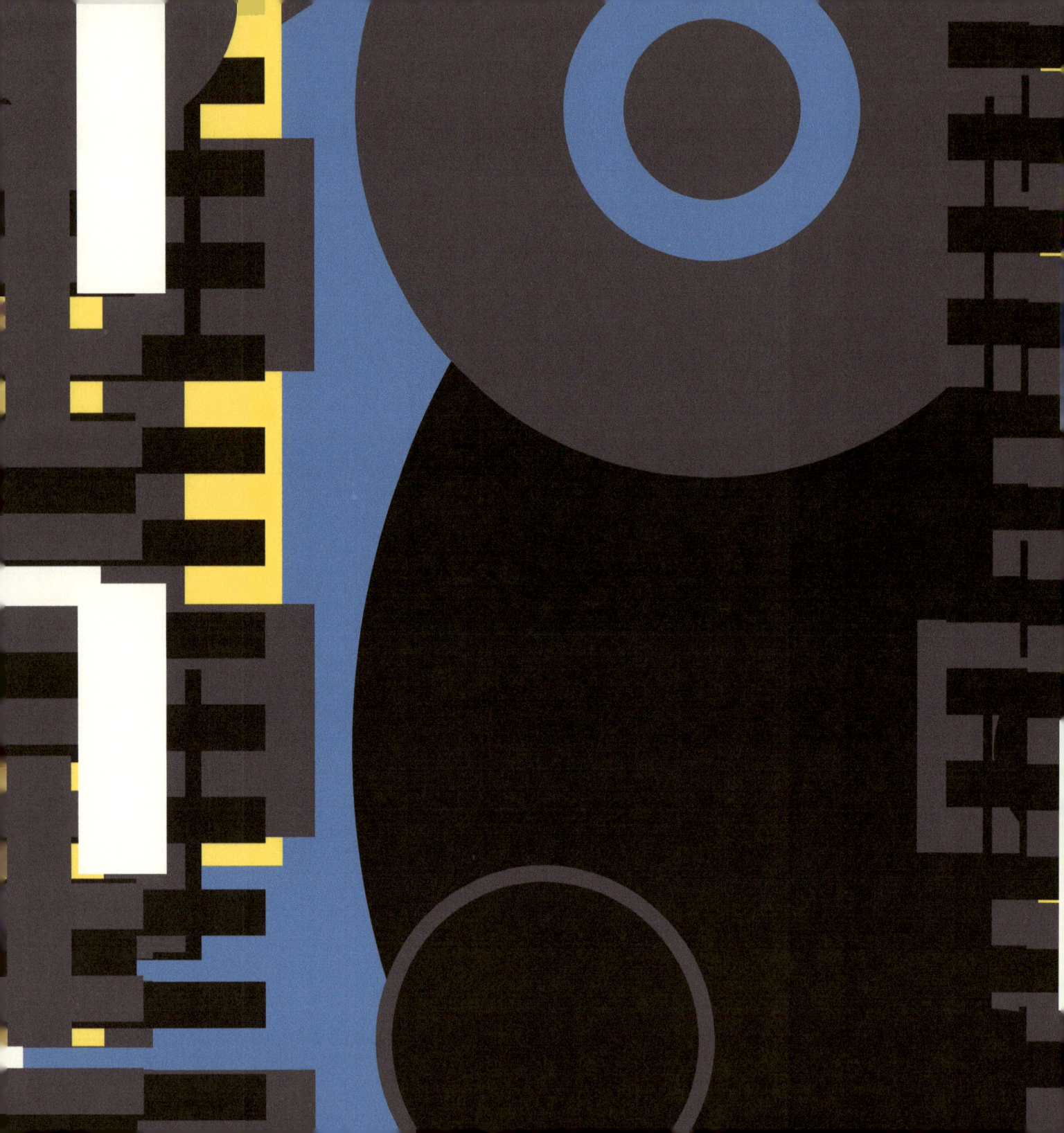

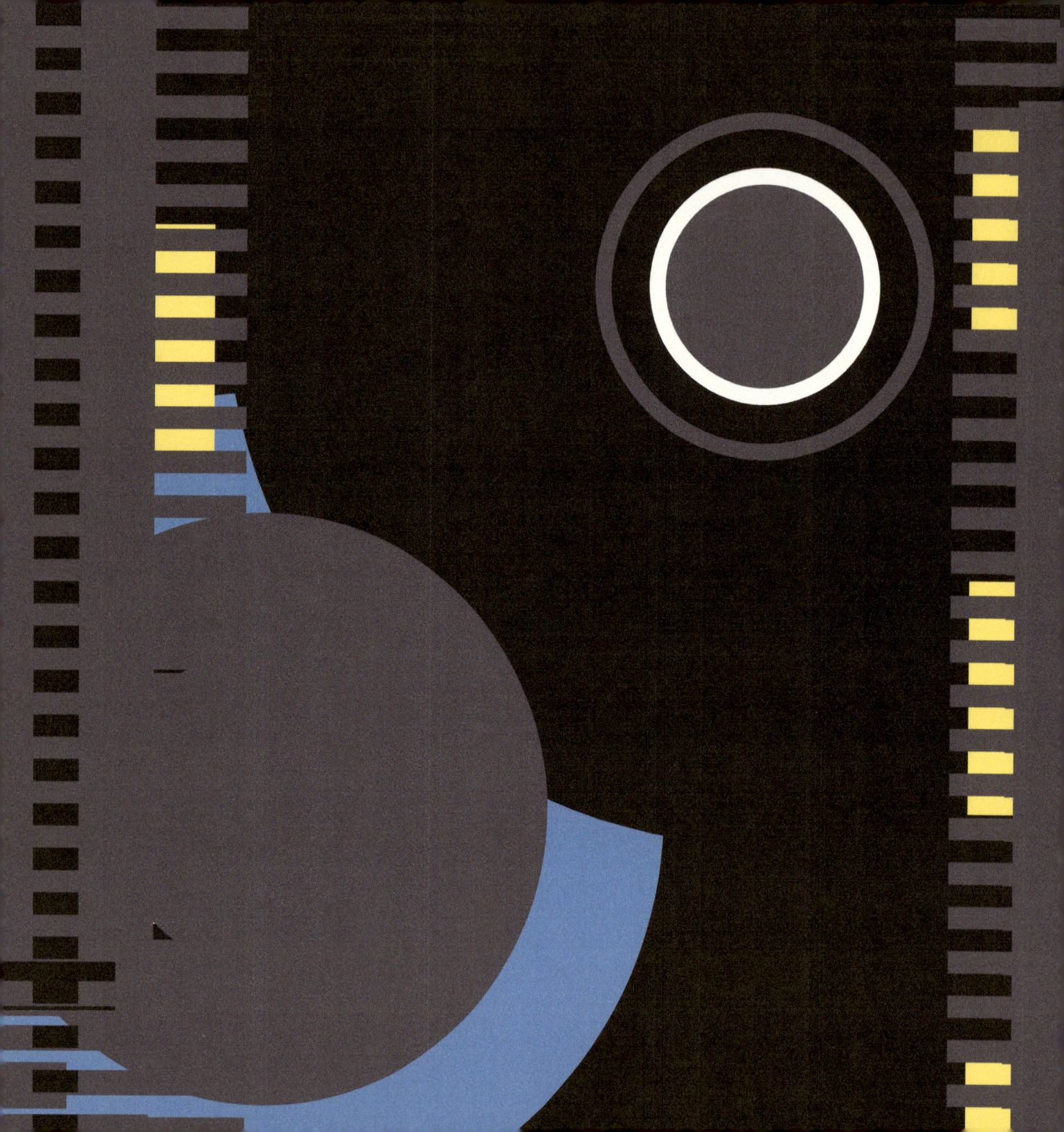

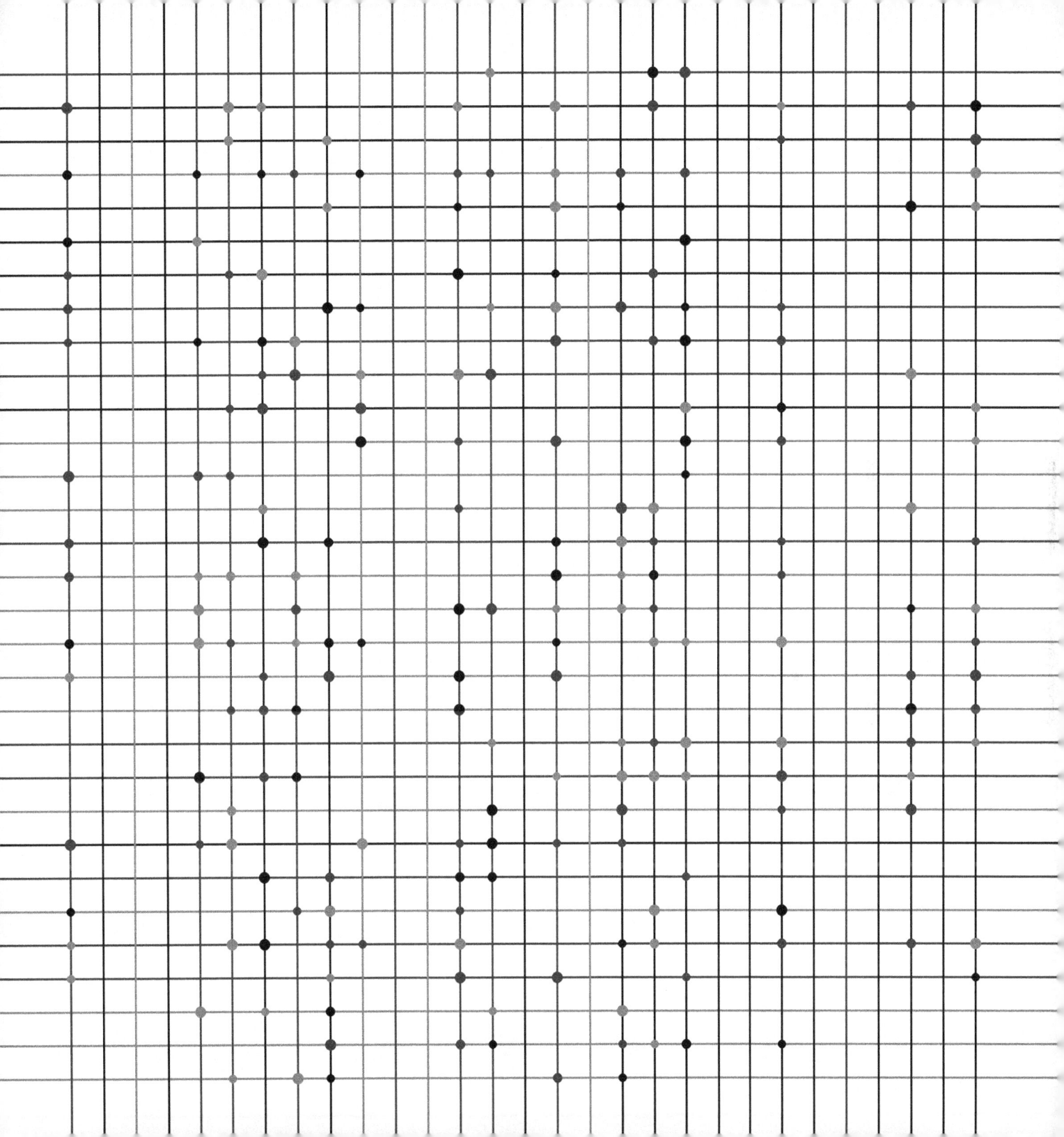

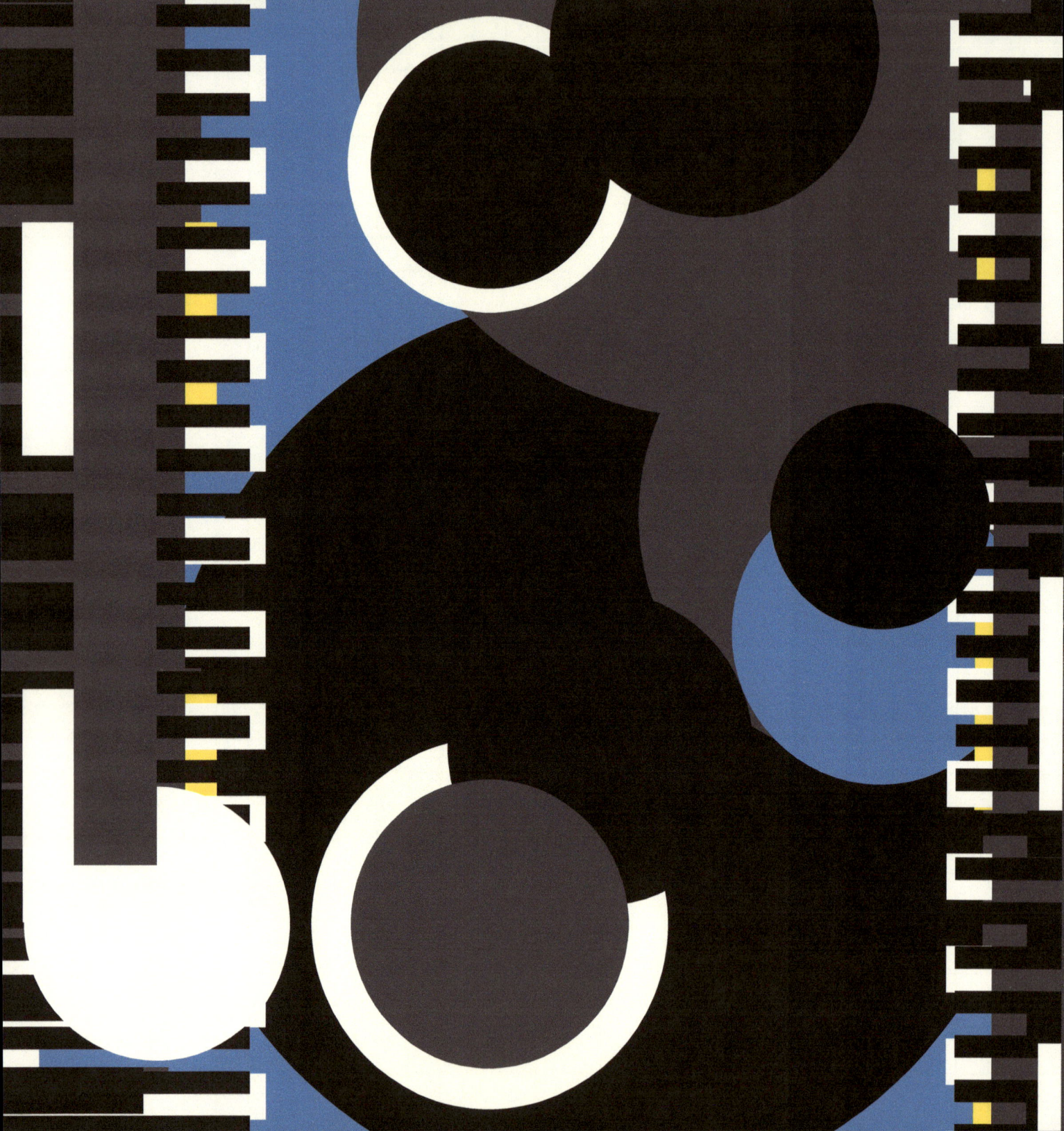

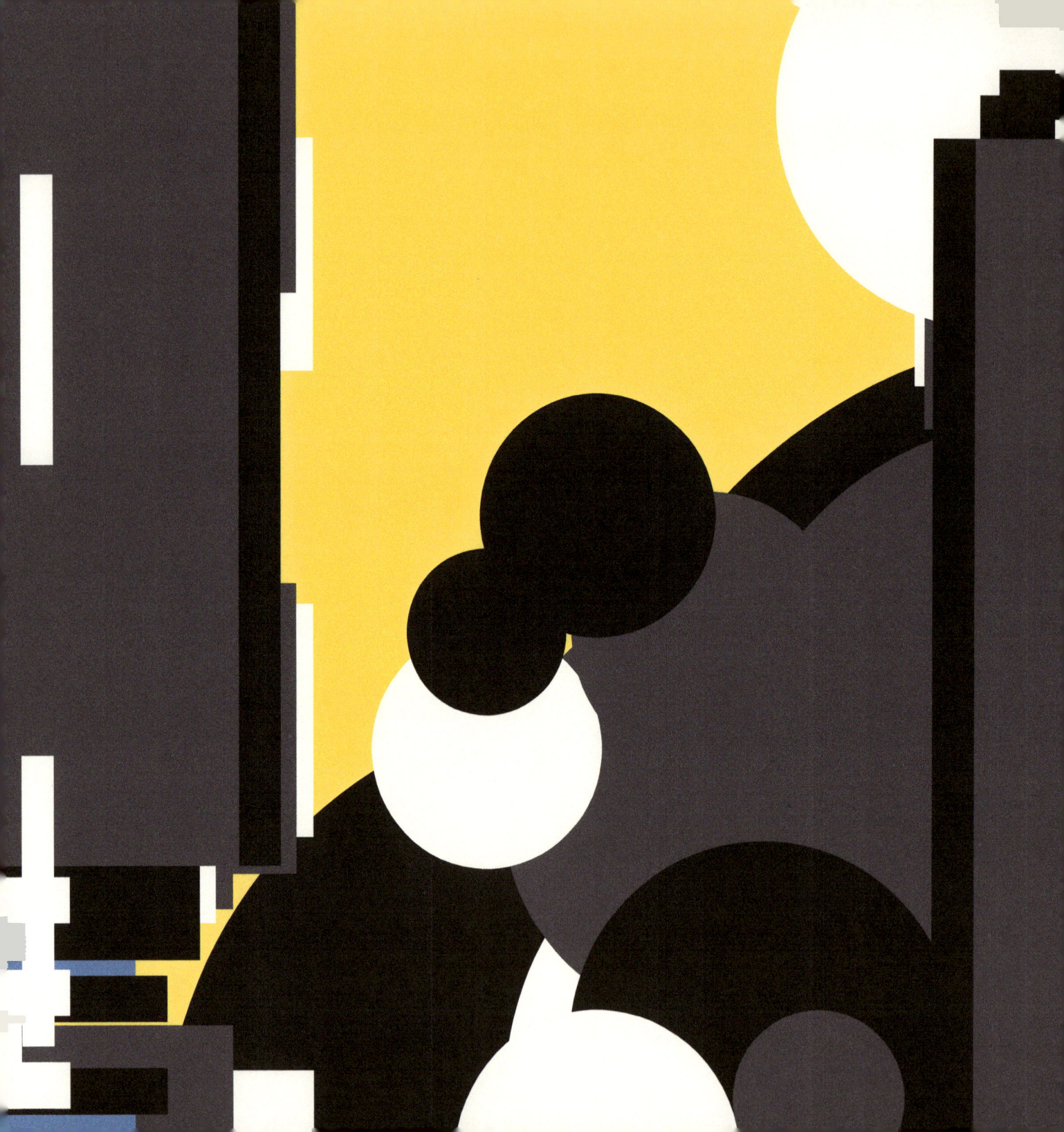

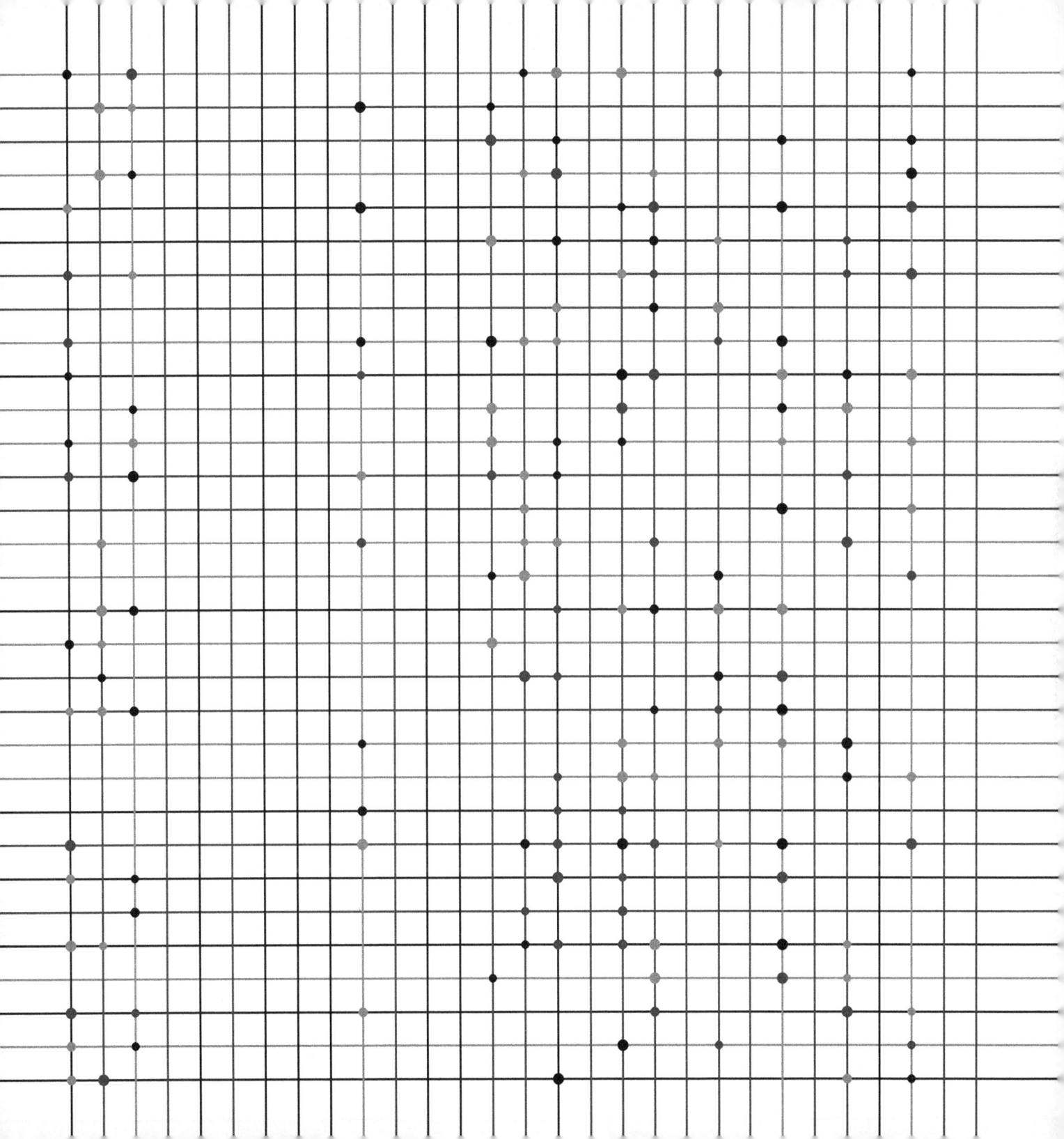

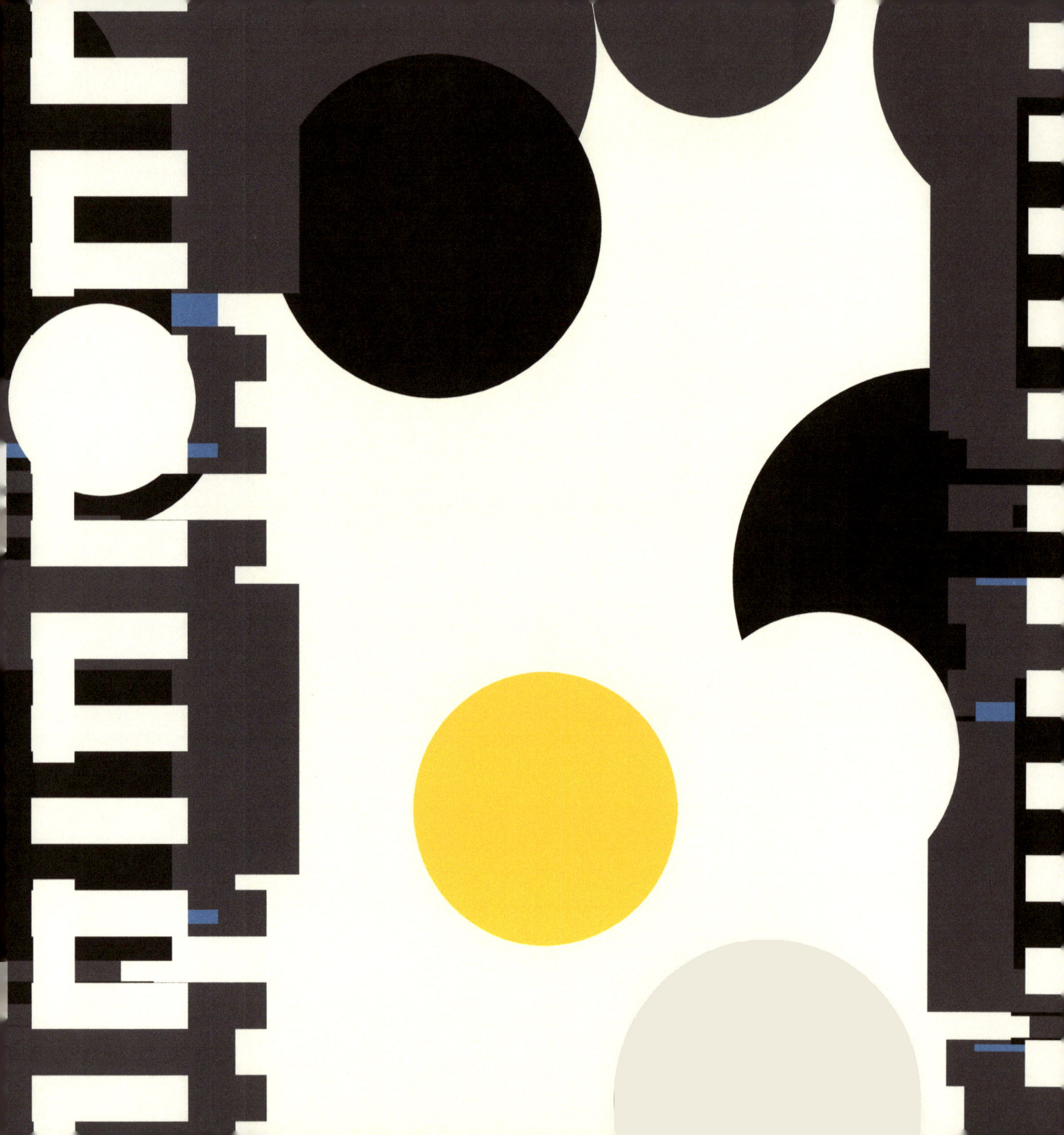

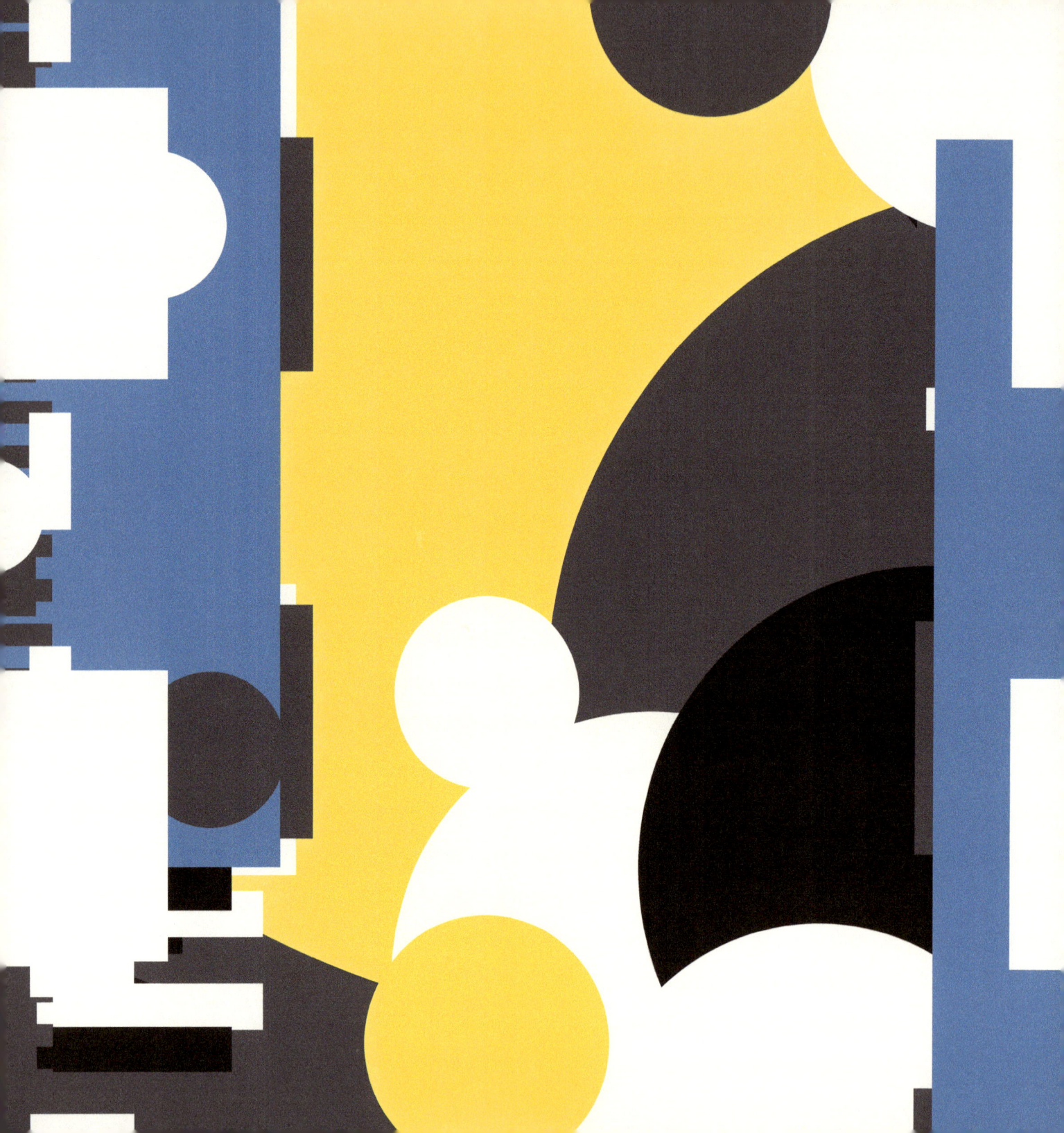

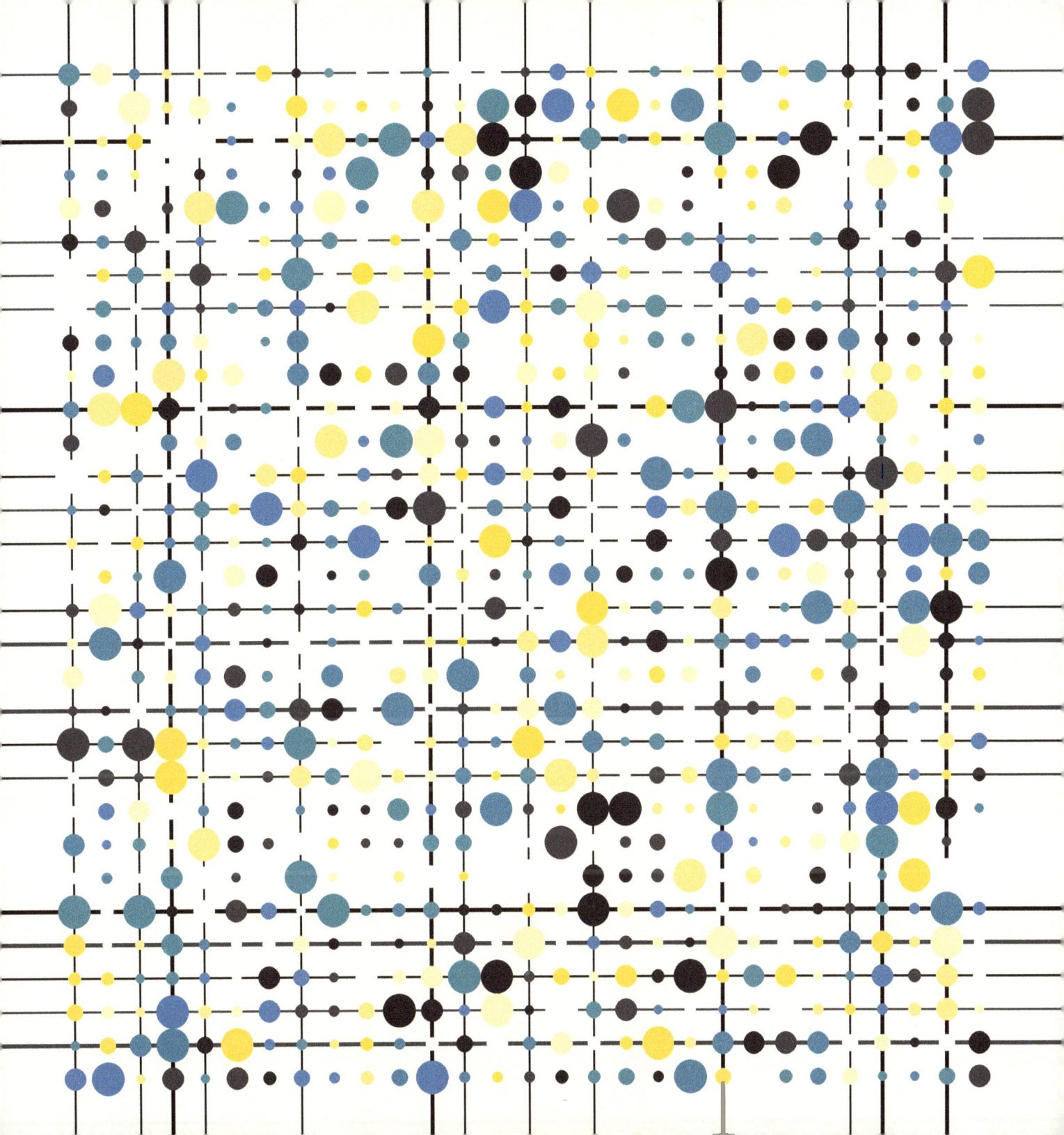

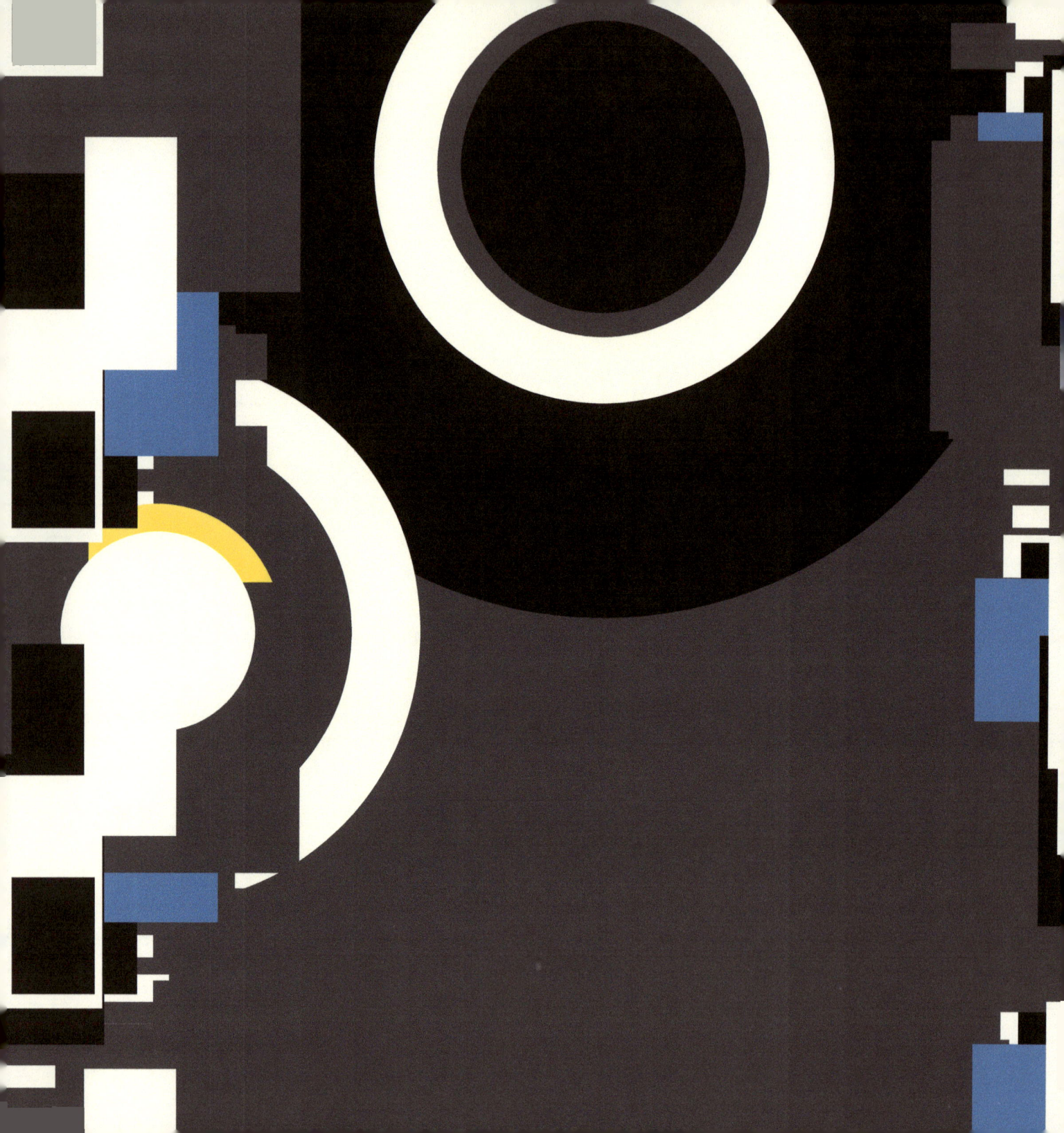

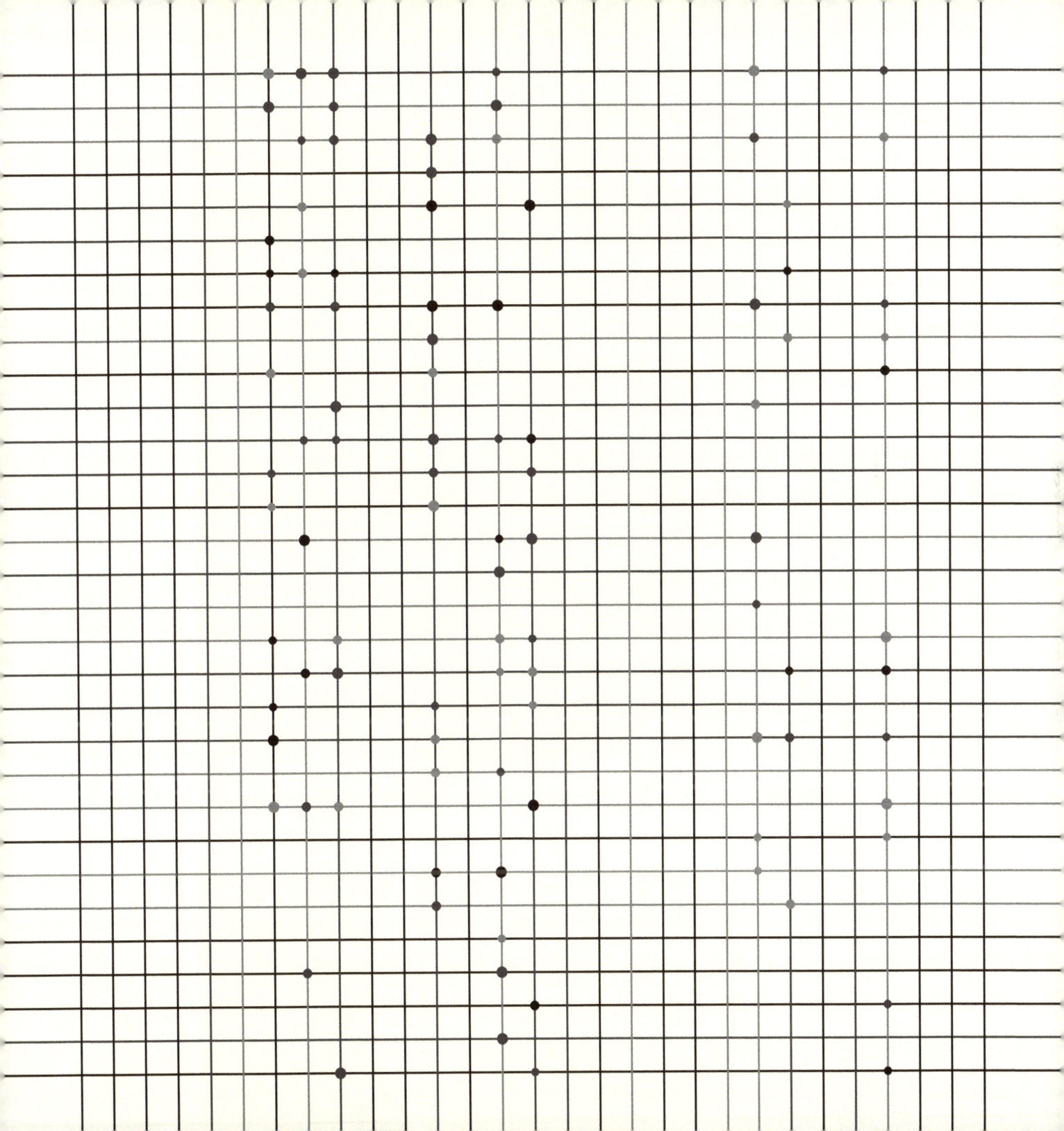

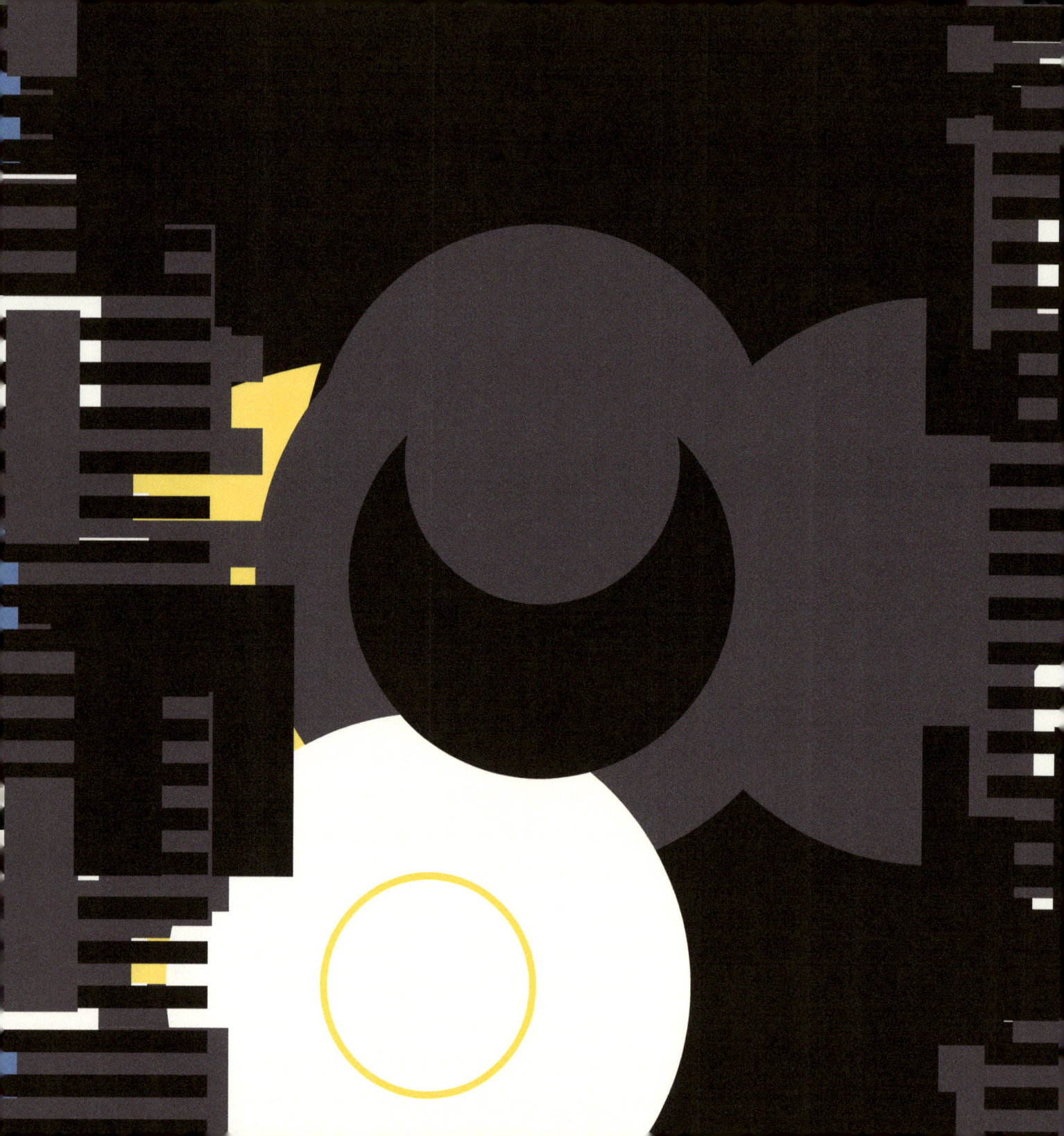

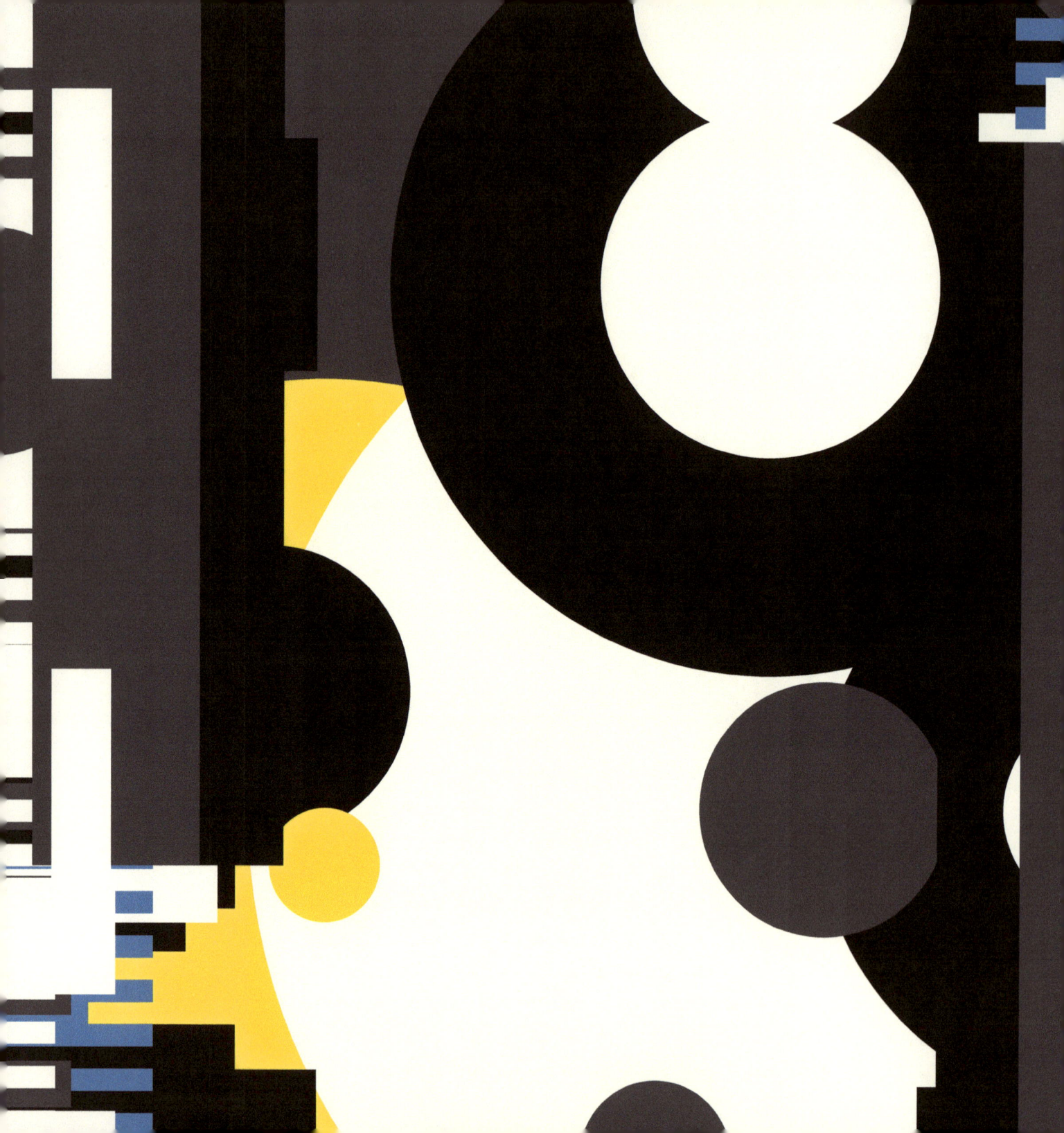

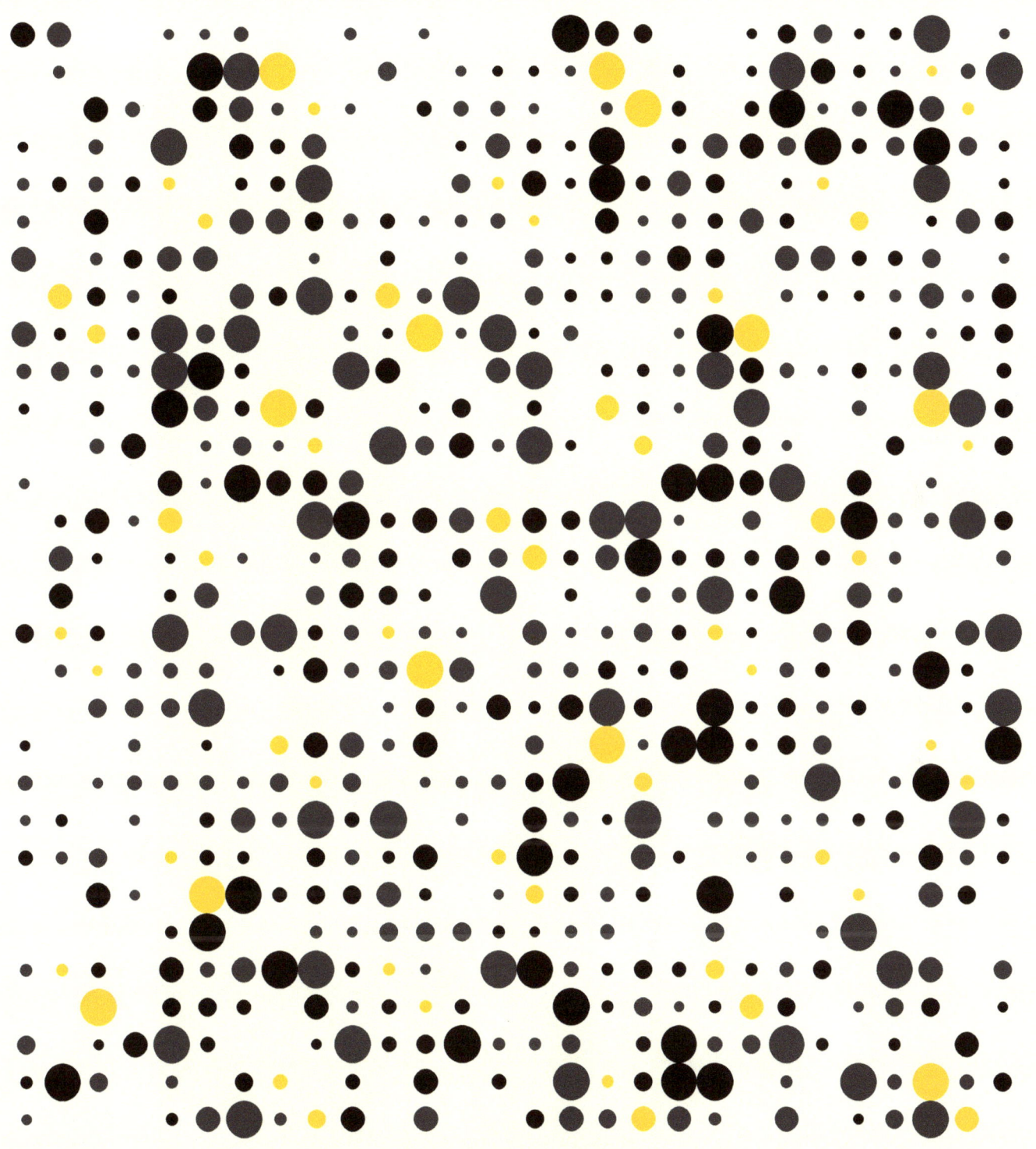

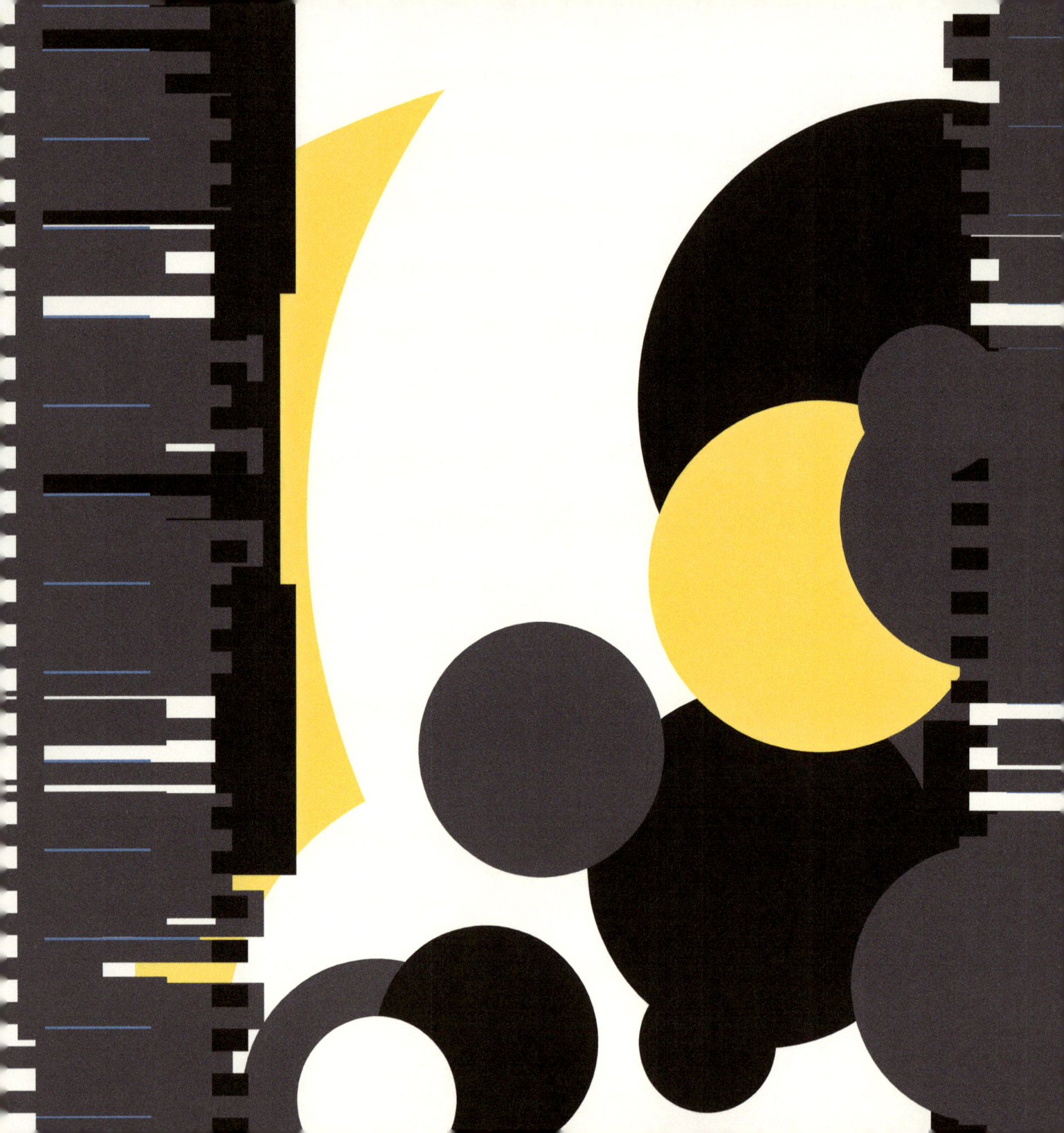

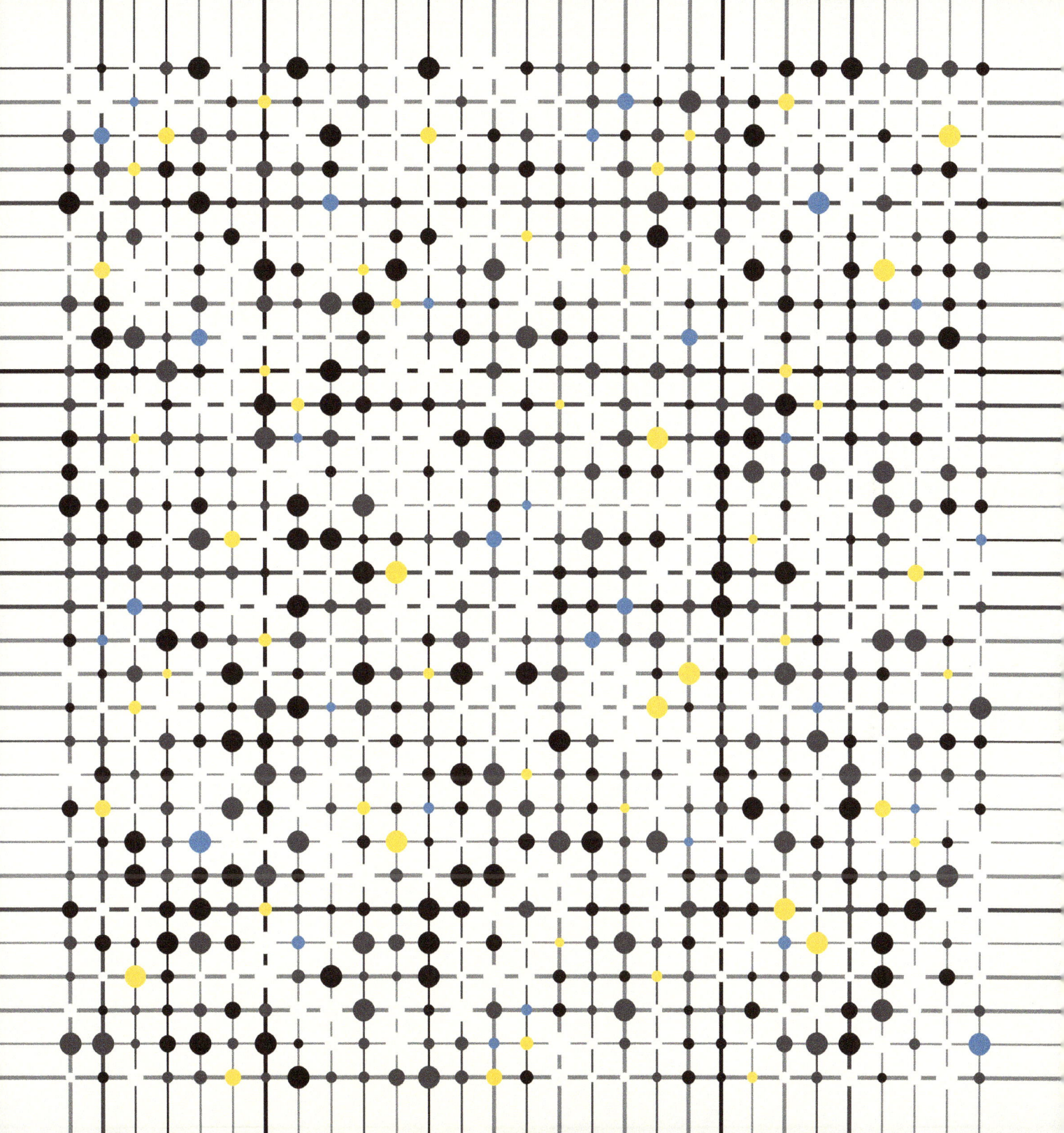

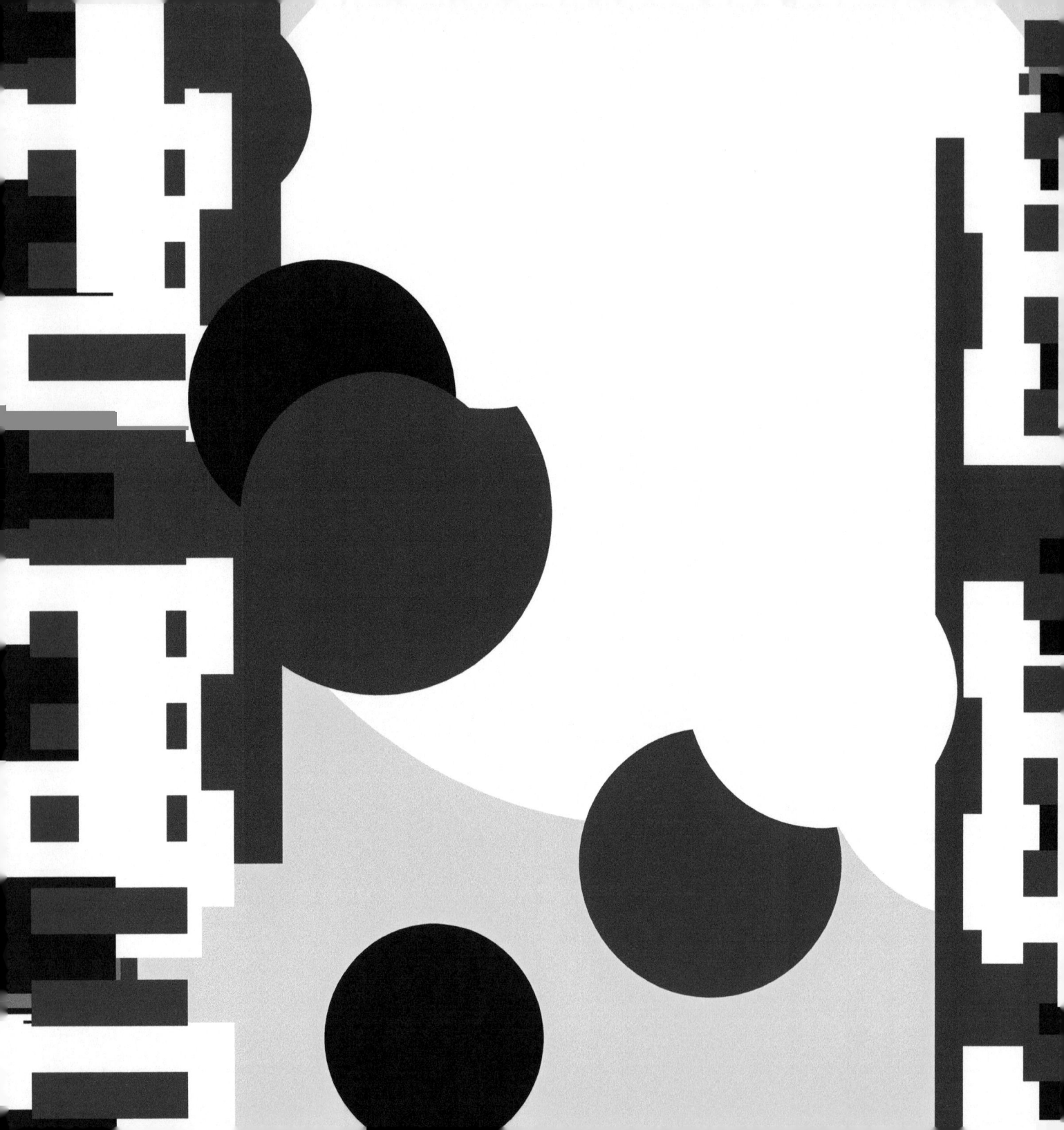

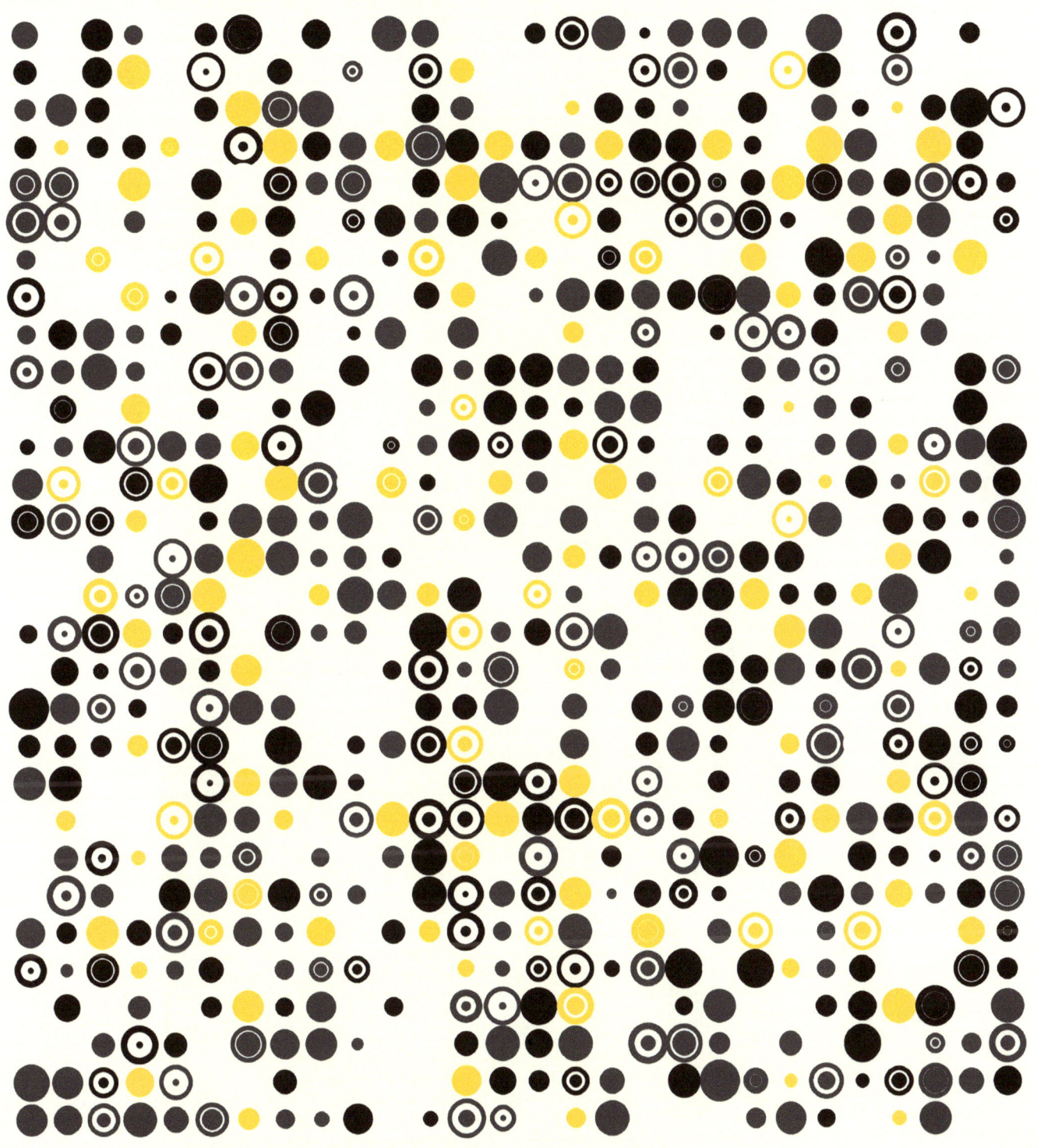

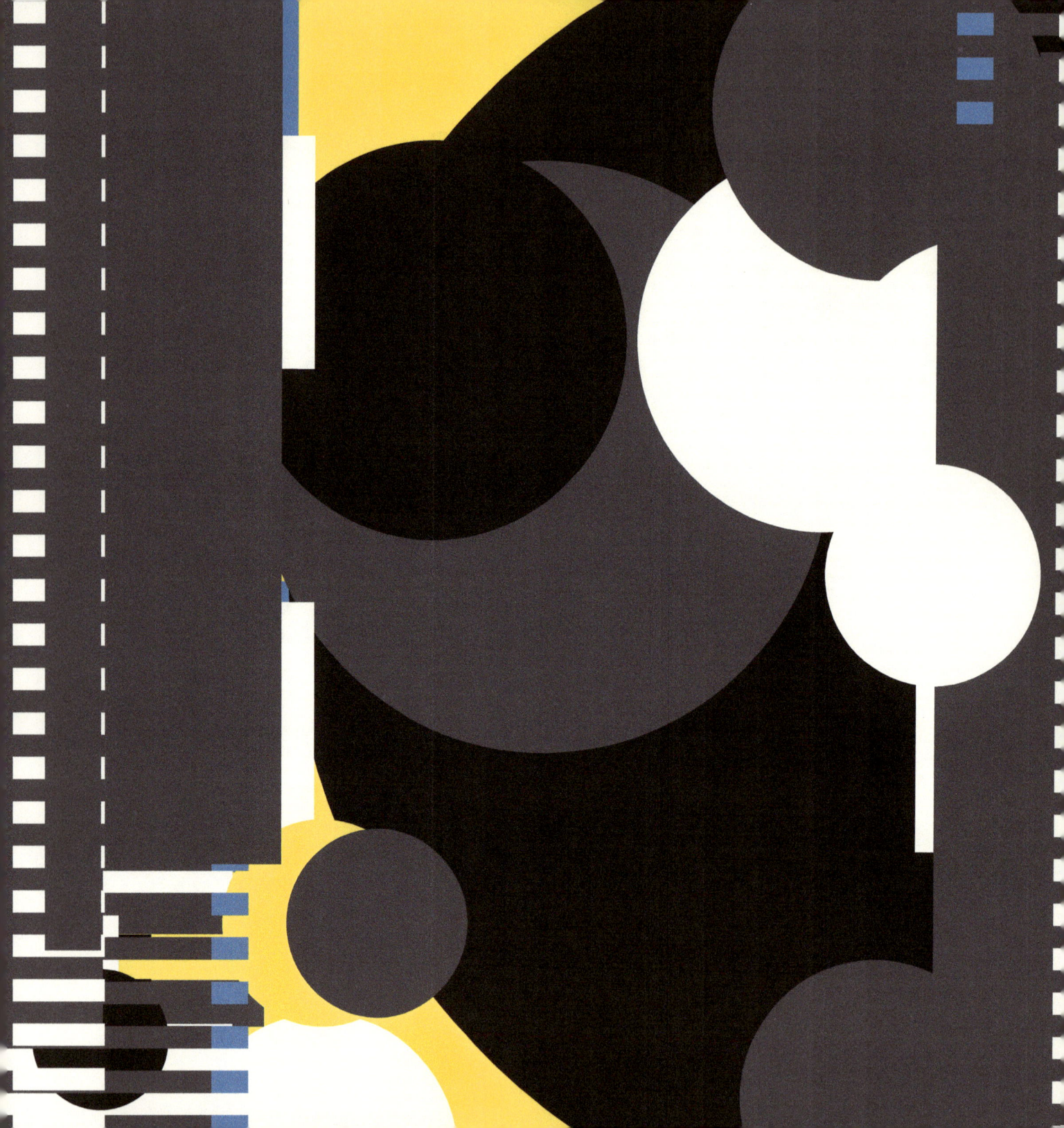

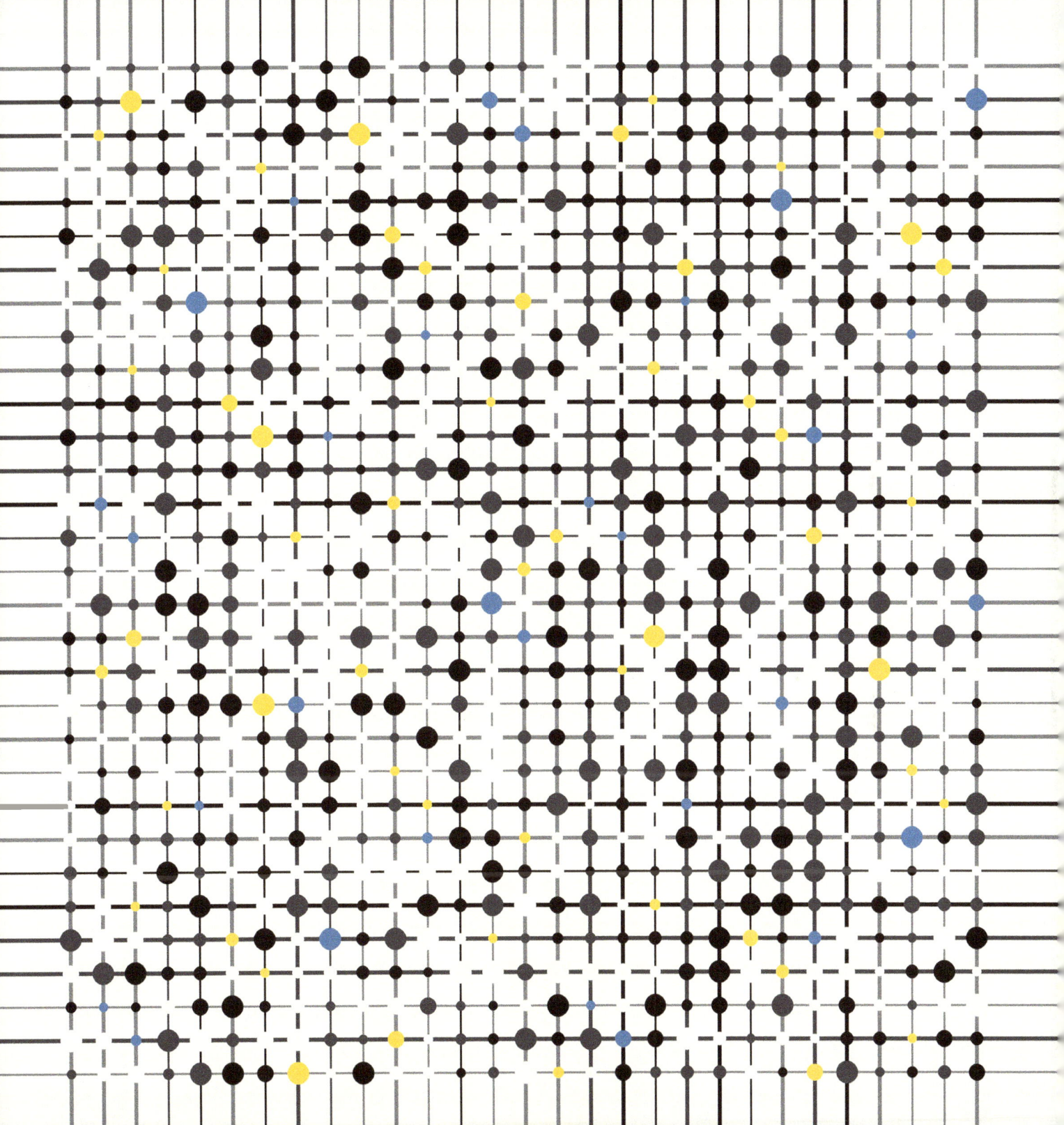

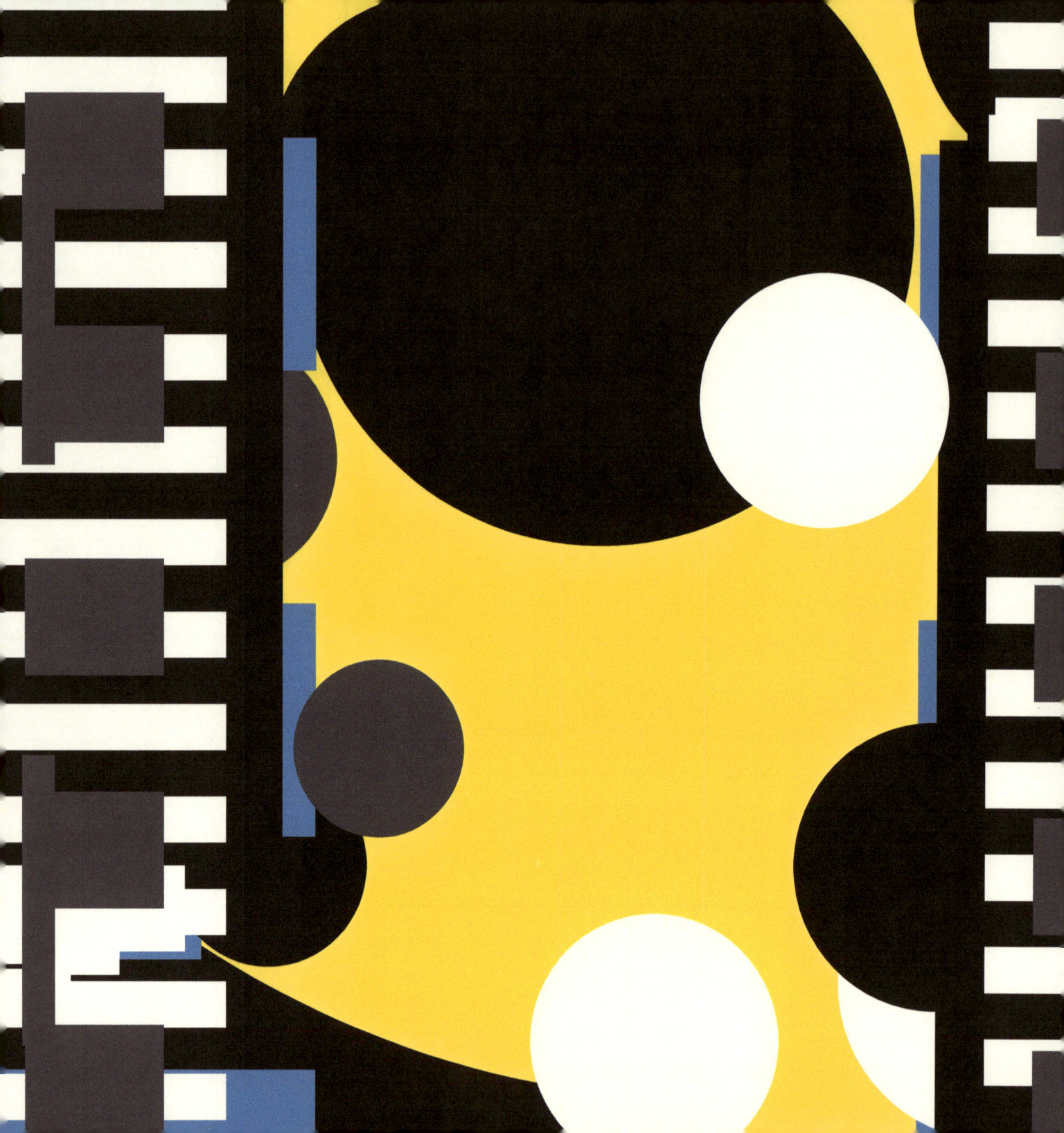

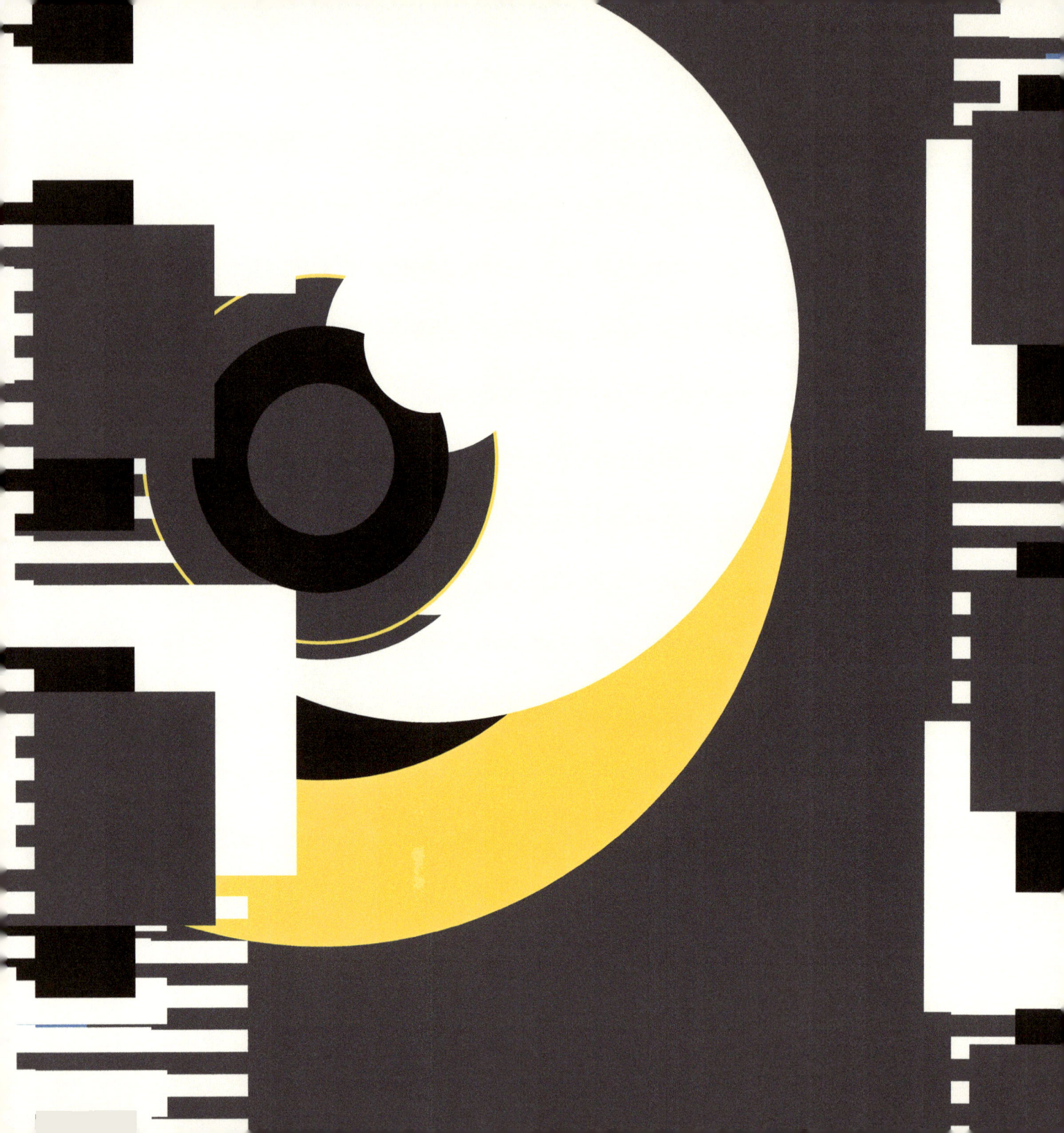

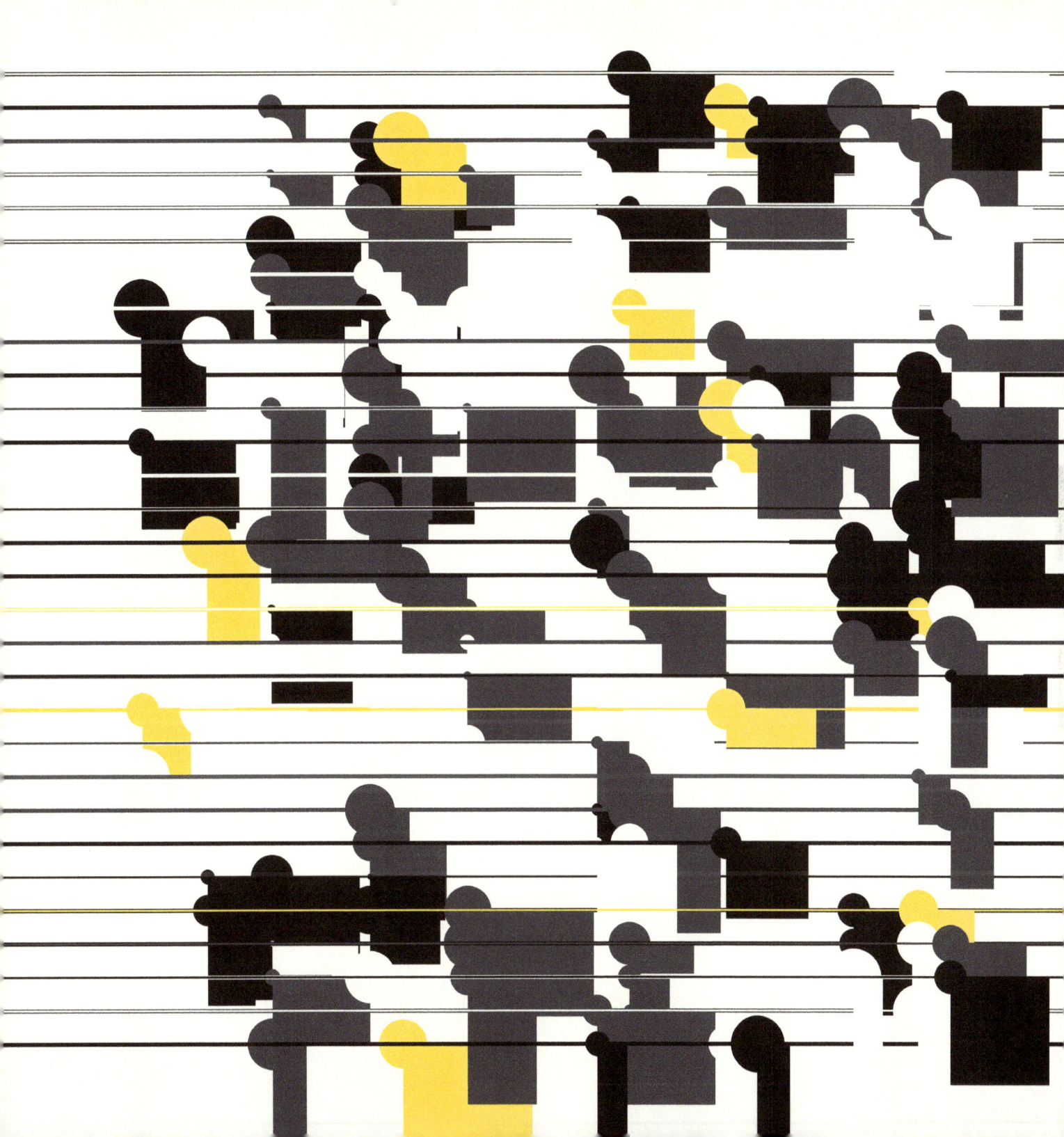

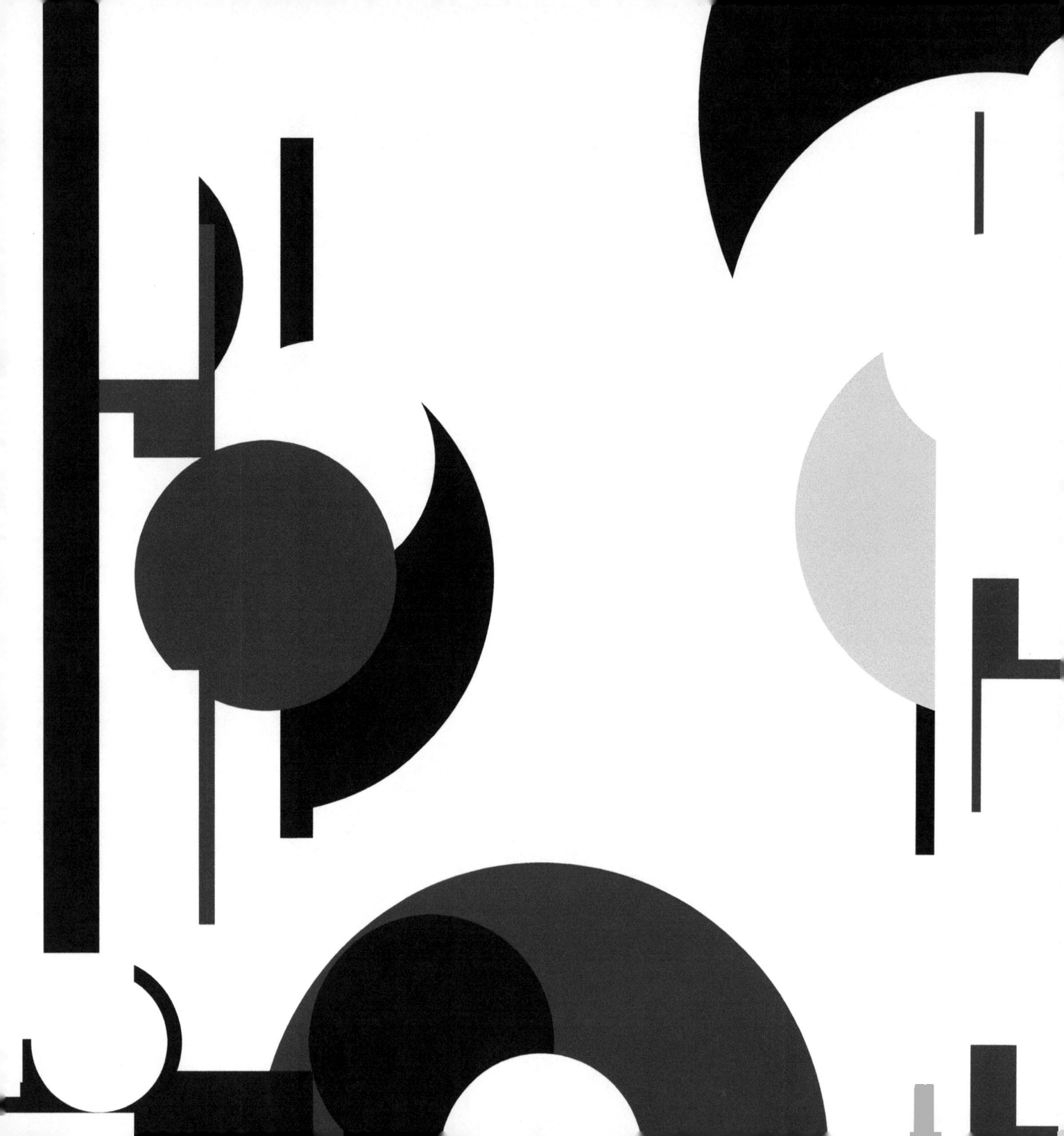

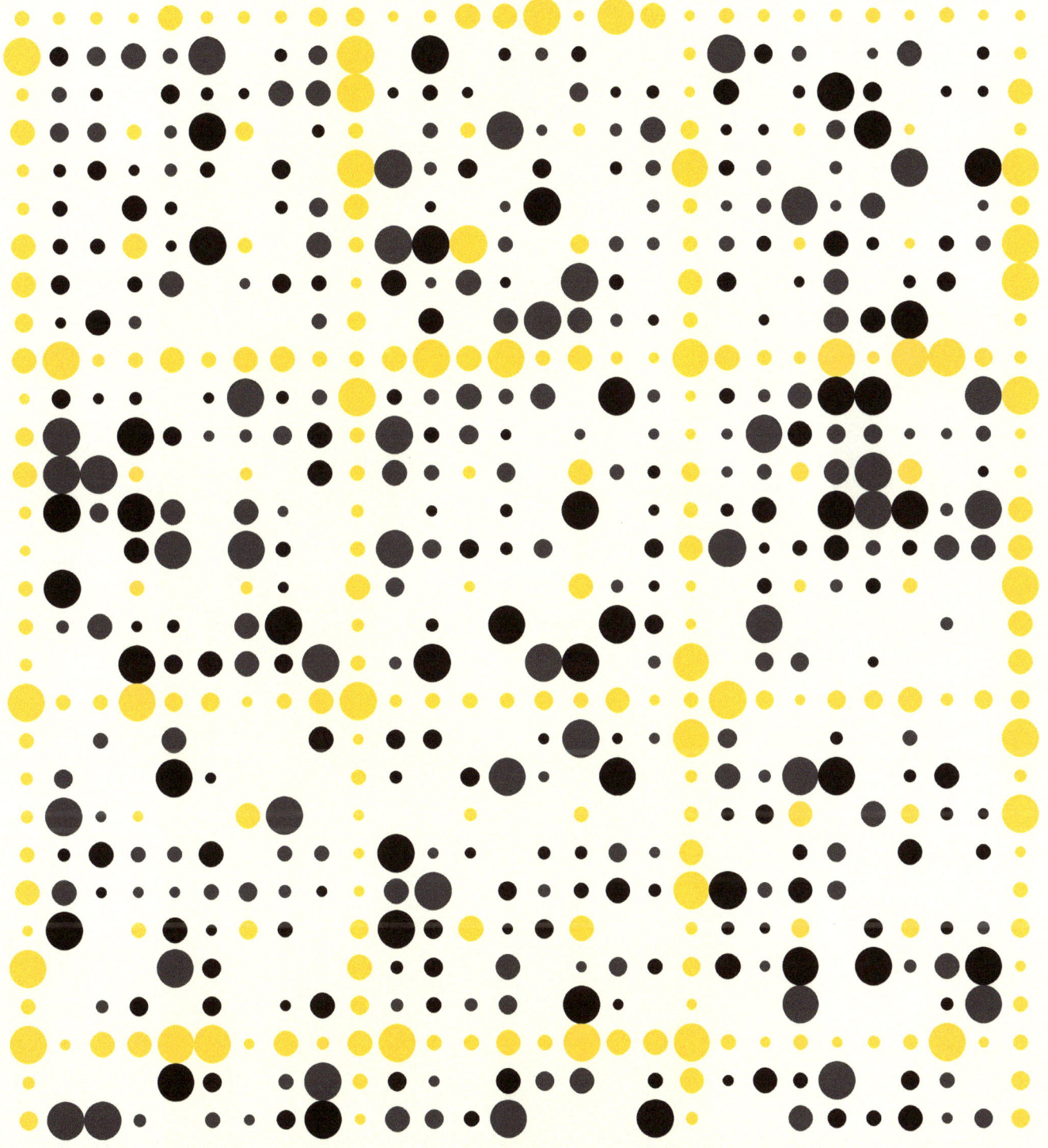

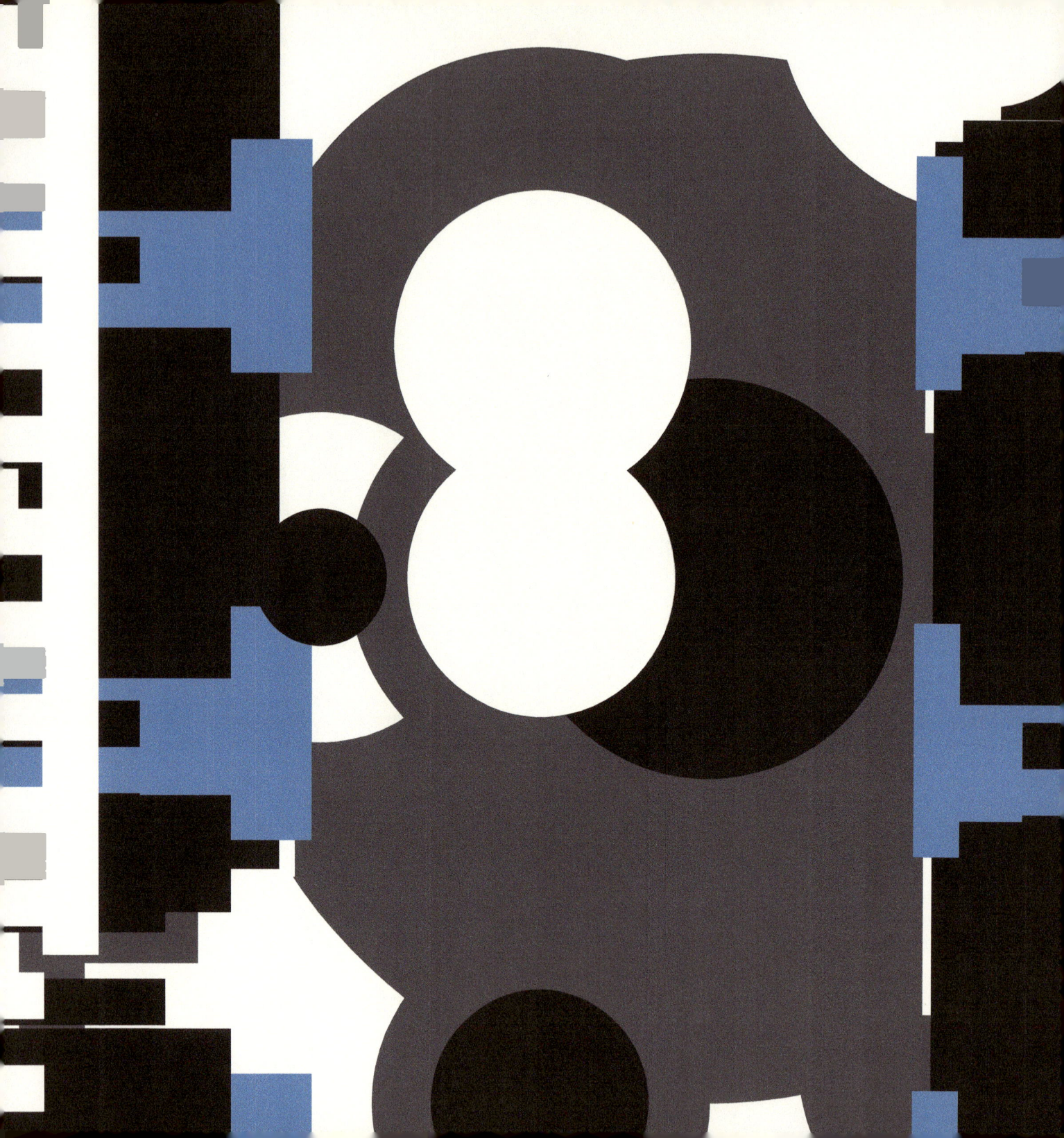

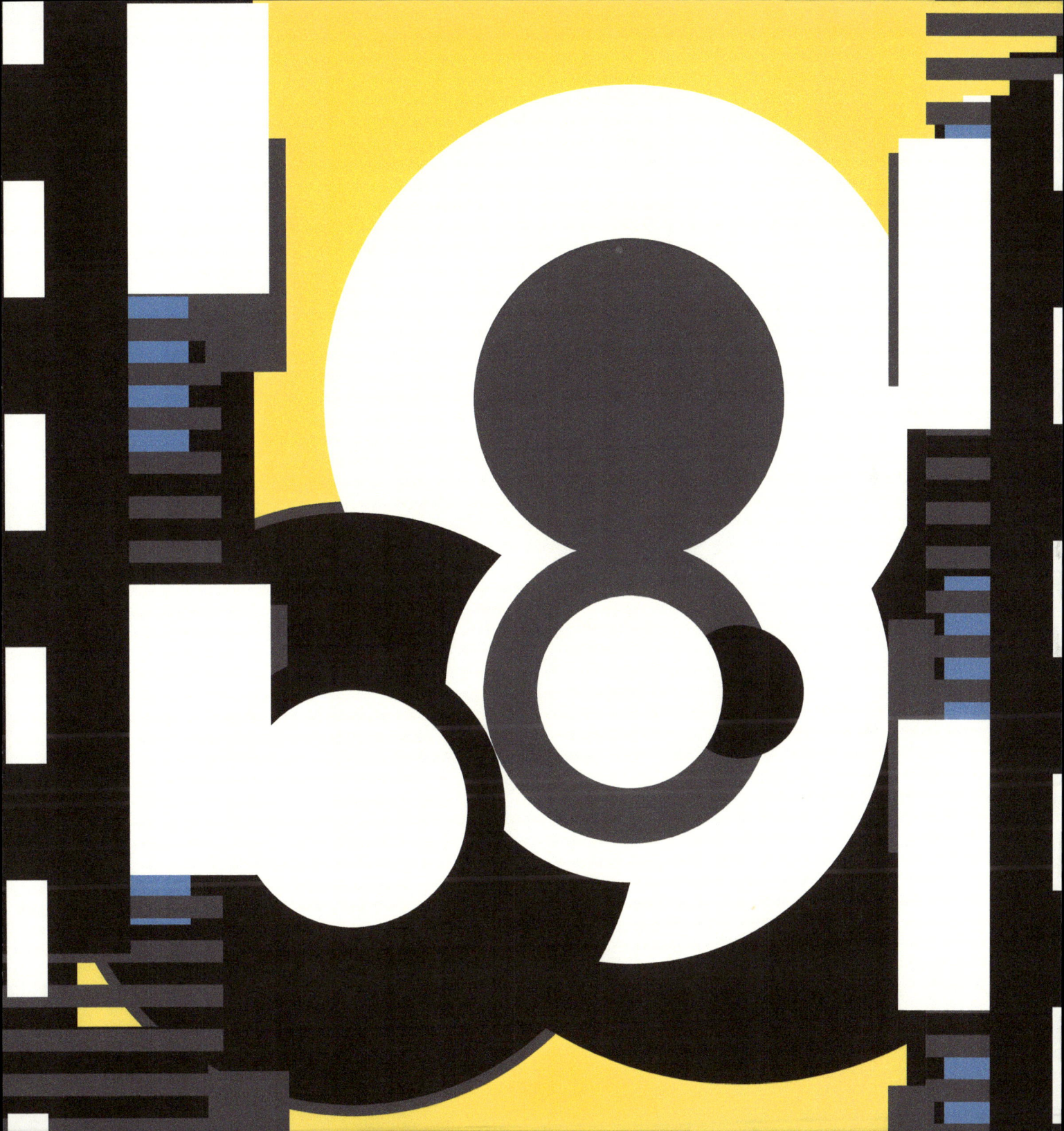

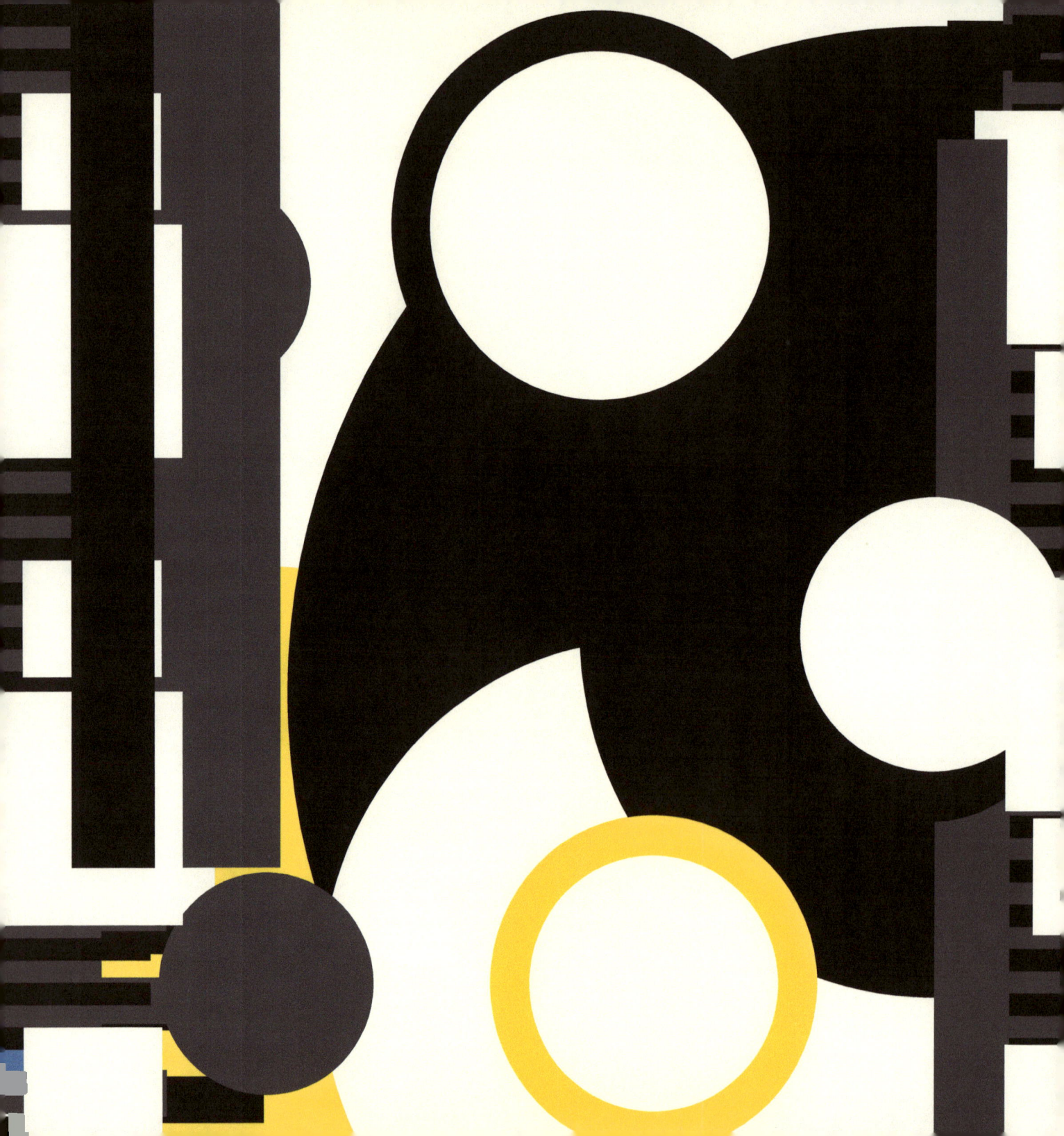